S. H. Nesbit

The Sabbath of the Bible

S. H. Nesbit

The Sabbath of the Bible

ISBN/EAN: 9783743325425

Manufactured in Europe, USA, Canada, Australia, Japa

Cover: Foto ©ninafisch / pixelio.de

Manufactured and distributed by brebook publishing software (www.brebook.com)

S. H. Nesbit

The Sabbath of the Bible

The Sabbath

OF THE

Bible.

BY S. H. NESBIT, D. D.

PITTSBURGH:
MYERS, SHINKLE & CO., PRINTERS, STATIONERS, BINDERS, 523 WOOD STREET.
1890.

DEDICATION.

The battle on Sabbatism began yesterday; goes on to-day; will continue to-morrow. Over the vast theater of history where the conflict has raged—where the strife was hot—where the forces were in hand to hand encounter—I have wandered as a spectator; and, in my own day, participated some little as an actor. The survey has dissipated some former personal hesitancies as to exact and abundant proofs of the ancient divine Sabbath and of the change of day. Three things have specially risen before me as great historic verities: Sabbatism, giving birth to the week, stands as the most notable miracle of ancient history; its divine origin is one of the widest facts lying at the very sources of history; and its change from Seventh to First day, by the Lord of the Sabbath himself, is a clear New Testament teaching and institution. It may be that the thoughts, so helpful to me along these lines, will be helpful also to others. In such faith and hope I send forth this volume. I dedicate it to all who are seeking Sabbath light, and who, in their place and day, are laboring to promote Sabbath sanctity. I invoke upon the work the blessing of the Divine Sabbath-Maker.

Table of Contents.

The Sabbath of Creation	5
The Sabbath of the Ancient World	16
The Sabbath of the Decalogue	36
Sabbatism of Gentile Nations	50
The Sabbath of Judaism, (Old Testament Period)	60
The Sabbath of Judaism, (The Dispersion)	68
Jesus and the Sabbath	88
The Risen Jesus and the Sabbath	96
The Ascended Jesus and the Sabbath	115
Sabbath of the Apostles	126
Sabbatism and the Apostolical Fathers	144
Sabbatism and the Church Fathers, (Second Century)	153
The Sabbath in History	168
The Sabbath a Natural Law	178
Sunday and the State	188
Appendix	203

THE SABBATH OF CREATION.

> "Hail to the day, which He, who made the heavens,
> Earth and their armies, sanctified and blest,
> Perpetual memory of the Maker's rest."
>
> BISHOP MANT.

The divine Worker, who planned and built the heavens and the earth, and impressed upon them hues of beauty and laws of order, was the first Sabbatarian. So the text of Creation, as given by Moses, pronounces:

"And on the seventh day, God ended his work which he had made; and he rested on the seventh day from all his work which he had made. And God blessed the seventh day and sanctified it, because that in it he had rested from all his work which God created and made." Gen. 2 : 2-3.

This is a graphic view, a pictorial illustration, of God when his Creation-work was ended; when the heavens and the earth stood complete; and when man appeared as the most finished specimen of creative skill and power. I study to know and to make known the divine portrait which the words paint.

GOD AS A SABBATH KEEPER.

"He *rested.*" The Divine Worker rested. He followed at the very outset, a two-fold line of action; was a Worker; then a Sabbatarian. The Work and the Sabbatism are alike his actings. The Mosaic narrative is distinct and emphatic; he rested when work was done; he Sabbatized when creation stood complete. Whatever this may mean, yonder it stands as a most remarkable fact in this Bible portrait of God.[1]

God, like man, may *need* rest, may *need* Sabbatism. Creation-work did not indeed overtax and exhaust his energies. It was easy for him to create; to roll worlds from his omnipotent fingers; to people them with forms of life and beauty. It required but his fiat. "He spake, and it was done, he commanded, and it stood fast."[a] And he certainly did not need rest, in the sense of utter cessation from activity—in the sense of idling—in the sense of dolesness. He is a pure spirit, and activity is as essentially an attribute of spirit, as inertia is of matter. He is lifted far above all possible sense of fatigue and weariness. "For the Lord God, the creator of heaven and earth, fainteth not neither is weary."[b]

God's Sabbatism then is not a cessation from activity, but a change of activity; not a cessation from work, but a change of work. His rest is not inaction. He suspended activity in but one direction. He quit *creating*. He quit creating as to our earth. The Mosaic record relates to our earth alone; or, at farthest, to our solar system; certainly not to the universe. God is still enriching the universe with new creations; launching starry worlds and their

---

[a] Ps. 33: 9.   [b] Isa. 40: 28.

[1]
"From work
Now resting, blessed and hallowed the seventh day,
As resting on that day from all his work."—MILTON.

"Moses says that in just six days, the world and all that is therein was made; and that the seventh day was a rest and a release from the labor of such operations; whence it is that we celebrate a *rest* from our labors on that day, and call it the Sabbath, which word denotes rest in the Hebrew tongue."—JOSEPHUS. *Antiq.*, 1: 1: 1.

"After the whole world had been completed according to the perfect nature of the number six, the Father hallowed the day following, the seventh, praising it and calling it holy. For that day is the festival, not of one city, nor of one country, but of all the earth; a day which it is alone right to call the festival for all people, and the birth-day of the world."—PHILO JUDÆUS. *Creation of the World*, ch. 30.

planetary retinues into the fields of infinite space; and peopling them with new and various forms of life. But, as to our earth, his creation-work ended when man appeared. He did not cease from upholding and superintending terrestrial affairs—from supplying life to pulsing things—but he ceased from creative acts—he paused from world making.[1]

He quit creating *matter;* for not since has a particle of matter been added to, or taken from, our world. He quit creating *vegetable life;* for the grasses, shrubs, plants, trees, already made, and made reproductive in kind, were sufficient to fill and beautify the earth in its ever-revolving seasons; and new vegetable creations were unnecessary. He quit creating *animal life;* for the beasts, birds, fishes, reptiles, and animalculæ, already planted in being with power to propagate themselves, were sufficient to fill and throng earth's hills, valleys, rivers, and oceans through time's appointed cycles; and new animal creations were

---

[1] "The rest however was not an entire cessation from activity. He had done *creating*, but he continued to sustain and bless his creatures."—SMITH's *Old Test. Hist.*, 21.

"Cessation from previous occupation is all that is implied in the figure, and is quite compatible with continuous activity in other directions."—*Pulpit Com.* Gen. 2: 3.

"God rested from the work that he *had* made, not from all work. The word Sabbath means resting from the work immediately preceding, because now complete. We have a very incomplete idea of God's Sabbath, unless we realize that he therein entered upon a new and higher kind of work. And this constitutes the clearest and sublimest illustration of what the Sabbath is."—BISHOP WARREN. *Sabbath Essays.*

"Since the beginning of this day no new creation has taken place. God rests as the Creator of the visible universe. The forces of nature are in that admirable equilibrium, which we now behold, and which is necessary to our existence. No more mountains or continents are formed; no new species of plants or animals are created. Nature goes on steadily in its wonted path. All movement, all progress, has passed into the realm of mankind, which is now accomplishing its task."—GUYOT, ON CREATION, as quoted in *Butler's Bible Work* on Gen. 2: 1-6.)

unnecessary. He quit creating *intelligent life;* for man, made in his own image, and made to reappear along the line of countless generations, was able to subdue and rule the earth and its living forms; and other intelligent creations were unnecessary. The earth was complete and fully peopled. Other living forms were not needed. The work of creation ended. God rested. "He rested and was refreshed." [a] Divine Work issued in Divine Sabbatism.

"He rested on the *seventh* day." An outline view of God in creation-work and Sabbatizing, gives a picture of *six* work days and of *one* rest day; or of *six* work periods and of *one* rest period. This is the Divine Model for work and rest. Six days or periods, were employed in creating, beautifying, vitalizing; then followed a rest day or period

The days of creation were, presumably, not days of twenty-four hours each, but great geologic periods. That would make God's Sabbath, not a twenty-four hour day, but a geologic Eon or age. This statement could hardly have a second side, but that the word "day" in the fourth commandment, is used equally of God and of man. And it is argued that if it means a period of twenty-four hours for man, it must also mean a like period for God. But this argument has in it the fallacy of attempting to measure God by man—God's day by man's day. God's day may be longer than man's day; precisely as God's wisdom, though expressed by the same word, is higher and broader than man's wisdom; or as God's power, though expressed by the same word, is mightier and vaster than man's power. We blunder when we attempt to measure God by man; God's day by man's day; God's creation day by man's twenty-four hour day. "A thousand years in thy sight are but as yesterday when it is past."[b] "One day is with the Lord as a thousand years, and a thousand years as one day."[c] God's time periods are evidently different

---
[a] Ex. 31: 17.   [b] Ps. 90:4.   [c] II. Pet. 3: 8.

from man's. The work done in each creation day bespeaks more than a twenty-four hour day—bespeaks a great geologic Eon. So too must be God's rest day—his Sabbath. It is a vast period. It began when world-making stood complete, and will only end with time. It embraces the whole human period. It is already six thousand years old; and the divine Sabbatarian has not yet resumed creation work upon our earth. He still rests. His seventh day has not yet reached its evening. His Sabbath goes on. Time's Great clock is still ticking off its revolving hours.[1]

But God's creation days and Sabbath are held by some to be literal twenty-four hour days. This theory makes him work six literal days in every weekly cycle, and rest the seventh. Man's Sabbath, in that case, cannot be an exact copy of God's, *as to its place in the weekly cycle.* For man was made on God's *sixth* creation day. God's seventh day—his Sabbath—would be man's second day of life and history. Now if man's Sabbath is on the same twenty-four hour day as God's, then it is on the *second* not

---

[1] "The morning of the seventh day is not followed by any evening. The day is still open. When the evening shall come the last hour of humanity will strike."—GUYOT, as quoted in *Butler's Bible Work on Gen.* 2 : 1-6.

"He has put forth no creative energy since he brought man into being; but at the end of the world, in the changes that shall produce a new heaven and a new earth, God will resume that creation activity, which is now in suspense. Till then he rests."—DR. J. P. THOMPSON, *Ditto.*

"When the last man has been born, and has arrived at the crisis of his destiny, then may we expect a *new creation,* another putting forth of the divine energy, to prepare the skies above and the earth beneath for a new stage of man's history, in which he will appear as a race no longer in process of development, but completed in number, confirmed in moral character, transformed in physical constitution, and so adapted to a new scene of existence."—DR. J. G. MURPHY, *Ditto.*

"The six periods of creative and formation work were followed, according to the narrative, by a period of rest, which, it is implied, still continues."—ALDEN's *Man. Cyc.*, Art. Cosmogony.

the *seventh* day in the weekly cycle of historic time. Or, if man's Sabbath is on the seventh day of his own weekly period, then it does not agree, as to the day of the week, with God's. The two Sabbaths—God's and man's—do not synchronize. They run parallel but do not unite in history. I avow my belief—it cannot in any case amount to knowledge—that the day originally given to man for Sabbatism was the seventh in the human weekly period—the seventh in historic time.

What God *does*, and does, as an *example* for man, must be something in the very nature of God and of man. The divine life, as a revealed basis of human duty, is a supreme law. There is, there can be, no higher law. God's example is permanently authoritative. It reports something in the very constitution of God—of man—of the universe. It expresses a natural, necessary, universal law. "Be ye holy, *for* I am holy;" "Be ye therefore perfect, *even* as your father in heaven is perfect;" are enactments of the highest and changeless law. It makes the good in God the basis of required good in man. This is the revealed law for world Sabbatism. Sabbatism in God is the basis of the Sabbatic law for man.

What God *appoints*, as to the time of Sabbath-keeping, is also a revealed basis of human obligation, but has the character of mutability. *Appointment*, like *example*, is authoritative. But example has permanence; appointment may change. Essences are eternal; forms mutable. The appointment of any particular twenty-four hour day, in the human weekly period, belongs to mere forms, and is changeable at the will of the Law-Maker.

Now on the theory that makes God's creation and rest days great geologic Eons, no known unit of time, as a day, a month, a year, is in the Divine Model. All that is fairly in it is: the septenary period; with work in its first six-sevenths; and rest in its last seventh. The unit of time for man must be a divine selection and appointment. If a day be chosen as the unit, then the particular day is not of the very substance of Sabbatism—is not in the Divine Model—is of the nature of mere forms—is alterable at the will of the Sabbath Maker.

On the theory that God's creation and rest days are literal twenty-four hour days, the divine example *is* an exact Model for human Sabbatism as to the time period. But, as seen, it leaves *the particular day* for Sabbath, in man's weekly period, open to doubt—clouded with uncertainty. The day must still be a divine selection and appointment; a changing form, if God will; a shrining husk that, at His fiat, may disappear in a successor.

On both theories, the Divine Model puts a seventh-of-days for holy time into the World's Constitution. But the particular day is an alterable By-Law. Its change would be only a change as to forms.

He "*blessed* the seventh day." The creations of the six work days were pronounced "good" and when man appeared "very good;" but the seventh day, God's rest day, was enriched with the divine blessing.[1] Sabbatism is thus crowned and sceptered with celestial benedictions. God's blessing distinguishes its day among days; differentiates it from secular or work days; makes it a day select and privileged. It bestows a real good, invests the day with divine favor, and imparts a happifying endowment. What God blesses is blest indeed. He has put his blessing upon the Sabbath; has spoken well of the day; has lifted it above its fellows. The day of the Sabbath, because of the divine blessing, is given a celestial elevation, where it crowns and overlooks the whole vale of time; its

---

[1] Inanimate things are blessed of God. "He blesseth the habitation of the just," Prov. 3 : 33. "He shall bless thy bread and thy water," Ex. 23 : 25. "Thou blessest the springing thereof," Ps. 65 : 10.

summit bathed in transfiguring light and glory; its slopes peopled and picturesque with all the Beatitudes and Graces.

He "*sanctified*" the seventh day. The six creation days were freighted with work—with formative words and deeds. The seventh was made sacred. It was appointed to be the holy of holies in the Temple of days. God separated it from common and set it apart to holy uses. He hallowed it in himself. He ceased from creation work. He rested—is resting. And he fills his Sabbath cycle, not with idling, but with well-doing; not with inactivity, but with works of necessity and mercy. He fills it with works of necessity; upholding and governing all terrestrial things; keeping the currents of life, vegetable, animal, and intelligent, moving in ceaseless appearings and disappearings. He fills it with works of mercy; loving and redeeming sinful man; and forever sending to him the all-helping Holy Spirit. Throughout all his Sabbath cycle, on our Sabbaths as on our secular days, he is the God of Providence. "My Father worketh hitherto," says Jesus; and it is of the all-pitying and all-loving Father, in his divine Sabbath cycle, that he thus speaks. The Model Sabbatarian makes works of necessity and mercy essential belongings of holy time. His Sabbath sanctity is as old as creation and as fresh and new as the last smile on the dimpled cheek of the little babe.

This pen sketch of God as a Sabbatarian is now complete. Divine Sabbatism, as traced in the Mosaic record, has four, and but four, essential elements: *rest;* a *holy* rest; a *blessed* rest; and a *septenary* rest, in the last seventh of the period. This is Sabbatism—its very substance—its Alpha and Omega. It is a photograph of God as a Sabbath keeper. The day to be kept in man's weekly period is a subject of divine appointment.

Some Suggestions Remain.

Divine Sabbatism lies imbedded in the Mosaic creation-narrative; a narrative entitled to be considered old even among the most ancient historic records; coming down to us indeed from the very sources of history. The document is as old as Moses, who lived and wrote ten centuries before Herodotus, "the father of history;" six centuries before Hesiod, who sang of "Works and Days" when the world was yet young; and five centuries before Homer, whose "Iliad" and "Odyssey" were first chanted by the blind old minstrel among very primitive peoples. It is older than Moses; for the Genesis Sabbath-record was gathered by him, under divine supervision, from a still older document. That still older document did not come from Egypt; for Egypt had then no seventh-day Sabbatism. The prehistoric elements out of which the Genesis Sabbath arose were not Egyptian, but Chaldaic. The Sabbath came from Chaldea, the early home of Abraham, the now known cradle of the seventh-day Sabbath. Abraham grew up among Chaldaic Sabbath records—inscribed on baked clay tablets—transcripts themselves from still older Accadian Sabbath records—and he undoubtedly preserved and transmitted them to his posterity. They thus came to Moses. They came from the banks of the Euphrates rather than from the Nile. Their aspect is Assyrian, not Egyptian—Asiatic, not African. Our ideas as to the beginnings of the Bible need revision. The world has never been without inspired documents—an inspired Bible. Its beginning records were pre-Mosaic and pre-Abrahamic. Moses, under special divine direction, gathered and reissued them in the book now known as Genesis. Thus the Mosaic Sabbath record is traceable back to the very remotest times. There is nothing that is known to be older. The oldest of all known writings are the Mosaic Genesis records and the inscriptions of Accad.[1]

In this most ancient document there appears the weekly cycle with the last day of the cycle as a day of rest. This is simply wonderful. A finished picture of the weekly period and seventh day Sabbatism lies yonder in a divine frame at the very sources of history. God, not

---

[1] "The sexagesimal division of the circle, the signs of the Zodiac, a week of seven days, named as we now name them, and the seventh as a day of rest, are all Accadian."—*Lib. Univ. Knowledge.* Art. Chronology.

"It was from the Semites of Babylonia—perhaps the Chaldeans of Ur—that both the name (Sabbath) and the observance passed to the Hebrew branch of the race, the tribe of Abraham."—RAGOZIN. *The Story of Nations.—Chaldea*, 256.

"It (the 7 day week) shall be considered rather as an ancient Babylonian institution which the Hebrews brought with them from their stay in South Babylonia, at Ur Kasdim."—SCHRÆDER. *The Cuneiform Ins. and the Old Test.*, 18.

"He (Abraham) communicated to them arithmetic, and delivered to them the science of astronomy; for before Abraham came into Egypt, they were unacquainted with those parts of learning; for that science came from the Chaldeans into Egypt, and from thence to the Greeks also.—JOSEPHUS. *Antiq.*, 1 : 8 : 2.

"In Europe the system of weeks and week days is comparatively of modern origin. It was not a Greek, nor a Roman, nor a Hindoo, but a Jewish or Babylonian invention."—MAX MULLER. *Chips from a German Workshop*, 5 : 116.

"The week . . . The Egyptians were without it . . . The Hebrew week therefore cannot have been adopted from Egypt; probably both it and the Sabbath were used and observed by the patriarchs."—McCLINTOCK & STRONG. *Cyclo.*, Art. Chronol.

"From recent discoveries of Assyriologists, it seems certain that the Assyrians, and through them probably the other Semitic nations, derived their week of seven days from the Accadians or early Turanian inhabitants of Babylonia, who also observe the seventh day as a day of rest."—*The Inter. Cyclo.*, Art. Week.

man, is the builder of the week and its Sabbatism, even as he is the builder of the day, the month, the year.[1]

In the Mosaic record, Sabbatism appears as a memorial of creation-work. A memorial is a monument that recalls and preserves the past; a picture that we hang up to help us keep fresh some notable event. God's Sabbatism is monumental—a remembrancer—a memento. It makes creation-work memorable forever. Sabbatism is the first monument ever built, and God the first monument builder. He is a monument builder as well as a world builder and a man builder. And the monument built was to be worthy of the Builder; was to run parallel with the world and man; to antedate and survive pyramids and pillars of brass; and to move, changeless like himself, through the wastes and vicissitudes of Time and History.

---

[1] "He who breaks the Sabbath denies creation."—*Jewish Teacher.*

"The Sabbath was instituted from the beginning, and was designed to be of universal and perpetual obligation."—HODGE. *Sys. Theol.*, 325.

"The institution of the Sabbath is thus as old as creation; and the fact of its high antiquity, its being coeval with the human race, demonstrates the universality and the permanence of its obligation.—JAMISON, FAUSSETT & BROWN. *Com. Gen* 2: 2-3.

"The first Scriptural notice of the weekly Sabbath, though it is not mentioned by name, is in Gen. 2: 3, at the close of the record of the six days' creation. And hence it is frequently argued that the institution is as old as mankind, and is consequently of universal concern and obligation."—SMITH. *Dict of the Bible.* Art. Sabbath.

"The seventh part of time is holy for man. God blessed it and hallowed it. Such is the deduction from the language of Gen. 2: 3." LANGE. *Com., Gen.* 2: 3.

SABBATH OF THE ANCIENT WORLD.

> "Sweet is the toil of tranquil holy day,
> Hallowed e'en from the birth of time to rest;
> To purest joys and contemplations blest:
> The cares of this vain world put far away."
>
> ALLEN.

The Sabbath is coeval with man, and, like Song and Marriage, is fragrant with thoughts and memories of Eden. Its holy light and unbroken quiet rested upon Adam and Eve when they came fresh from the creative hand of God. Its original institution, on the authority of the divine example, and by express law spoken in Eden but long lost to history and the world, antedates sin and the expulsion of the primal man and woman from their Edenic home. I seek to show this high antiquity for the Sabbath; that it has existed as a divine institution from the beginning; that it was given to man as man; and that its boundaries are therefore Time and Man. Proofs of such a seventh-day Sabbath from the very beginning abound in the remains of antiquity.

THE SABBATH ANTE SINAITIC.

The Fourth Commandment introduces and names the Sabbath, not as a new institution, but as already well-known in the world. Its opening word—"Remember" is not merely monitory, does not merely enjoin a future recollection of the precept, but also recalls something past and known. It sets forth the institution as a pre-existent one as having come down out of the past, the Sinaitic legislation merely confirming and investing it anew with divine authority. Moses, by this word, distinctly declares that he is not beginning but only renewing the Sabbath; that his is not an original publication of the institution, but only a re-enactment of an older law. Sinai then did not witness the first promulgation of the Sabbath law. It had a pre Sinaitic life and history.

The Sabbath was known and observed among the Israelites before Sinai was reached. Sinai was reached in their third month out from Egypt, and was the fifth stage in their journeyings from the Red Sea. But in their second month out from Egypt, and in their third stage, from the sea, the camp was pitched in the Wilderness of Sin. There began the miracle of manna. The law for its coming and its gathering is Sabbatic. God, in sending it, was a Sabbatarian. He sent it six consecutive mornings; a double portion on the sixth; none on the seventh. Man, its gatherer, was also required to be a Sabbatarian. He was to gather it six consecutive mornings; a double portion on the sixth; none on the seventh. "Six days shall ye gather it," says Moses, "but on the seventh which is the Sabbath, there shall be none." The day of no-manna is called "the rest of the holy Sabbath unto the Lord."[a] The Sabbatic name and institution are both here; and sabbath-keeping too. And this is before Sinai was reached; before the giving of the law; before the Sabbath was made part and parcel of the Decalogue. The Sabbath, by authority of Holy Scripture, is ante-Sinaitic.[1]

Israel in Egypt knew such associated Sabbatic ideas as "seven days," "seventh day," "holy convocation," "feast unto the Lord," and "sacrifice unto the Lord"—phrases with which the people appeared to be familiar. And

---

[a] Ex. 16 : 11-31.

[1] "The celebration of the seventh day as a day consecrated to Jehovah is first mentioned after the Exodus from Egypt, and seems to have preceded the Sinaitic legislation, which merely confirmed and invested it with the highest authority." *The Inter. Cyc.*, Art. Sabbath.

Pharoah, addressing Moses and Aaron respecting the Israelites, said, using the Hebrew Sabbatic word: "Ye make them rest (Sabbatize) from their burdens." The Chaldaic language was at that time the Court language of Egypt, and of Western Asia—the language of diplomacy. There were in many places libraries and schools where it was taught. This explains its use by the Egyptian Pharoah—his use of the Hebrew Sabbatic word.[1]

It throws a flood of light upon the scene. It shows the Israelites as Sabbatizing; Moses and Aaron restoring among them known but neglected Sabbath-keeping; and Pharoah denouncing their Sabbatizing as idling. The Sabbatic war is already on in history; an oppressed people seeking to keep the day; greed and despotism wresting it from them. This interpretation—the very best possible—establishes the Sabbath as known and observed by the Israelites in Egypt. The name was there. The Sabbath-keeping people were there. This broad Sabbatic trace antedates the Decalogue and Sinai.

The Sabbath Ante Mosaic.

The Septenary number is crowned above all other numbers in the Bible. It is used over three hundred times. The oldest Bible writings—the ante-Mosaic—are specially

---

[1] Prof. A. H. Sayce in a paper on The Tel-el-Amarno Tablets, read July 1, 1889, before the Victoria Institute, London, says: "From them we learn that in the fifteenth century before our era—a century before the Exodus—active literary intercourse was going on throughout the civilized world of Western Asia, between Babylon and Egypt, and the smaller states of Palestine, of Syria, of Mesopotamia, and even of Eastern Kappadokia. And this intercourse was carried on by means of the Babylonian language. This implies that all over the civilized East there were libraries and schools where the Babylonian language and literature were taught and learned."

"That the Babylonian was the language of diplomacy and society in the fifteenth century B. C., all over the civilized East, is the greatest of archæological surprises."—Prof. Taylor. *Andover Rev.*, Feb. 1890, p. 221.

full of the word in some of its forms. We are told of the "sevenfold" vengeance to be visited on any one slaying Cain. We are told how things were taken into the ark in classes of "sevens." We are twice told of "the seven ewe lambs" given as a token of the covenant between Abraham and Abimelech. We are twice told how Jacob served "seven years" for Rachel, and then "seven other years" for flocks and herds. And we are told how Pharoah dreamed, and saw "seven well-favored" then "seven ill-favored" kine; "seven rank and full ears" then "seven thin ears" of corn; and that each class represented "seven years." These are samples of the Bible use of the word in ante-Mosaic times and writings. Its use runs clear back through Noah to Cain and Abel.[1]

Reverence for the septenary number also perpetually appears in the most ancient records of all earliest peoples.

---

[1] Special interest belongs to certain numbers—always has—always will. They are used as symbols of important ideas. Here are samples:

Three is the *mystical* number: Man's trinity of natures, body, mind, soul; God's trinity of substances, Father, Son, Holy Ghost; and Time's trinity of parts, past, present, future, or the Was, the Is, and the Will Be.

Four is the *world* number: Our globe's four quarters, East, West, North, South; and the year's four seasons, Spring, Summer, Autumn, Winter.

Twelve, the product of three and four, seems a symbol of arrangements to meet *world needs*. Ishmael had twelve princes; Jacob twelve sons and tribes; and Christ twelve Apostles. The New Jerusalem has twelve gates, and its temple twelve foundations. This number is written on the sky, from the earliest times, in the twelve signs of the Zodiac; and it is incorporated in all chronologies in the twelve months of the year.

Seven, the sum of three and four, is the *sacred* number. It ranges, as seen above, widely through the Bible and in all primitive literature. Its impress is upon nature as well. The rainbow, God's chosen emblem of promised good, is painted on the sky in seven colors. Seven is the symbol of sufficiency. It is called the number of perfection. The word in Hebrew expresses fullness, completion. A sacred character has attached to it from the earliest times.

It was among very primitive peoples that the tales began of the "Seven Sages," the "Seven Wise Men," the "Seven Masters," and the "Seven Wonders of the World." No reliable astronomic histories go back so far as to tell us when men first began to speak of the "seven planets" and the "seven stars" in the Pleiades. The Indian cosmogony speaks of the "seven worlds," the "seven continents," and the "seven seas." Among the earliest Greeks "seven" was sacred to Apollo and Dionysius. Homer sings of the "seven tripods" and the "seven maids" that Agamemnon offered to Achilles for the return of Briseis.[a] "With the desire to purify myself," says one of the ancients, "I bathe in the sea, dipping my head seven times in the waves; for this number, as the divine Pythagoras tells us, is the proper one in all matters of religion."[b] These samples, outside of the Abrahamic family, show the septenary word in wide use as far back as the lights of history and tradition take us.

Now it is impossible to explain this high antiquity and wide currency of the septenary number—an associate Sabbatic idea—on any theory that does not trace it back to God's seventh day rest, when his creation work was ended. The creation "seven," completing divine work and rest, is its only fairly known source and archetype. This accounts for its origin and prevalence, and nothing else does. The primeval origin of the Sabbath is suggested and confirmed by the early and world-wide sacredness of the number.

The septenary division of time—the week—seven days—has an equally venerable antiquity and currency. It was, after day and night, the earliest known of all time-markers—indeed a primal and universal time-marker. Primitive Hebrews and Arabians found it in the world and used it. Joseph appointed "seven days of mourning"

---

[a] Iliad 19: ls. 243–6.
[b] CUNNINGHAM GEIKE, "Oriental Mode of Covenanting," S. S. Times, Oct. or Nov., 1888.

for Jacob. "Fulfill ye her week," said Laban to Jacob, enjoining upon him seven years' service for Rachel. Job's three friends sat down in silence with him "seven days and seven nights." And Noah, in the ark, twice stayed "seven days" before sending forth his exploring dove. Thus in the Bible, the weekly period, always implying Sabbatism, is pre-Mosaic, pre-Abrahamic, coeval with Noah.[1]

The week was indeed known and of world-wide use among all primitive peoples. It is seen, and in its purest form, at their very beginnings. The dwellers in the earliest seats of mankind—Accadians, Assyrians, Babylonians—had the week and the seventh-day Sabbath. Marvelous and convincing is the testimony of their sculptures and inscriptions. They are as so many witnesses, risen from the

---

[1] "The week is perhaps the most ancient and incontestable monument of human knowledge."—LAPLACE ŒUVRES, *tom. vi, liv. i, ch.* 3.

"The septenary arrangement of days was in use among the orientals from the remotest antiquity." SCALIGER. *De Emend. Temp. lib. i.*

"The week, whether a period of seven days, or a quarter of the month, was of common use in antiquity."—MCCLINTOCK & STRONG, *Cyclo.*, Art. Chronol.

"The week .... has been employed from time immemorial in almost all eastern countries."—*Cycl. Brit.*, Art. Calendar.

"We have reason to believe that the institution of that short period of seven days, called a *week*, was the first step taken by mankind in dividing and measuring their time. We find from time immemorial, the use of this period among all nations without any variation in the form of it. The Israelites, Assyrians, Egyptians, Indians, Arabians, and, in a word, all the nations of the East have in all ages made use of a week, consisting of seven days."—PRESIDENT DE GOGUET, *The Origin of Laws*, (1761,) 1 : 230.

"From time whereof the memory of man, and history and mythology, run not to the contrary, the division of time into the week of seven days has been almost the universal law. It prevailed among peoples far removed from each other, and remote from as well as near to the Asiatic center whence the nations of men radiated—among Persians, Chaldeans, Egyptians, Hindoos, the ancient Chinese on the farthermost East, and the Scandinavians on the Northwest. In most of these instances it is certain that the week revolved on a day of rest." REV. W. W. ATTERBURY. *Sabbath Essays.*

dead. Their testimony, going back to the utmost borders of Historic Chaos, is final—conclusive—cannot be gainsaid—or resisted.[1]

Egypt, like her own Sphinx in the Nile Valley, keeps stern watch and guard over her most distant life and customs. Her very ancient eras are fabulous. Mists are everywhere; and it is only through occasional rifts that we catch glimpses of first things. In the earliest hieroglyphs, antedating perhaps the pyramid kings, usually located by the critics in Manetho's Fourth Dynasty, appears the revered number seven; the septenary cycle or week, with its name given as *uk*, perhaps the original of our work week; and the seventh day as a day of rest. Thus beyond the certainly known historic dates, there appear in Egypt traces of the weekly period and of Sabbatism.[2]

---

[1] "The sacred Babylonian seven and seven-day week."—GEORGE SMITH. *Chaldean Acc. of Creation*, 308.

"The number seven was a sacred number among the Accadians, who invented the week of seven days, and kept a seventh day Sabbath."—GEO. SMITH. *Assyrian Discoveries*, 56-7.

"They (the Chaldeans) appear to have used the month of 30 days, and the year of 12 months, from immemorial antiquity, as also the week of 7 days, the nomenclature of which from the 7 chief heavenly bodies, coincides with the seven stages of the temple-towers, and seems on other grounds also to have been invented by them."—P. SMITH. *Anc. Hist. of the East*, 401.

[2] "Rest being enjoined by the Egyptian priests on the seventh day."—PROCTOR. *The Great Pryamid*, 246.

"That the Egyptians dedicated the seventh day of the week to Saturn, is certain. And it is presumable this day was a day of rest in Egypt."—*The Great Pyramid*, 266.

"Weeks are mentioned in company with months in some of the oldest hieroglyphs; and, curiously enough, they are called *uk*, which may be the origin of our Anglo-Saxon word."—TREVOR. *Anc. Egypt*, 168-9.

"In Egypt, where the number seven was held in great reverence; and it is more probable that it had prevailed there in ancient times, than that it had been introduced subsequently to the age of Herodotus."—JOHN KENRICK. *Anc. Egypt*, 1: 283.

Hindoo literary remains are abundant to very distant times. We have trustworthy knowledge of their primitive institutions in the Puranic, the Epic, and the Vedic periods. The still older literature has traces of the sacred seven—of the weekly period—and of Sabbatism. These traces appear only at the most distant sources of history and in the mythical period.[1]

Chinese civilization has been peculiar and philosophic, and without Sabbatism, from the time of Confucius and Lao-tse. But the still older and simpler forms of religion reveal wide traces of the seven day period, ending in a day of rest and sacrificial worship.[2]

---

[1] Prof. Wilson on "Hindoo Festivals."—"Every seventh day is considered sacred."—*Jour. of the Royal Asiatic Soc.*

The god Vishnu to Satyavrata: "In seven days all creatures.... shall be destroyed by a deluge.... Together with seven holy men... enter the ark without fear..... After seven days the floods descended and drowned the world."—SIR WM. JONES. *Asiatic Researches*, 2: 116-17.

Ancient Hindoo Prayers: "Mother of all creatures, Saptami, who art one with the lords of the seven courses and the seven mystic words." ..... "Glory to thee, who delighteth in the seven chariots drawn by the seven steeds, the illuminators of the seven worlds. Glory to thee on the seven lunar days." .... "It is impossible to avoid inferring from the general character of the prayers and observance, and the sanctity evidently attached to the recurring seventh day, some connection with the Sabbath, or the seventh of the Hebrew Heptameron." H. H. WILSON's *Works*, 2: 201.

"When the great king of glory, on the Sabbath day, (uposatha,) on the day of the full moon, had purified himself, and had gone up in the upper story of his palace to keep the sacred day." NOTES 3.— Uposatha, a weekly sacred day : being full-moon day, new moon day, and two equidistant intermediate days."—*Sacred Books of the East*, 12: 251, 254.

"In Buddhism the same word (*uposatha*) has come to denote a Sabbath, observed on the full moon, on the day when there is no moon, and on the two days which are eighth from the full and new moon respectively."—*Cycl. Brit.*, Art. Sabbath; CHILDER's *Pali. Dict.*, 535; KERN, *Buddhismus*, 8, Ger. trans.; MAHARAGGA, 2: 1: 1.

[2] "The Emperor offered sacrifices to the Superior Unity, Tog-y, every seven days."—*Annals of Sec. Masico.* Quoted from PROUDHON.

The historic Greek had the decade, not the hebdomad. But earlier Greek writers, as Linus, Homer, Hesiod, and Pythagoras, mention and eulogize the seventh day and its sacred character. These traces of the week and of an associated rest day, belong to the most distant Greece—to the golden age of the poets—when religion was simple in its forms—and when great sanctity attached to temples and festivals.[1]

Thus the week—the seven day period associated with Sabbatism—stands out clearly in the most ancient and silent deserts of time. It appears as a primitive and universal institution; as an incontestable monument of the very earliest civilization; as at its very best in the earliest times. Now this division of time into weeks —an arbitrary not a natural arrangement like the day, the month, the year—could not have been an invention of primitive man. It is not a natural division of time, nor yet an accident in human affairs. It must have arisen from some remarkable event in history—and at its very beginning. It is a primitive tradition springing from some divine Genesis

---

"All the ancient Emperors on the seventh day, called the Great Day, caused the doors of houses to be closed. No business was done that day, and the magistrates judged no case."—CHIN KING. Quoted from PROUDHON.

[1] "By the same arm my seven brave brothers fell."—ILIAD 6: 421.
"Seven golden talents to perfection wrought,"
Ulysses in cave of Polyphemus

"But now arose
A well-towered city, by seven golden gates enclosed."
—HESIOD. *Shield of Hercules.*

"Early Athens had to send 7 youths and 7 maidens yearly to Crete to be devoured by the Minotaur."—SMITH. *Hist. Greece,* 6.

"It was the gods themselves who communicated the fact that the septenary, an intelligent number, existed after the ternary. Orpheus taught it as well as the Pythogoreans."—LENORMANT. *The Beginnings of History,* 536.

"The seventh day is observed among pious persons,
The seventh day is the festival of the world's nativity;
The seventh day was kept by our forefathers,
The seventh day is the most perfect of days."
—LINUS, 10 *cent. B. C.* Quoted by EUSEBIUS, *Evan. Præp.*, 3: 13.

narrative. It is impossible, indeed, to explain its high antiquity, its wide prevalence, its deep impression upon emerging nations, on any theory that does not trace it back to God's "seven days" of work and rest. It was this that started the weekly period on its travels among mankind. This is its only sufficient source and authority. It can have no other.[1]

The Book of Job twice speaks of "a day when the sons of God came to present themselves before the Lord." That must have been an appointed day, a fixed day, an understood day, in order to the assembling of the sons of God at the same time and place. Their name is odorous of saintship; and their assembling to present themselves before the Lord is an obvious act of worship—an act of social or public worship. Worship and an appointed day for worship are suggestive of Sabbatism—are legible traces of an ancient Arabian Sabbath.

Noah, on quitting the ark, built an altar and offered burnt offerings; and the Lord smelled "a sweet savor"—

---

[1] "Seven natural days constituted a week. This division of time appears to have been observed by all nations, probably from the beginning of the world; and it originated with God himself."—*Cottage Bible*, 1: 10.

"We find from time immemorial the knowledge of the week of seven days among all nations—Egyptians, Arabians, Indians--in a word all the nations of the east have in all ages made use of this week of seven days for which it is difficult to account without admitting that this knowledge was derived from the common ancestors of the human race."—*Kitto's Cycl. of Bib. Lit.*, Art. Sabbath.

"The measuring of time by day and night is pointed out to the common sense of mankind by the diurnal course of the sun. Lunar months and solar years are equally obvious to all rational creatures; so that the reason why time is computed by days, months, and years, is readily given. But how the division of time into weeks of seven days, and this from the beginning, came to obtain universally among mankind, no man can account for, without having respect to some impressions on the minds of men from the constitution and laws of nature, with the tradition of a Sabbatical rest from the foundation of the world."—*Cycl. Rel. Knowl.*, 10: 39.

marginal reading, "savor of rest." Sacrificial worship and rest—Sabbatic elements—here go together, and are traces of an ancient Sabbath. For this is that Noah who gathered clean animals into the ark by "sevens" and who observed "seven day" periods in sending forth his exploring dove.[1]

Worship and sacrifice are as old as man. Cain and Abel brought an offering unto the Lord "in process of time"—marginal reading, "in the end of days." In the end of what days? Man was then but newly created and placed upon the earth. Time divisions, the growth of study and experience, could not as yet have been formed. But in some way he knew creation's story; its six work days; its seventh day rest. He knew this for it is part of his transmitted history. To him then the end of days, as connected with offerings unto the Lord, would be the end of week days—the end of secular or work days—giving way to the altar and the sacrifice—to Sabbath rest and worship. This "offering unto the Lord" then is a large and plain trace of an ante-diluvian Sabbath.

Thus the ante-Mosaic world had in it all the Sabbatic elements: *rest;* a *sacred* rest, as the sons of God appearing before the Lord; a *blessed* rest, as Noah's thank-offering on quitting the ark; and a *septenary* rest, as Cain and Abel's offering in the end of days. This establishes, by indirection, a pre-Mosaic Sabbath, a pre-Abrahamic Sabbath, an ante-diluvian Sabbath. The proofs, though but circumstantial, are wholly one-sided. There is nothing on the other side, nothing to oppose them—to weaken them—to make them doubtful.

---

[1] "Noah, with all his family, and all the animals, were but seven days embarking; which seems to intimate the division of time into weeks, and the observance of a Sabbath."—DR. WM. PATTON. *Cottage Bible.* Com. on Gen. 7.

The Assyrian, Babylonian, Accadian Sabbath.

The Sabbath of the ancient world is in the Cuneiform inscriptions, as well as in the Mosaic records. This story had perished; but one of its lost chapters has been recovered. The pick and shovel have broken the long silence of the undreaming dust. Oriental researches are turning up before us the fleshless faces of the first men who walked the earth after the flood; are exhuming records and monuments of their taste and genius; are recovering their histories, teachings, beliefs. Long buried cities are yielding their mighty secrets. At Kouyunjik, the ancient Nineveh, the pick and shovel laid bare, in the palace of Sennacherib, two "Chambers of Records." Their floors were covered, a foot deep with tablets of baked clay, having inscribed upon them *histories* and *legends* of the earliest times—early literature of Chaldea —of Accad. Like records have been found at other places, as at Babylon, at Calneh, and at Erech, the oldest of all cities.

The "*historic* tablets" contain very wonderful Sabbatic records. One—"A Religious Calendar of the Assyrians" —forbids work every seventh day and enjoins rest and devotion.[1] Another—"A Babylonian Astronomic Record"

---

[1] "In the year 1869 I discovered, among other things, a curious religious calendar of the Assyrians, in which every month is divided into four weeks, and the seventh days, or Sabbaths, are marked out as days in which no work should be undertaken."—*Assyrian Discoveries*, Geo. Smith, 12.

Assyrian Calendar. Translated by Rev. A. H. Sayce. The rubric of the 14th day, the 21st day, and the 28th day is the same as for the 7th day, here given:

The seventh day. A feast of Merodach and Zir-Panitu—A festival. *A Sabbath.* The Prince of many nations
The flesh of birds and cooked fruit eats not.
The garments of his body he changes not. White robes he puts not on. Sacrifices he offers not. The King in his Chariot rides not.
In royal fashion he legislates not. A place of garrison the
  General (by word of mouth) appoints not.
Medicine for his sickness of body he applies not.
To make a *sacred spot* it is suitable.
In the night in the presence of Merodach and Istar
The king his offering makes. Sacrifices he offers.
Raising his hand the high place of the god he worships.
—*Records of the Past*, vol. 7, pp. 157–170.

—divides the month (lunar) into septenary periods, and ends each period with a day of rest. The day is, in substance, the Sabbath of Moses. It has also the Mosaic name; is called *Sabatu*—"a day of rest for the heart.[1] This historic Sabbath, exhumed by Assyriologists, reaches back to the earliest Assyrians, and beyond them to the Accadians, the eldest blood of earth after the flood. Sabbatic ideas, institutions, and practices are thus historic verities back fairly to Noah.

The "*legendary* tablets" are all very old. The "Genesis Legends"—"the story of beginnings"—are assigned, by that eminent Oriental scholar, George Smith, to two thousand years before Christ; and as copies then, by Assyrian scribes, of still older Accadian documents. This makes them five centuries older than Moses, a century older than Abraham, and still reaching indefinitely beyond.

Their "story of beginnings" is in very fair agreement with the Mosaic narrative. The Accadian Sabbath is essentially the same as the Mosaic Sabbath; and the "Genesis Legends" trace the institution to the divine appointment.

---

[1] BABYLONIAN ASTRONOMICAL TABLET, compiled for Sargon, King of Agane, in the sixteenth century before Christ. "The moon a rest—on the 7th day, the 14th day, the 21st day, the 28th day—causes."—*Trans. of So. of Archæ.*, vol. 3, p. 145.

"The very word Sabatu, or Sabbath, was used by the Assyrians, and a bilingual tablet explains it as a day of rest for the heart."—*The Chal. Ac. of Crea.* GEO. SMITH, p. 308.

"The Sabbath was known to the Babylonians and Assyrians . . . Like the Hebrew Sabbath it was observed every seventh day.—*Hibbert Lectures*, 1887. SAYCE, 82.

"Its recurrence every seventh day—its character, 'a day of rest for the heart'—its very name '*Sabatu*'—are given in a way which leaves but little to be desired, when taken in connection with other testimony, so abundant in our hands from other sources."—*The Primitive Sabbath Restored by Christ.*

"The week of seven days was in use from an early period, indeed, the names which we still give to the days can be traced to ancient Babylonia; and the seventh day was one of *sulum*, or rest."—*Encycl. Brit.*, Art. Babylonia.

Thus the Mosaic and the Cuneiform records agree as to the origin and import of the Sabbath, and as to its high antiquity.[1]

Proofs, in abridged form, of an ancient Sabbath—a patriarchal Sabbath—an ante-diluvian Sabbath—are now before the reader. The proofs, now dim and shadowy, anon plain and luminous, are gathered from the remains of the earliest peoples, as far back as the lights of beginning histories take us. They had the septenary number, an associate Sabbatic idea, appearing everywhere in the grey mists of antiquity. They had the weekly period, also an associate Sabbatic idea, and an incontestable monument of history at its very sources. They had worship, and an appointed day for worship. They had the Sabbath itself; Hebrews had; Babylonians and Assyrians had; and Accadians, their remotest known predecessors, had. They had its name. They had its very substance. They were Sabbath keepers. And the primal human Sabbath was a fair copy of God's creation Sabbath. An ancient Sabbath, in presence of Assyrian and Accadian records supplementing the Mosaic records, ceases to be debatable ground. It is a verity to the uttermost line of historic vision—and of legendary vision. Exact history,

---

[1] The fifth tablet is much mutilated. The first part alone remains perfect. The following is an extract:

"He constructed dwellings for the great gods.
He fixed up constellations, whose figures were like animals.
He made the year. Into four quarters he divided it.
Twelve months he established, with their constellations, three and three,
And for the days of the year he appointed festivals.
 . . . .
In the center he placed luminaries.
The moon he appointed to rule the night,
And to wander through the night until the dawn of day.
Every month without fail he made holy assembly days.
In the beginning of the month, at the rising of the night,
It shot forth its horns to illuminate the heavens.
*On the seventh day he appointed a holy day,
And to cease from all work he commanded.*
—*Records of the Past,* vol. 9, p. 117.

with legendary supplements, proclaims and verifies the institution as existing from the beginning.

Some Conclusions Follow.

Sabbatism, with its weekly period, is traced by some thinkers, to lunar changes, because found in association with such changes in Babylonia. The theory is incredible—bristles with impossibilities. New moon attracts notice; full moon also; but not the quarters; they are vague and inconspicuous. Moon phases might therefore suggest a dual but hardly a quaternion division of the lunar month. Then the seven-day week is not an aliquot part of the lunar month; is not an exact fourth; is less than a fourth. The moon's phases are not exact seven-day cycles. How could they give birth to such cycles?[1] If the week with its Sabbatism was born of lunar changes, it would not only have been universal in beginning histories, as it was;

---

[1] "The unfitness of the week as an astronomical measure of time."—PROCTOR. *The Great Pyramid*, 240.

"The ancient Hebrews, who had the week and the Sabbath long before they had any acquaintance with the planetary science of the Babylonian priests."—*Cycl. Brit.*, Art. Sabbath.

"The week. * * * As it forms neither an aliquot part of the year nor of the lunar month, those who reject the Mosaic recital will be at a loss, as Delambro remarks, to assign to it an origin having much semblance of probability."—*Cycl. Brit.*, Art. Calendar.

"That the week should be conditioned by the planets seems barely credible. It was not until after the people had got the seven days, that they began to call them after the seven planets. The number seven is the only bond of connection between them. Doubtless the week is older than the names of the days."—WELLHAUSEN. *History of Israel*, 113. *Edinburg*, 1885.

"As the Sabbath corresponds with no cycle or natural division of time, it must have been impossible for any man, or number of men, to single out one day and set it apart authoritatively. Man could neither have decided rightly the proportion of time to be set apart, nor have guarded the sanctity of the day by penalties. If the division of time into weeks were wholly unknown, it would be impossible that it should be introduced by man."—*Butler's Bible Work*, Gen. 2: 1-6.

but it would have remained in all history, as it has not; and it would not have disappeared in *nundinæ* and *decades*, as it widely did. The association of the week with lunar changes was the later and corrupt, not the earlier and purer record. Mosaic Sabbatism has no society whatever with lunar changes. The oracles of the Hebrews always ascribe the institution to God. The Accadian "legendary" Sabbath also appears as a divine appointment. The fifth "Creation Tablet" says:

"On the seventh day he appointed a holy day;
And to cease from all work he commanded." [1]

Such testimonies are final. History and legendary lore alike declare, from the most distant witness box, that the week originated from religious, not from astronomical influences; that the Sabbath was born of God, not of the moon. It is really wild, unhistorical, unphilosophical to trace the institution to lunar changes. The earliest known histories and legends name the World-Maker, not the moon, as its author. They report the seventh-day used as sacred time from the very beginning, and so authenticate its divine origin.

Sabbatism, with its weekly period, is regarded by other thinkers as a human contrivance. The assumption is without reason, even as it is in violent conflict with history and legendary lore. The Sabbath, so proverbial among the earliest peoples—a primitive and universal institution—could not be of man. It is such an institution as the best man could not make, if he would; and as the worst man would not make, if he could. The weekly period of six

---

[1] "The last lines of the fifth tablet are intensely interesting, as containing probably the oldest monumental evidence of the institution of the Sabbath, and that, too, almost in the very words of Genesis. It is here affirmed, moreover, that the institution of the Sabbath was coeval with the creation. We find the same fact mentioned on other cuneiform inscriptions."—PROF. J. L. PORTER. *The Prince. Rev.*, July, 1878, p. 10.

work days and one rest day—without any exact archetype in nature—was not possible to human invention. To determine originally the due proportion that work should have to rest was above his wisdom; and to fit holy time into the framework of society above his power. He has not the genius to frame, nor the authority to appoint, a natural, universal, and unchangeable institution, such as the Sabbath is. The institution is not of man.[1] It is of divine order and appointment. It stands in history and legend, not as a human discovery, but as a revelation from God himself. It is not possible in reason to think otherwise of the weekly day of hallowed rest, that is incorporated in our very nature, and enters into the World-Maker's plan of the universe.

Sabbatism is not an evolution, like written language, like science, like art. It is not an unfolding from the simple to the complex, from the lower to the higher and better,[2] like a growth from seed or bulb to plant, and flower, and fruit. The world has not reached its Sabbatism by steps. The institution rises up at once—starts off immediately. It stands out in complete form at the very sources of history; appearing there at its very best; as perfect as it is to-day. It is as full-featured in the Cosmogony as in the

---

[1] "Many vain conjectures have been formed concerning the reasons and motives which determined all mankind to agree to this primitive division of their time. Nothing but tradition, concerning the time employed in the creation of the world could give rise to this universal, immemorial practice."—PRESIDENT DE GOGUET. *The Origin of Laws* (1761), vol. 1, p. 230.

"The gods, pitying the laborious race of men, have ordained for it remission from labor, the return of feast days, in honor of the gods."—PLATO. *De. Leg.*, 2: 1.

[2] "The alternation of working and resting days appeared, even to the ancients, as something so primeval in its origin, so indispensable, and so closely connected with religion, that they perceived in it, not an innovation of human cleverness, but a divine ordinance."—PROF. ERNST CURTIUS. *Alterthum and Gegenwert*, Berlin, 1875, p. 148.

Legislation of the Hebrew—in the Cosmogony as in the Legislation of the Accadian. It is not an Evolution but a Revelation. It is a divine Mercury springing full-grown from the head and brain of our divine Jupiter. Its perfection in the beginning and always makes it, like the Ancient of days, "the same yesterday, to-day, and forever"—makes it God-born.

The great temple of our world, reared, roofed, and complete, was at last peopled with its intelligent Worker and Worshiper. Sabbatism sprang from God—from his example—from his appointment—establishing a septenary rest day for all time. The Sabbath of God gave birth to the Sabbath of man. Out of the Creator's rest and appointment has sprung all the Sabbatism in the world. Thinkers, in whose creed God, the Creator, gave to newly-formed man no instruction as to how he should live, deal unnaturally with the question. They make him an unnatural father. The Bible, whose God walks in Eden, communes with the primal man and woman, instructs them, and appoints them duties, is a better teacher. The "Genesis Legends" of Accad, whose World-maker addresses his late-born creatures, teaches them duties and privileges, and points out the glory of their state, are a better teacher. This was fitting and natural. The highest reason—the reason of the heart—endorses it. God was man's first teacher, and the law for holy time must have been one of his themes and appointments. His creation Sabbath would not be kept secret. It would be part of the creation narrative rehearsed by divine lips to the first man. It must have been so. There must have been some unfolding of the divine plan. Otherwise the institution of six days work and one day rest—impossible to human invention—never would have appeared in human history. But it is in history—history the most ancient—history at its very fountains. The institution was therefore God-proclaimed as well as God-born. It was revealed to Adam. It was commanded to be kept. It wears upon its face in history such primal celestial credentials. A primeval revelation, announcing the truth to the first man, made it the property of all early men.[1]

From Eden—from the era of primeval innocency—issued two hallowed institutions, surviving the wreckage of the Fall and all the wastes of Time. They are Sabbatism and Marriage; unchanged and changeless divine appointments; meeting deep and abiding human needs. They rival and parallel each other in the good they do. One builds the home; the other the church; both society. Neither can be abrogated without involving human affairs in social and moral disorder.

Near the gates of Eden—within and without—are glimpses of that divine trinity of social regenerators: the Day, the Word, and the Temple; or the Sabbath, the Bible, and the Church. Eden had the Sabbath: its bowers heard the first Word of Promise: and, immediately outside its gates, appears the Tent of Meeting—Cain and Abel building its altar, and offering sacrifice. These have been steadier lights in the world than any

---

[1] "In the state of innocence, God gave the law of the Sabbath."—McClintock & Strong. *Cycl.*, Art. Law.

"The antiquity of the division of time into weeks is so great, its observance so widespread, and it occupies so important a place in sacred things, that it has been very generally dated from the creation of man, who was told from the very first to divide his time on the model of the Creator's order of working and resting. The week and the Sabbath are, if this be so, as old as man himself; and we need not seek for reasons, either in the human mind, or the facts with which that mind comes in contact, for the adoption of such a division of time, since it is to be referred neither to man's thoughts, nor to man's will. A purely theological ground is thus established for the week, and for the sacredness of the seventh day."—*Smith's Dict. of Bible*, Art. Week.

incandescent torches lighted from the King of Day. To the more than orphaned exiles from Eden, it was no light alleviation of their lot to have labor—an entailment of sin—suspended one day in seven; to have the Word of Promise overarching their sky as a rainbow of hope; and to have the Tent of Meeting, with its altar and sacrifice, as a help and means of return to God. With such divine equipments, mankind, fallen, began its mighty march along the shores of Time and History.

SABBATH OF THE DECALOGUE.

> "The cheerful Sabbath bells, wherever heard,
> Strike pleasant on the sense, most like the voice
> Of one who from the far off hills proclaims
> Tidings of good to Zion."—CHARLES LAMB.

The Sabbath, born of the divine example and appointment at creation, known and observed in the ancient world, was re-enacted by express law at Sinai. Its text, as written by the finger of God on one of the two tables of stone given to Moses, stood then and will forever stand in words of which these are a fair translation:

Remember the Sabbath day to keep it holy. Six days shalt thou labor and do all thy work; but the seventh day is the Sabbath of the Lord thy God; in it thou shalt not do any work, thou, nor thy son, nor thy daughter, thy man servant, nor thy maid servant, nor thy cattle, nor thy stranger that is within thy gates; for in six days the Lord made heaven and earth, the sea, and all that in them is, and rested the seventh day; Wherefore the Lord blessed the Sabbath day and hallowed it."—Ex. 20: 8–11.

The Creation Sabbath is the day on its God-ward side; the Fourth Commandment Sabbath, the day on its man-ward side. The Sabbath for man is the exact counterpart of the Sabbath for God; Godward it is appointed; manward it is to be observed. The Fourth Commandment gives a graphic view—a pictorial illustration—of man in his relation to the Sabbath. I seek to know and to make known the Sabbath portrait that it paints of man.

A REST DAY; NO WORK.

The Commandment forbids Sabbath *work*. "In it thou shalt not do any work." The work prohibited is "*thy* work"—not divine work—not humane work—not works of necessity and mercy.[1] It is secularities that are

---

[1] "You do not, however, consider the law of the Sabbath; they are human works, not divine, which it prohibits."—TERTULLIAN, *Against Marcion*, 21. *Ante-Nicene Fathers*, 3: 313.

forbidden. Worldly business, worldly cares, worldly pleasures are all to be laid aside. The pulse of industry is to be stilled; the ships and railway trains of commerce are to be anchored and stationed; the marts of trade are to be closed; and the toil life of man and beast is to cease. The Sabbath is God's antidote in breaking the curse of ceaseless labor. It is a God-given heritage to toiling man. Listen to the Sabbath bells! They forever ring out: "No work! no work! no work!" They confront the traffic and travel that whirl through the day, and still ring on: "No work! no work! no work!"

The Commandment prescribes Sabbath *rest*. Man is to rest. Rest is of the very substance of Sabbatism. The word Sabbath means rest. A Sabbath day means a rest day.[1] Now the Creation-Worker, in making rest periods for man, shows his care of the human worker. Ceaseless toil—"labor in the treadmill of an eternal round, the hands and feet forever on the go, the brow forever sweating, the loins forever aching"—would fill the world with weariness and sadness. A Sabbathless world! What a world it would be of wails and moans! What a sunless world! But rest periods for man are God's appointment, and enforced by the divine example. Human life is not

---

[1] A Sabbath-keeper, meeting a neighbor hauling a load of hay on a Sabbath day, suddenly called out: "There, there! It's broke! You've run right over it." "Run over what?" gasped the neighbor stopping his team in alarm. "The Sabbath" was the reply. "You've run over God's Fourth Commandment, and broken it all to pieces."

Years ago, in a Midland County, in Old England, an orphan boy, a church goer, worked in a factory where he earned five shillings ($1.25) a week. The overseer of the factory ordered him to work on Sabbath. James went to church. Next morning the overseer said: "Where were you yesterday?" "I went to church, sir." "Then you may go to church again to-day," said the overseer, and paid him his wages. James immediately sought work in other factories. A merchant heard of his dismissal, and its cause, and engaged him, at increased wages, in his stores where he rose to wealth by his correct and steady habits.

meant to be all toil. Pauses from secularities are divinely arranged for all worn and weary ones. The Sabbath, with trailing garments of light, brings rest and refreshment. O, if all tired people would but let themselves know the sweetness of real Sabbath rest; business toils and ventures put aside; sordid cares and perplexities barred out; and fellowship with pure thoughts invited! This is divine Sabbatism. This is restful.

The prohibition of work, and the Commandment to rest, in holy time, are broad and sweeping. They relate to thee, O man, to thy son, to thy daughter, to thy manservant, to thy maid-servant, to thy guest, and to thy cattle.[1] Does God care for cattle? Yes. He mentions them with tenderness, and provides rest periods for them in his Sabbath law. In all this I am only a reporter and interpreter of divine words. If the Fourth Commandment means anything at all, it means that all secular work is forbidden to man and beast in holy time; and that to do it then is sin. The day is not for common uses —for personal gains and ambitions. Secularities, because an invasion of the day and an assault upon the Sabbath-maker, are all placed under ban. To work is sin. To rest is duty.

SIX DAYS WORK AND ONE DAY REST.

The Commandment prescribes *six days* work. "Six days shall thou labor and do all thy work." Thus six days out of seven are set apart and given to man for his own uses—for secularities—for business pursuits and pleasures. Man, after God's example, is required to work as well as rest. He is to work six days in seven. Work six

---

[1] "It was designed to prevent the emancipated Israelites from practising the hard and bitter lessons they had learned as slaves, on those who should afterwards serve them."—Bishop H. W. WARREN, *in Sabbath Essays.*

days out of seven is the divine appointment and a human duty. This is the Commandment. All idlers, sluggards, do-nothings, during this work-period are breakers of the Sabbath law.[1]

The Commandment also prescribes a *seventh day* rest. Rest, one day in seven, is the divine appointment and a human duty. A seventh of our time is reserved by the Divine Giver of all time. "The seventh day is the Sabbath of the Lord thy God." It is his—his day—his institution—his property; even as the altar is his, or as the Church is his, or as I am his.[2] He has set it apart for himself; to be his day, not man's; to be used for rest, not for secularities. It is to be employed, not according to our inclinations, but according to his directions. Heaven's boon to the six days' worker is this seventh day rest. Blessed day! Divine gift to toil doomed man! This is the patrimony of every man. He has a God-given right to a seventh day rest. Resting one day in seven meets the

---

[1] The rich who do no work—idle time away—are breakers of the Sabbath law, even as the poor who will not work six days in seven. An employer dismissed a workman, telling him that it was because he broke the Fourth Commandment. The workman denied, and said he always rested on the Sabbath. "Repeat the Commandment," said the employer. "Remember the Sabbath day to keep it holy," said the workman, and stopped. "Go on," said the employer. He would not. "Then I must do it for you," said the employer: "Six days shalt thou labor and do all thy work." That's the part I complain of. You rest readily enough on the Sabbath; but you don't work faithfully on the other six days."

[2] "Did you ever hear of the meanest of pickpockets? A man, who had but seven dollars, gave him, in his apparent poverty, six of them; and he, watching his opportunity, picked his benefactor's pocket of the seventh. Sabbath-breaker, thou art the man. God has given you six days for your own interests, to speak your own words, and go your own ways, and think your own thoughts; and then you have turned about and robbed him of the seventh. But not only that, *you have robbed yourself*, your body, and mind, and pocket, as well as your soul."—*Sab. for Man*, pp. 215–16.

requirements of Sabbatic law, and nothing less does. All Sabbath workers are breakers of the Commandment.

The divine frame is complete in six work days and one rest day; and this divine method for working and resting is the model for human working and resting. Human life so spent is in harmony with the life of God.[1] Man, a pilgrim, moves in toilsome marches from the cradle to the grave. Six days' journeying brings him weariness, but also brings him to a divinely arranged Sabbath arbor, where he may find rest and refreshment. Freshened forces equip him for other toilsome effort. Journeying and resting are both God's appointment; the journeying as much as the resting; and the resting as much as the journeying. The Commandment enforces equally six days' work and a seventh day rest. The divine example imparts a tenderness to the whole duty. God created and then rested. In the domain of morals, example teaching is supreme; higher than precept; superior to express law. "Actions speak louder than words." God's example, as a World-Maker and as a Sabbath-Keeper, appoints six days' work and a seventh day rest to man. Man, in all his generations, is

---

[1] "Six days' work and the seventh day's rest conform the life of man to the method of his Creator. In distributing his life thus, man may look up to God as his Archetype."--FRANCIS GARDEN, *in* SMITH's *Dict. of the Bible*, p. 2761.

"What statesman could have first discovered that in ordinary time the period of labor ought to be to the period of rest as six to one? Moses, then, having to regulate the labors and the days, the rests and the festivals, the toils of the body and the exercises of the soul, the interests of hygiene and of morals, political economy and personal subsistence, had recourse to a science of numbers, to a transcendent harmony which embraced all space, duration, movement, spirits, bodies, the sacred and the profane. The certainty of the series is demonstrated by the result. Diminish the week by a single day, the labor is insufficient relative to the repose; augment it in the same quantity, it becomes excessive."--PROUDHON, *De la Celebration du Dimanche*, p. 67.

required to mirror forth in himself the Creator's work periods and his rest period.[1]

A Holy Day.

The Commandment prescribes that the rest day shall be kept *holy*. "Keep it holy." Every day is holy, but the Sabbath holiest of all. As Horeb was holy to the feet of Moses, because of God's presence in the burning bush; as the inner sanctuary was holiest of all because of its indwelling Shekinah; so the Sabbath is holy because it is a day of special divine manifestations by the self-revealing God. It is consecrated *time*, even as the Mount of Transfiguration was to Peter consecrated *ground*. It soars above the mere commonplaces of every-day life, and is marked off from other days even as the Tabernacle was marked off from all the tents of Israel.[2]

Man's hallowed rest, like God's, is not to be a cessation from activity, but a change of activity; not a cessation from work, but a change of work. Holy rest is not inaction—idling—loafing—sleeping away sacred time. This is the Sabbath of a brute, not of a man. The day is not only separated from common but set apart to sacred uses. It requires worship as well as rest—divine work in the way of meditation and devotion. It demands from all,

---

[1] "We are to account the sanctification of one day in seven a duty which God's immutable law doth exact forever."—HOOKER.

"There is no middle ground between keeping the Sabbath holy unto God and its utter licentiousness. Compromise is treason. Surrender is cowardice. To fight for the right is heroism."—DR. J. O. PECK, *Sabbath Essays*.

[2] "If the day is at all holy time, it is *all* holy time. Compromise to-day of half the Sabbath means the capture of the whole to-morrow. The only way we can defend the citadel is to fight for the whole of it." DR. J. O. PECK, in *Six Days Shalt Thou Labor*.

"The Decalogue .... is a law exclusively religious and moral, which only twines itself about the duties of man to God, and to his fellow-creatures."—GUIZOT, *Medita. on the Essence of Christ.*, 218.

not only a sacred pause from the humdrum of ordinary toil, but its employment in spiritual thoughts and holy pursuits. Sacred meditations, free from secularities, are its suitable furniture and befitting deeds. This sanctification of the day is enforced on a higher plane than that of mere expediency, or because it is a law of the land. It is a duty which God's immutable law exacts from every one. Neglected Sabbaths imperil both soul and body. He who made the world and us gave us the Sabbath and the law that should govern its use; and he bids us keep it holy.[1]

A Blessed Day.

The Commandment appoints the Sabbath to be a *blessed* day. "The Lord blessed the Sabbath day."[2] He makes

---

[1] "Come on Sunday," said an elderly gentleman to little six year old Bob; "for I am at home all day, and want to see you."

"Why," said Bob; "do you really stay at home all day on Sunday?"

"Yes," said the elderly man; "don't you?"

"No, indeed; I go to church and Sunday-school; and so does papa. It is wicked not to go to church, if you are well."

It was a little word—a little seed thought. It did its work. The elderly gentleman became a steady church-goer.

[2] "I feel as if God had, by the Sabbath, given fifty-two springs in the year."—COLERIDGE.

"In the ring and circle of the week, the Sabbath is the jewel, the most excellent and precious of days."—BISHOP HEZEKIAH HOPKINS.

"Sunday is the golden clasp
That binds the volume of the week."—LONGFELLOW.

"Through the week we go down into the valley of care and shadows: our Sabbaths should be hills of light and joy in God's presence."—HENRY WARD BEECHER.

"A blessed Sabbath! The ladder set up on earth whose top reaches to heaven, with angels of God ascending and descending on it."—REV. JAS. HAMILTON, D. D.

"O day most sweet, most calm, most bright,
The bridal of the Earth and Sky."—HERBERT.

"This is the day which the Lord hath made; we will rejoice and be glad therein."—Ps. 118: 24.

"O what a blessed day is the Sabbath, which allows us a precious interval wherein to pause, to come out of the thickets of worldly concerns, and give ourselves up to heavenly and spiritual things."—WILBERFORCE.

it overtop other days, even as Saul and Jonathan overtopped by the head and shoulders the men of Israel in their times. He freights the day with special blessings, even as the Virgin Mary is blessed above women. This divine endowment makes the day satisfy deep human needs, and minister grace and help to all Sabbath keepers. Holy-day is a season not of stern privation, but of special privilege; not of restricted liberty, but of recreation and happiness. It is our best day; the jubilee of man; a cooling and refreshing spring to the traveler through the desert; the brightest page in the volume of the week. It conducts us among the wells and palm trees of sacred rest.

The World-maker, O man, employs his Sabbath in blessing others—the living forms that he keeps pulsing in life—man whom he has redeemed and is seeking to save. So thy Sabbath should be made a blessing to thy neighbor. To do good—to give help to the needy—to do works of necessity and mercy—is of the very essence of Sabbath keeping. What can fairly be done on Saturday, or deferred till Monday, is indeed no work of necessity; as social visits; journeyings begun or ended to save time; or reading secular newspapers. But all well-doing, lying in the realm of essential right, or of human need, is not merely permissible but obligatory in sacred as in secular time. Even secularities, employed for divine purposes, not for personal ends, are suitable Sabbath deeds. So keeping the day never hurts, but helps and blesses, the individual—the community—the nation.

Arguments and Conclusions.

The travesties of genius and learning seem inscrutable. Some scholars have held that the Decalogue, others that the Fourth Commandment, including in each case the

Sabbath, is for the Jew alone. Is the Old Testament—is the Messiah—for the Jew alone? Why then the imperishable Decalogue? Or the equally imperishable Sabbath? This is the pivotal point of a long contention—an extended battle—among the reformers. It is a very Gibraltar of unreasoning prejudice. Its advocates climb no Sinai, nor even camp at its base. Theirs is but the logic of doubt. It had its little hour. It created a ripple on the surface of thought. It has drawn its last gasp. Its warriors have all trooped by. The restatement of the Sabbath, as revised by accumulating evidence, has routed them "horse, foot, and dragoons."

The Sabbath is not a Judaic ordinance in any sense in which it is not an ordinance for man as man. The Fourth Commandment, as already seen, forbids such an idea, by beginning with the word "remember."[1] It calls on Israel to keep in mind an old commandment which had been in the world from the beginning. It was not the first promulgation of the Sabbath law. It was but a re-enactment of an older institution; an institution coeval with man in Eden; an institution dating back to God's Creation Sabbath. It recognizes, republishes, and enforces the Sabbath, but did not originate it. It did not invent it. It merely discovered it in the world, and put it anew under the form of express law. The Sabbath came to the Jews from the ages before. Septenary holy time belonged to the first man, and will be the property and privilege of his latest

---

[1] "The law of the Sabbath is universal, and not peculiar to the Jews."—WATSON. *Institutes*, 2 : 520.

"The form of the Fourth Commandment—'*Remember* the Sabbath day'—points not to the ordaining of a new day, but the sanctioning of an old one."—FRANCIS BROWN. *Pres. Rev.*, Oct. 1882, p. 686.

"'Remember the Sabbath day'—implying it was already known and recognized as a season of rest."—JAMIESON-FAUSSET-BROWN. *Com* Ex. 20 : 8-11.

descendant. It is of world-wide authority and obligation.[1]

The Creation Sabbath and the Decalogue Sabbath are one. They have the very same elements; a *rest* day; a *seventh-day* rest; a *holy* rest; and a *blessed* rest. This is the very substance of the Sabbath of God and the Sabbath for man—of the Creation Sabbath and the Decalogue Sabbath. The Sabbath of the Decalogue is a unit with all preceding Sabbatism; with the Sabbath of creation; with the Sabbath of the ancient world; is a copy of it and its continuation; is its re-enactment in the form of express law. It is impossible then in fairness to regard the Decalogue Sabbath as a mere Jewish institution—as a Jewish institution in any sense in which it is not also an institution for man as man. There ain't a Judaism in it, or a Judaic form about it. It is wider, and greater, and more durable than any mere Jewish law. It has not a word peculiar to the Jewish people. It does not start from a Jewish foundation. It antedates Judaism and survives it.[2] If the Jew needs a seventh-day for rest and worship, so does man everywhere and in all time. The Decalogue Sabbath has this air of wideness and perpetuity. Within the plan and

---

[1] "God gave the Sabbath, *his first ordinance*, to man while he stood the father and representive of the whole human race; therefore the Sabbath is not for one nation, for one time, for one place."—DR. ADAM CLARKE.

"If the divine command was actually delivered at the creation, it was addressed, no doubt, to the whole human species alike, and continues, unless repealed by some subsequent revelation, binding upon all who come to the knowledge of it. This opinion precludes all debate about the extent of the obligation."—PALEY's *Mor. Phi. Book* 4, *Chap.* 7.

[2] "We do not owe the Sabbath to the Jew; we received it from God. It was thundered indeed from Sinai to the Jew, but it was whispered to us from Paradise, when the heavens and the earth were finished, and God blessed the day of rest."—H. J. BROWN.

"Whether or not the Sinaitic Sabbath was ordained for Gentile as well as Jew, the original rest-day was made for the human race."—PROF. J. T. TUCKER, *in Sabbath Essays*.

ordering of God, it is not for a single period, or for a single people, but for time and man. These are its divine boundaries.

The Fourth Commandment is part and parcel of that wonderful epitome of moral law—that complete summary of human duty—the Decalogue—that was given, not merely to the Jew, but to man as man. It was written by the finger of God on the same tables of stone on which were traced the sublime precepts, forbidding image worship, profanity, and covetous desires; commanding children to honor their parents; and making it the duty of every one to hold sacred the life, the chastity, the reputation, and the property of others.[1] The Sabbath, thus appointed, and in such society, must be as universal, as permanent, and as binding, as those other great and imperishable principles, that, interpenetrative like the air, and surviving all change, appear everywhere in the civil and religious laws of society. "*Noscitur a sociis*"—it is known by its allies. It is in excellent company. As its associates are, so is it. As they are binding upon all men, everywhere and for all

---

[1] In 1858 a Sunday school worker was, on Sunday morning, on a ferry boat going from Brooklyn to New York, to his Sunday school. He noticed a bright-eyed boy on the boat with books under his arm, evidently on the way to Sunday school. He thought he would test the boy, and asked him if he would go with him to Harlem, a pleasure resort.

"Sir," said the lad, "did you never read the commandments?"

"The Commandments! what are they?" said the gentleman.

"Well, sir, there is one which says, 'Remember the Sabbath day to keep it holy.'"

"Well, what of that, my boy, will it not be keeping it holy to go to Harlem?"

"No, sir; and I shall not go with you."

After farther testing the lad, with an offer of twenty-five cents if he would go, and meeting with refusal, the gentleman made known his real character, and found means to help the lad—a son of intemperate parents—in life.

time, so is it. It, even as they, is not ceremonial, but moral. It, like they, is of universal and perpetual obligation—a primitive and unchangeable natural law. The Sabbath has forever and aye all the sanctions of the Decalogue.[1]

The reason assigned in the Fourth Commandment for Sabbath-keeping belongs, not merely to the Jew, but to man as man. That reason is the divine example of six days' work and one day's rest. The divine example establishes duty, not merely for the Jew, but for man as man—for all men in all time. God kept the weekly period of six work days and one rest day; therefore such a period is appointed to man. God rested on the seventh day; therefore man should have a seventh-day rest. Now all this is in the Fourth Commandment, and makes its reason for Sabbath keeping universal and perpetual. It is the example of God that vitalizes the Sabbath; that makes it obligatory upon the Gentile as upon the Jew; that makes it binding upon all. One and all are, at their peril, under obligation to keep a seventh-day rest.[2]

The Ten Commandments, as a code of morals, are adapted to man in all ages, countries, climes, and circum-

---

[1] "There it stands with nothing to differentiate it from the other Commandments. It is as strong as they, or as weak; as transitory, or as enduring. Have they been fulfilled by Jesus? So has it. Has Jesus exhausted the curse following on transgressions of the nine? So has he exhausted the curse due to Sabbath-breaking. Has the Law-fulfiller left the nine to guide the feet and rule the life of his people? So does he leave the law of weekly sacred rest for like ends. It stands between the three which have their faces towards God, and the six which look towards man. As Jehovah's Sabbath, it binds man to God; and as man's Rest Day, it unites him to his fellows."—GRITTON. *Time's Feast, Heaven's Foretaste.*

[2] "The Sabbath was not smuggled into the Calendar of the week by a crafty church, neither is it sustained by designing priests. God established the Sabbath; and the hand that upholds the sun and revolves the seasons, secures the recurrence of the Holy Day."—DR. E. B. WEBB. *The Sabbath.*

stances. They are so perfect, that, like nature itself, there has been given no second edition of them. Science, art, language, has, each, enlarged its boundaries, and is ever modifying its forms of expression. But the Ten Commandments, dating back to distant times, have come across the ages without alteration or improvement; not one new duty added; not one fallen into disuse. They are widely the laws of modern thought and civilization. Time and experience neither annul or improve them. The Ten, though engrossed for the Jews, are laws for all mankind. The Sabbath is one of the Ten; is enshrined in the very heart of the Ten; and has all the high sanctions and obligations that belong to the Ten. It is a universal and imperishable law.

The very atmosphere of the Sabbath, as incorporated in the Decalogue, is suggestive of permanence and universality. It was written, not on parchment, a symbol of the perishable, but on stone, a symbol of the imperishable. It was written, not among the ceremonial and civil laws of the Jews, that had national limitations, but among the moral laws that relate to all people and to all time. And it was preserved as remarkably as it was promulgated; among associated moral laws; in an ark prepared by special directions of God; and in the Holy of holies that shrined and guarded the most sacred things. I stand in profound reverence before the Decalogue Sabbath. Its majesty overwhelms me. Its high divinity commands my fealty and obedience. It is God, the High and Holy One, who here gives express charge to all men everywhere, to work six days, and then rest one day. This Sabbath law is authoritative over individuals, corporations and communities. Sabbath keeping is duty; Sabbath breaking sin. And the Sabbath-maker, O man, seated upon the circle of the heavens, keeps a forever watch and guard over his own day—over its keeping—and over its desecration.[1]

---

[1] "A father said to his son, who was a Sunday school scholar, "carry this package to——place."

"It is Sabbath," replied the boy.

"Put it in your pocket," said the father.

"God can see in my pocket," was the instant reply.

A little Sunday school girl, for repeating well from memory the Twenty-third Psalm, was presented, by a visitor, with a dime. Her father was present and said:

"A great many shops are open, though it is God's day. You must not go into them to spend the dime to-day; but keep it for to-morrow. Now I won't be with you to see you, but there is One who will see you if you break the Sabbath. Who will see you?"

"Myself will see me," was her reply.

It was expected she would say, "God will see me." Her addition to this Scriptural idea is good. We are witnesses of all our doings.

SABBATISM OF GENTILE NATIONS.

> "The Golden Age was first, when man, yet new,
> No rule but uncorrupted reason knew,
> And, with a native bent, did good pursue.
> * * * * * * *
> Succeeding times a silver age beheld.
> * * * * * * *
> To this came next in course the brazen age.
> * * * * * * *
> Hard steel succeeded then,
> And stubborn as the metal were the men."—OVID.

From Abraham to the close of the Old Testament, seventh day Sabbatism, among Gentile nations, changed for the worse—suffered decay—fell into disuse. The ancient divine forms in which it tabernacled—the weekly cycle—the seventh of days—and which stand out clearly in the morning sky overarching post-diluvian man, were slowly but steadily obscured and mutilated. They grew corrupt; and, at last, nothing of Sabbatism remained among Gentile peoples but multitudinous effigies. The reason for this decadence of the institution is plain.[1] Mere tradition, that opens not but shuts all the gates of progress, is insufficient to preserve and perpetuate the purer ideas, and institutions. Change comes, but not in the way of improvement, always in the direction of degeneracy—of decay. It was so with the ancient divine Sabbath; historic with Moses and Abraham; historic with Babylonians, Assyrians, and Accadians. It appears in

---

[1] Pres. Seelye traces to "an inherent law of deterioration" the Sabbath declension now going on among us. And says: "It only represents a universal tendency among men. Singular as it may seem, the fact is clear that human nature is far more active in throwing away its privileges than in preserving them."—*The Princeton Review*, Nov., 1880, p. 338.

later times entangled with the astronomic element; its weekly cycle merging into other periods; its holy day into holidays; its blessed rest and devotion into sensual and corrupting rites; and, in cases, it entirely disappears.

Silent spaces in distant history, so brief and fragmentary, are as clouds upon the scene, under which the light that we seek disappears. They are as great gaps that make the steps of Sabbath change and decay indistinguishable. But the fact of change for the worse remains.[1] The marchings of early nations, unguided by a special divine revelation, took everywhere routes of deterioration. When the Old Testament ended—or when the Babylonian captivity ended—Gentile nations had no weekly period, no seventh day Sabbath, no regularly recurring holy and blessed rest day. These institutions do not anywhere fairly appear among them in that far away period. All Gentile nations, indeed, by the movings of tired and restless human nature, devised some poor substitutes for the week and its Sabbatism, as *nundinæ, decades,* and annual *festal* days.[2] But the week dropped out of their history. A seventh of days ceased to

---

[1] Historic silences are stumbling blocks to ignorance, and have many misinterpretations. They abound in the oldest and fragmentary records of the Bible. The law of sacrifice must have been instituted before Cain and Abel made their offering; and yet the Bible is silent as to its institution; and it is not mentioned again till after the Flood. The distinction between clean and unclean animals was known to Noah; but its origin is nowhere reported. From Moses to Jeremiah there is no allusion to circumcision. And there is no mention of the Sabbath from Moses to David. Bossuet, in his universal history, does not, it is said, mention the Sabbath. Arguments from historic silences are uncertain. Silent spaces in history hide the steps of Sabbath decay; and they can only be seen by comparing the later with the earlier records.

[2] "That the heathen, nevertheless, from time immemorial, have known certain festive periods, appears from their mythological systems."—*Lange's Comment. on Gen.* p. 192.

be kept for hallowed rest. Sabbatism was dead. The proofs of this are fairly complete and satisfactory.

The researches of science point to the highlands of Armenia, breaking away into the valleys of the Tigris and the Euphrates, as the primitive seats of post-diluvian man—of Accadians, Assyrians, Babylonians. There Babel, "the temple of the Seven Spheres," arose. There human speech was confused. Thence mankind scattered, to people the earth as races and nations. Those first men were all Sabbatarians. They knew the weekly period. The historic and legendary week and Sabbath are inscribed in their resurrected clay tablets. But their primitive beliefs and customs were changed. The Sabbath and the week do not appear among later occupants of those primal seats of civilization. At the time of the Babylonian captivity, they were clearly not Sabbatarians; they did not have the week. For they mocked at the Sabbaths of the captive Jews. They antagonized Jewish *customs* and *laws*, chief of which was the Sabbath. And they were in the habit of selecting Sabbath days for attacking the Jews in battle.[1] These historic facts report them Sabbathless. Their

---

[1] "The anti-Sabbatic spirit comes out subsequently in the conduct of the Babylonian 'adversaries of Jerusalem,' who not only 'mocked at her Sabbaths,' but compelled her people to labor without any rest."—Lam. 1: 7; 5: 5. GILFILLAN. *The Sabbath*, 2.

"Babylonians and Jews were almost always at variance, by reason of the contrariety of their laws."—JOSEPHUS. *Antiq.*, 18: 9: 8.

"Mithridates (Babylonian and Parthian Commander) . . intending to fight them on the day following, because it was the Sabbath, the day on which the Jews rest."—JOSEPHUS. *Antiq.*, 18: 9: 6. See also 18: 9: 2.

"It is practically certain that the Babylonians at the time of the Hebrew exile cannot have had a Sabbath exactly corresponding in conception to what the Hebrew Sabbath had become."—*Cycl. Brit.*, Art. Sabbath.

"We have no evidence of the establishment of set festivals in Assyria. Apparently the monarchs decided of their own will when a feast should be held to any god."—RAWLINSON. *Seven Great Monarchies*, 1: 365.

Sabbath and week were in ruins; entombed in buried "Record Chambers." It is fair history that, in those ancient seats of life where Moses locates the first kingdom, and where Berosus regarded a Chaldean monarchy as existing two thousand years before Christ, they had ceased from keeping the seventh-day Sabbath. Syrians were Sabbathless. Historic Persia had no Sabbath. And historic Media had no known Sabbath.[1]

The chronology of ancient Egypt—land of myths and many gods—is much in dispute among critical scholars. The Manetho Dynasties, prior to the Eighteenth, are all uncertain. The Egyptian kingdom, antedating Abraham, a nomad chief, looks very primitive in his day.[2] The Pharoah's wealth is estimated in flocks and herds.[a] The Egyptians seem dwellers in shifting tents; to become later builders along the Nile. It may yet be found that the Nile monuments, all dateless, were built since that known period; that the extreme dates of enthusiastic Egyptologists will have to be abandoned; and that even the more sober

---

[a] Gen. 12: 16.

[1] "Neither was it lawful for a man to keep Sabbath days."—2 Macc., 6: 6.

"Others had run together into caves near by to keep the Sabbath secretly."—2 Macc., 6: 11.

"Her feasts were turned into mourning, her Sabbaths into reproach.'—1 Macc., 1: 39.

"Antiochus had sent letters . . . that they should profane the Sabbath."—1 Macc., 1: 45.

"Made war against them on the Sabbath day."—1 Macc., 2: 32.

"So they rose up against them in battle on the Sabbath."—1 Macc., 2: 38.

"Nicanor . . . resolved without any danger to set upon them on the Sabbath day."—2 Macc., 15: 1.

See also 1 Macc., 1: 43; 2: 34; 2: 41; and 2 Macc., 5: 25-6; 15: 3-4.

[2] "They found a Pharoah on the throne, at the head of an organized government. The Egyptians, however, were a scattered and weak people compared with what they came to be afterwards."—POND. *Con. on the Bible*, 126.

dates of cautious authorities will need toning down. Joseph, it is known, converted the kingdom into a despotism; the people into serfs; and exacted a fifth of all their yearly earnings for the Pharoah. This mighty bondage, never lifted, made possible all the Nile monuments. Later the building instinct appears. Israelites were drudges as brickmakers, and built for Pharoah treasure cities, as Pithom and Rameses. But Egypt, with sensibly reduced dates, will rank, after Chaldea, as the oldest known seat of life, civilization, art. The temples and palaces that, in ruins, still dot the Nile valley, evoke the ghosts of very ancient times. The pyramids, the "books of kings," connect us with the fabulous past—with fabulous learning—with a mystical priesthood. In that most ancient Egypt was veneration for the number seven—was the seven-day cycle—was the week's name *uk*—was the seventh-day rest. These are in the oldest hieroglyphs. Then they disappear. They do not belong to later periods; to the golden age of art and letters; to the Egypt reported by Grecian travelers and writers. The people outgrew their traditional religion. The Pharoah of the Exodus denounced the Hebrews for Sabbatizing. The week disappeared. The Calendar was changed.[1] The decade was enthroned. It is the month of thirty days, divided into three decades, that appears on the monuments.

---

[1] "The old Egyptians had a week of ten not of seven days."—*Cycl. Brit.*, Art. Sabbath.

"The Egyptians, however, were without it (the week), dividing their month of 30 days into decades."—McCLINTOCK & STRONG. *Cycl.*, Art. Chronology.

"The week, consisting of seven days, was unknown to the Egyptians, . . . who had a week of ten days."—SCHRADER. *The Cuneiform Ins., and the Old Test.*, 18.

"The Egyptians . . . divided their solar month into . . . three parts of ten days each. . . . The decade division was a later introduction."—RAWLINSON. *Hist. Herodo.*, 2: 282.

"Wilkenson, (*Manners and Customs of Ancient Egypt*), shows that the week of seven days existed in the earliest times in Egypt, though afterwards superseded by the decade."—*The Sab. for Man*, 527.

From Manetho's Eighteenth Dynasty to the Ptolemaic kingdom—when the Jews were colonized in Alexandria—Egypt had the decade, not the week.

Hindoos and Chinese, derivative but very ancient peoples, possessed, in earlier histories and legends, the seven-day period and an associated Sabbatism. But these institutions do not appear among their later inheritances.[1] The Hindoo literature, a noble monument of an ancient civilization, has had, from the beginning of the Vedic period, no recognized septenary cycle or Sabbatism. And these institutions have also disappeared from Chinese literature and customs, since the fall of the Tscheu Dynasty and the appearance of Confucianism. Somewhere the gates of progress were closed, and the gates of decay opened for the disappearance of their ancient divine institutions.

Prehistoric Greece, a probably still later people, shows but diminished traces of the primal week and Sabbatism. Among the earlier writers, the number seven was widely current and venerated; and suggestions appear of the seventh-day as sacred. But these things cease from special currency, or entirely disappear, in later literature. It is the decade, not the hebdomad—the annual festival, not the seventh-day rest—that reigns in all the historic period—the classic Greek period. When Jews and Greeks, in the fourth century before Christ, began to commingle in history, the Jewish seven-day week and Sabbath became

---

[1] "According to the best authorities, long ages before our era, there existed in China a deep-seated conviction that the idolatry existing was a corruption of a purer faith."—J. L., in *Nation. Repository*, May 1877, p. 453.

"In a work ascribed to Fuh-he, who is supposed to have lived considerably more than four thousand years ago, the following remarkable sentence is to be found:—'Every seven days comes the revolution'—that is, of the heavenly bodies, as generally explained by Chinese scholars; and it is a singular fact, that in the Chinese almanacs of the present day, there are four names applicable, during the course of each lunar month, to the days which answer to our Sundays."—GILLESPIE's *Land of Sinim*, pp. 161-2.

known to the Greeks; and Greek writers, like Polybius, Plutarch, and Strabo, speak of the Sabbath as a new and surprising arrangement.[1]

The ancient Romans, appearing later in history, never had the week or the Sabbath. They divided their month into *Calends, Nones,* and *Ides.* They had *nundinæ*—a nine day period closing with a fair or market day. Annual festal days, when they abstained from business, were many, and were held to be important. Cicero commends them. Seneca applauds the wisdom of their institution. When Jews and Romans began to commingle in history, Roman writers, as Appian, Cicero, Ovid, Horace, and Juvenal, mention the Jewish Sabbath, to doubt its expediency—to oppose it—to satirize it.[2]

This corruption of the seven-day week and of its Sabbatism is part of that mighty downward trend of Pagan nations, after the flood, that is recorded by themselves, and that appears as a descent from a primal Golden Age to an

---

[1] "The Greeks divided the month into three decades, or periods of ten days."—*Encyc. Brit*, Art. Calendar.

"The ancient Greeks.... had no division properly answering to our weeks.... had their decades of days."—ANTHON. *Man. Class. Lit.*, 61.

"Every month was divided into three decades of days."—*A Cat. of Grecian Antiq.*, 79.

"The week, consisting of seven days, was unknown to.... the Greeks who had a week of ten days."—DR. SCHRADER. *The Cuneiform Ins. and the Old Test.*, 18.

[2] "The Roman calendar knows absolutely nothing of a hallowed seventh-day."—*The Inter. Cyc.*, Art. Sabbath.

"The Romans divided their months into three parts, viz.: *Kalends, Nones, and Ides;* and not as we do into weeks in imitation of the Jews."—*Cat. of Rom. Antiq.*, 74,

"The ancient Greeks and Romans had no division properly answering to our weeks; although the former had their decades of days, and the latter their nundinæ, or market days, occurring every ninth day."—ANTHON'S *Man. of Class. Lit.* p. 61.

"The Nundinæ occupied every ninth day and market days."—OVID. *Fast. i,* 54.

age of Silver—to one of Brass—and at last to one of Iron.¹ All primitive peoples had traditions of a Golden Age and of the Fall. The confession of decadence does not come from disappointed characters—from social failures—but from Persian Magi, from Hindoo Sages, from Eminent Greeks and Romans, as Hesiod, Plato, Aratus, and Ovid. It was a farther descent into the wilderness which man's sin had made out of his native Paradise. Nature tends to run wild. A plant, neglected, changes into a worse plant; a garden into weeds; a domestic animal into wild forms. So man, self-neglected, becomes a worse man and a lower man; disuse of functions leading to decay of faculty; unimproved talents taken away. The law is universal. Institutions and customs bow to it. Without the care of eternal vigilance, they drop into other and worse forms—reappear in new shapes—or entirely disappear. This is a historic picture of the seven-day week, and the seventh-day Sabbath, in the ancient Gentile world. Perfect in Eden, distinct and clear among all earlier men, only corrupt forms appear in later times.

Nothing is more certain in ancient history—among the earliest nations—in the earliest seats of mankind—than the universal prevalence, from the Nile to the Ganges, of an exact seven-day week, and the seventh-day Sabbath. This is historically true. But wider dispersions and later histories show steady departures from these ancient historic institutions;. Sabbatism disappearing in multitudinous festal days that Plato traces to the gods; and the exact seven-day week dropping into the inexact astronomical week—into a five-day period in Mexico—into a nine-day period

---

¹ "The Greeks thought there had been four ages—the Golden age, the Silver age, the Brazen age, and the Iron age—and that people had been getting worse in each of them."—*Pictorial Hist. of the Great Nations*, Vol. 1, p. 2.

" On earth of yore the sons of men abode
From evil free and labor's galling load."
HESIOD. *Creation of Pandora.*

in Peru and Rome—and into a ten-day period in Egypt and Greece. At the epoch of five centuries before Christ, all Gentile nations were without the seven-day week, and without the Seventh-day Sabbath. Romans had them not—never had—had *Nundinæ*. Greeks and Egyptians had them not—had lost them—had the *decade*. Hindoos, Chinese, Babylonians, Syrians, Medes and Persians had them not—had lost them—had no reported substitutes. The seven-day week was dead. Seventh-day Sabbatism was dead. The elder glory had disappeared in a vast eclipse.

Thinkers opposed to supernaturalism—rejectors of a special divine revelation—trace the ancient historic Sabbath to human invention, suggested by lunar changes. The theory is visionary, hypothetical, unphilosophical. But it's the very best these high sceptical scholars give us. They do not name the inventor; or suggest when he lived; or where; or tell how he accomplished the mighty work—invented and gave currency to a natural and universal law. They allow themselves to be easily satisfied. But their theory has one grace. It, in a way, lets them out of an insuperable difficulty. Another equal question now confronts them and us. The seven-day week among Gentile nations was dead; could it be revitalized? Seventh-day Sabbatism was dead; could it be given a new life? If a primitive man invented, a later Gentile man could recover, the week and its Sabbath. This would have to be their answer. But it is as faulty as their original theory. Self resurrections are absurdities. Spontaneous generation is an exploded scientific bubble. Living forms do not rise out of the realm of death. Life comes only from antecedent life. A Savior is ever from without; redemption from beyond; the new creature from above. The lost institutions could not grow out of the Gentile world, but must be brought to it. They could not be of human invention, but must be of divine Providence. The mighty gates of history, as they swing open before us, report the plan and steps of recovery. It is not human, but divine; not of man, but of God. Read yet on and see.

SABBATH OF JUDAISM.

(OLD TESTAMENT PERIOD.)

> "This transitory scene
> Of murmuring stillness, busily serene,
> This solemn pause, the breathing space of man,
> The halt of toil's exhausted caravan,
> Comes sweet with music to thy wearied ear;
> Rise, with its anthem, to a holier sphere."
> —HOLMES.

The Sabbath of the Hebrew people from Moses to Christ, and inclusive of their times, I call the Sabbath of Judaism. It is the ancient world-Sabbath, the Decalogue Sabbath, but with human additions and corruptions. The day was long preserved by a race which in its history and providential training has no parallel. The Hebrew—the Jew—is the most remarkable character among the nations —the most persistent, imperishable, enduring. His Sabbatism is as remarkable.[1]

Judaism and the Sabbath descended together along the centuries from Moses to Isaiah, from Isaiah to Malachi, and from Malachi to Christ—a time period of over fifteen hundred years. The Sabbath of Judaism is proverbial in history. Compressed into a single national or race stream, it was transmitted by special divine revelation as well as

---

[1] "Israel has been the stem on which the faith of the human race has been grafted. No people has taken its destiny so seriously as Israel; none has felt so vividly its joys and its sorrows as a nation; none has lived more thoroughly for an idea. Israel has vanquished Time, and made use of all its oppressors. . . . . I seemed to see before me the living genius of that indestructible people. Over every ruin it has clapped its hands; persecuted by all men, on all men it has been avenged."—*Etudes d'Histoire Religieuse.* Quoted from DRAPER'S *Civil Policy of America,* 210-11.

by tradition. It lies as a bright jewel on the breast of Judaism—a central fact in its history—hedged in by divine safeguards—and renewed in purity from time to time. This chapter will discuss the Judaic Sabbath of the Old Testament period.

Judaism is called a theocracy—a God-government. But was it any more a God-government, except as to special divine revelations then going on, than government is to-day? "All government is ordained of God." And He rules nations now just as He did then. His providential interpositions in these United States are the very same as in ancient Israel—but unreported by divine penmen.

Jewish Sabbatism had its *civil* code. It was administered by the civil arm. Its enforcement was of man, as well as of God; had its human as well as its divine side. The Jew himself interpreted and applied it; judged of its violation; and enforced its penalties. All additions made to the Decalogue Sabbath, and all special interpretations of it; as prohibiting fire-kindling in a warm country like Arabia; as stoning a stick-gatherer to death; as shutting the gates of Jerusalem to keep out Tyrian traders; and as refusing to march and fight on Sabbath day; all these were purely Jewish.[1] They belong to the Jew alone, and to special times in his history. They do not affect other times and peoples. With them we have nothing to do. The Jewish civil Sabbath puts no obligations upon us. [2]

Jewish Sabbatism had also its *ceremonial* code, as seen in its society with priests, altars, and sacrifices, and their directory rituals. The great annual festivals, some of them

---

[1] "The violation of this law of rest, was, as a crime of high treason against Jehovah, punishable with death."—*The Inter. Cyc.*, Art. Sabbath.

[2] "Those Commandments of the Old Testament, which were addressed to the Jews as Jews, and were founded upon this peculiar circumstances and relations, passed away when the Mosaic economy was abolished."—HODGE. *Systematic Theol.*, 3: 321.

called Sabbaths, were part of this ceremonial code. All festival Sabbaths were belongings of ceremonial Judaism. And Judaic ceremonials—its priesthood, altars, sacrifices, circumcision, festival Sabbaths, and their directory rituals—were but shadowy, preparative, perishable; giving way at last to abiding realities. They were manifestly not for all time, but only for the economy—the Eon—the age—to which they belonged. They resounded with the din and bustle of preparation; and were a temporary polity that was to wax old and decay. With ceremonial Judaism we have nothing to do. It was binding only on the people to whom given, and during the economy of which it was a part. Its day has passed. Its obligations have ceased. Its priests are gone; its altars and sacrifices have disappeared; so too its ceremonial Sabbaths. They are binding no more.

Jewish Sabbatism had also its *moral* code. It was God appointed and God administered. The Jew was responsible to God for its proper observance. This moral Sabbath, given to the Jew as a representative of mankind, is broader and more enduring than his civil and ceremonial Sabbath. It is always placed on a par, not with civil or ceremonial but with moral law.[1] As in the Decalogue, so throughout the entire Old Testament, the Sabbath is associated with natural and imperishable principles. It everywhere ranks high; not on the low plain of mere rites and forms; but far up among eternal verities. It is ever kept in view as the Sabbath of the Decalogue, unabridged, unamended, unchanged; not an iota added; not a tittle taken away. Its divine appointment and sacred character are never challenged. God cared for it; watched over it;

---

[1] "Though the threatened punishments for Sabbath-breakers never seem to have been carried out to the full during the times of the established commonwealth, in the scheme of Judaism it was placed on a par with the entire body of the law."—*The Inter. Cycl.*, Art. Sabbath.

preserved it in purity for centuries; frequently and urgently renewed its claims; and his ceaseless supervision is a remarkable attestation of its value.

See his care of the day in the frequency with which he enjoined its keeping and forbad its desecration.[1] Early and late he brought it to the attention of the Jew. The claims of the Sabbath were persistently and urgently restated and enjoined; nothing else so frequently; nothing else so urgently. God watched over the day as a chief bulwark of the state and of religion. It ranked other institutions.

See again his care of the day, in pronouncing so great blessings on Sabbath-keepers, and so great evils against Sabbath-breakers. His promises are great; his threats appalling.[2] There is a renewal of the splendid but awful scene when Israel stood between Mounts Gerizim and Ebal to hear the blessing pronounced upon the law-keeper, and the curse upon the law-breaker. The Sabbath is given

---

[1] The hallowing of sacred time is thus enjoined: "Verily my Sabbaths ye shall keep; for it is a sign between me and you."—Ex. 31: 13. "Ye shall keep the Sabbath therefore, for it is holy unto you."—Ex. 31: 14. "Keep the Sabbath day to sanctify it."—Deut. 5: 12. "Ye shall keep my Sabbath."—Lev. 19: 30. "They shall hallow my Sabbaths."—Ez. 44: 24. See also, Lev. 10: 30, Ez. 44: 24.

[2] To the Sabbath-keeper God says: "Blessed is the man that keepeth the Sabbath from polluting it."—Isa. 56: 2. "Thus saith the Lord unto the eunuchs that keep my Sabbath . . . . Even unto them will I give in my house and within my walls a place and a name better than of sons and daughters."—Isa. 56: 4-5. "If thou turn away thy foot from the Sabbath, from doing thy pleasure on my holy day, and call the Sabbath a delight, the holy of the Lord, honorable . . . then . . . I will cause thee to ride on the high places of the earth."—Isa. 58: 13-4.

To Sabbath-breakers God says: "Every one that defileth it shall surely be put to death. For whosoever doeth any work therein that soul shall be cut off from his people."—Ex. 31: 14. "My Sabbaths they greatly polluted; then I said I would pour out my fury upon them in the wilderness to consume them."—Ez. 20: 13. See also 2 Chron. 26: 21; Lev. 31: 31-4; Amos 8: 4-6, and Neh. 13: 15-21.

the investments that belong to the law. Words of blessing—divine words—are spoken over Sabbath-keepers; and words of malediction—divine words—against Sabbath-breakers.

See yet again his care of the day in the utterances that tell how Sabbath profanation is an occasion of strong and abiding grief to Him. It is *his* Sabbath that he pleads for. He bewails its desecration. His words have the sound of a sob—a wail. They are a divine lamentation over the profanation of something very dear to Him. The Sabbath—*my* Sabbath—his gift to the Jew—his gift to all toil-doomed men—seems as the very apple of his eye.[1]

Now this Sabbath of the Jewish moral code is a natural and universal institution. It belongs to us even as to the Jew. The Jew was a representative man. God deals with us as he dealt with him. Behold him punished for Sabbath breaking; kept out of Canaan; returned to wilderness wanderings; till a whole generation perished. The Mosaic record names rebellion against Jehovah as the crime that brought on this national calamity. But God in Ezekiel names Sabbath profanation as part of the crime. "But the house of Israel rebelled against me in the wilderness," he cries, "and my Sabbaths they greatly polluted; then I said I would pour out my fury upon them in the wilderness to consume them."[a] And Nehemiah ranked Sabbath desecration as one of the mighty forces of evil that wrecked Jerusalem, burned down the temple, and sent the Jews into captivity. "What evil thing is this that ye do," he cries, "and profane the Sabbath? Did not your fathers thus, and did not our God bring all this

---

[a] Ezek. 20 : 13.

[1] Plaints of God against priests and people for profaning his Sabbath: "My Sabbath have they greatly polluted."—Ez. 20 : 13. "Hast profaned my Sabbath."—Ez. 22: 8. "Have hid their eyes from my Sabbath."—Ez. 22 : 26. See also, Ez. 20 : 16, 21, 24 and 23 : 38.

evil upon us and upon this city? Yet ye bring more wrath upon Israel by profaning the Sabbath."[a] In the removal of the Sabbath, the national fabric crumbled into dust. When the people forgot their sacred day they went into captivity. Sabbath breaking thus stands as a violation of moral law—as treason against God—and as punishable with the greatest calamities.

Now behold the Jew as a Sabbath-keeper. The day was enclosed, as in a crypt, and committed to him for safe-keeping. He was faithful. He preserved it in history. He stood towards the Sabbath, as towards the Temple and the Law, not indeed without imperfection, but erect, steady, changeless. The Sabbatic institution was a belonging of all his Old Testament history. It remained as it came to him; perfect at Sinai; unchanged when the Old Testament ended. In that time period of a thousand years, he stood in history as a keeper of the seventh-day rest, often profaning but always clinging to the day.[1]

God's reward for Sabbath-keeping is not earthly preferment—not mere temporal emoluments—but better and nobler types of manhood—purer and loftier character. This was the compensation he bestowed upon the Sabbath-keeping Jew. He added cubits to his moral stature; hallowed all his powers and passions; and made him the best built man of his day. The religious culture of the Jew,

---

[a] Neh. 13 : 17-18.

[1] "The Jewish Church had been trained in an atmosphere of the most rigid exclusiveness, to preserve it from the tainted worship and foul morals of the heathen world. A unique discipline had achieved its object, and with all their faults the Jews were now the repositories of the finest theology and the best practical ethics the world had ever seen."—REV. JAMES HOPE MOULTON, M. A. *Sunday School Journal,* Jan., 1890, p. 4.

"The peculiarity of the Hebrew civilization did not consist in the culture of the imagination and intellect, like that of the Greeks, or in the organization of government, like that of Rome—but its distinguishing feature was *religion.*"—CONYBEARE & HOWSON. *Life and Epis. of St. Paul,* 1: 4. Also NEANDER. *Fflanzung und Zeitung,* 91.

working on and on for centuries, appeared in himself. Sabbatism was in him as a regenerating and transforming force; touching his life with new and celestial shapings; and creating around him the noblest civilization. Sabbath-keepers, touched by secret and invisible fingers, have the reward of a nobler self-hood. The Jew had. This was his character's coronation. Writers who talk of his narrow culture misread history. He was the Puritan of his day.[1]

Only things that are divine remain as they came to us, and descend in history. The divine in the old Testament Jew remains. It is imperishable. His bequest to posterity is remarkable. Three great religions—Judaism. Mohammedanism, Christianity—have come from him. Our gospel is his Pentateuch and Prophets in fulfillment. His ten Commandments resound forever in all Christian churches, and are the moral rule of all Christian nations.

---

[1] "The Jews, instead of being stationary like other Asiatics, were, next to the Greeks, the most progressive people of antiquity, and, jointly with them, have been the starting point and main propelling agency of modern civilization."—JOHN STUART MILL. *Considerations on Rep. Gov.*, p. 43. London.

"Modern civilization is in effect derived from the Jews and from the Greeks. To the latter it is indebted for its human and intellectual to the former for its divine and moral element. Of these two sources, we owe to the Jews, if not the more brilliant, at all events the more sublime and dearly acquired one."—GUIZOT. *Med. on the Essence of Christ*, p. 245.

"Take a skull of each of the different races of mankind, and, placing them at random on a table before an anatomist, ask him to select that which indicates the highest mental capacity. Without knowing anything of their history, from what graves they were obtained, or to what branches of the human family they belonged, he lays his hands at once on the skull of the Jew. This, take it for all in all, is the best on the table. . . . . It is visibly superior to the skulls of those Greeks and Romans that in ancient, and also of those Teutonic races that in modern times have marched at the head of civilization, and seemed destined to rule the world. The star of Abraham is in the ascendant here."—DR. GUTHRIE. *Gems of Illus.*, p. 104.

His ancient history is full of the noblest forecasts. Christianity itself, the leader for eighteen centuries in the world's best civilizations, traces its lineage back—not to the Greek—not to Greek culture—but to the Jew—to the Judaic Sabbath, Law, Synagogue. So God rewarded him—the Sabbath-keeper. He placed him on a conspicuous pinnacle, as a type of the superior souls that, in every age and clime, give to the world its heroes and its martyrs. He has granted him the immortality of conferring upon the race its richest inheritances. Ancient Judaism's bequests to posterity—the Sabbath, the Law, the Tent of Meeting—are monuments more durable than the silent pyramids.

SABBATH OF JUDAISM.

(THE DISPERSION.)

> "Now let us repose from our care and our sorrow,
> Let all that is anxious and sad pass away;
> The rough cares of life lay aside till to-morrow,
> And let us be tranquil and happy to-day."
> JAMES EDMESTON.

The Judaic Sabbath of the Old Testament had a royal place and history. It witnessed the coming and going of prophets, priests, kings; the rise and the fall of empires and nations; the growth and the decay of ancient civilizations. It survived the ruin of the State and Temple; was clung to in exile; and illumined the restoration. Malachi, the last of the prophets, died. The Old Testament ended. For four centuries God sent no special message to man. But the Sabbath sun remained brilliant in the Judean sky. The day was still to be mighty in history—in the era of political ruin—in the era of Dispersion.

The interspace between Malachi and Christ—between the Old Testament and the new—was filled with the greatest events of ancient history. World Empires came and went; the Medo-Persian disappearing; the Grecian sweeping clear across the stage; the Roman ascending to its zenith, and covering the civilized world. The greatest philosophic schools—the Platonic, Socratic, Aristotelian, and Stoic in Greece, the Zoroastrian in the East, and the Ptolemaic in Alexandria—were born and, the last alone excepted, died. The ocean of mind was widely stirred. The Greek language became the organ of civilization. The greatest events were struggling for birth.

It was a special epoch in Jewish literature. There was a fusion of Greek and Jewish thought. Jewish men of letters—thinkers in their own epoch—writers in the Greek language—were numerous. The Apocryphal books are nearly all of that period.[1] The Septuagint—"the Greek Bible"—"the First Apostle to the Gentiles"—then appeared; opened up the Old Testament to Greek-speaking peoples; gave birth to the New Testament dialect; and was a forerunner of the Christianity soon to shine upon the world.[2] Ezekiel, a priest, dramatized the Exodus. Aristobulus wrote an allegory on the Pentateuch. Theodotus versified the story of Dinah and Shechem. One Philo wrote an Epic on Jerusalem. Another Philo recast Jewish theology for Greek philosophers. Josephus and Jason of Cyrene wrote histories. And Hebrew prophets and kings were put into Grecian garb by Eupolemus,

---

[1] "The books termed the *Apocrypha*, . . . were all, or nearly all, composed before the Christian Era."—ANTHON. *Man. of Class. Lit.*, p. 541.

"Uncertain as may be the date of individual books, few, if any can be thrown further back than the commencement of the 3d century B. C. The latest . . . is probably not later than 30 B. C."—SMITH. *New Test. Hist.*, p. 154.

[2] "The Septuagint translation threw open to the Greek world the sacred books of Israel."—*Lux Mundi*, 84. New York, 1890.

"This version, therefore, which rendered the scriptures of the Old Testament intelligible to a vast number of people, became one of the most considerable fruits of the Grecian conquest . . . In this manner did God prepare the way for the preaching of the gospel, which was then approaching."—*Rollin's Anc. Hist.*, 2: 55. Harper Bros.

"In Greek strategy and Greek statesmanship, Greek learning and Greek refinement, they were ready and brilliant disciples; even their artisans and workmen were sent for by distant countries. From the number of Judeo-Greek fragments, historical, didactic, epic, etc., (by Demetrius, Malchus, Eupolemus, Artapan, Aristæus, Jason, Ezechialos, Philo, Theodot, etc.,) which have survived, we may easily conclude what an immense literature must have sprung up here within a few centuries in the midst of the Judeo-Egyptian community."—*The Inter. Cyc.*, Art. Jews.

Demetrius, Aristæus, and Cleodemus. Judaism was a notable factor in contributing to the spreading light and literature.

THE DISPERSION.

The era was distinguished for the Jewish Dispersion— a historic miracle—too little considered by historians.[1] The Dispersion—among all nations—for centuries—is a fact unique in the history of mankind. The Dispersed Jews were settlers, and yet aliens and foreigners, in all lands outside their own God-given Canaan; dwelling under all

---

[1] "The Jews of the Dispersion . . . was the general title applied to those Jews who remained settled in foreign countries after the return from the Babylonian exile, and during the period of the second temple."—*Smith's New Test. Hist.*, p. 145.

"Our nation of whom the habitable world is full."—JOSEPHUS. *Antiq.*, 14: 7: 2.

"The Jews since the Babylonian Captivity had been scattered over all the world."—NAST. *Com.* Intro. § 34.

"In the time of our Savior there was scarcely any land of the ancient world, in which Jewish residents were not to be met with."—McCLINTOCK & STRONG. *Cycl.*, Art. Dispersed.

"Now these Jews are already gotten into all cities, and it is hard to find a place in the habitable world, that hath not admitted this tribe of men, and is not possessed by it."—STRABO. Quoted by Josephus. *Antiq.*, 14: 7: 2.

"There is first the ubiquity of the race: testified alike by Josephus, Strabo, and Philo, and by the witness of inscriptions. They are everywhere and everywhere in force throughout the Roman world."—*Lux Mundi*, 152. New York, 1890.

"The holy city of Jerusalem, not merely . . . because of the colonies led out . . . in the neighboring countries, such as Egypt, Phœnicia, Syria, and Cœlosyria; but also into those that are remote, such as Pamphylia, Cilicia, and the chief parts of Asia as far as Bithynia, and the innermost parts of Pontus; also into the regions of Europe, Thessally, Bœotia, Macedonia, Ætolia, Attica, Argos, Corinth, and the principal parts of Peloponessus. Not only the continents and provinces are full of Jewish colonies, but the most celebrated isles also, Eubœa, Cypress, Crete, not to mention the countries beyond the Euphrates. All these are inhabited by Jews."—*Philonis Opera*, (Mongey. Edit.) 2: 587.

governments; traders and artisans in all cities. Their coming and going among the nations was remarkable. They were "scattered to the utmost parts of heaven." The Babylonian Captivity—perhaps the more remote captivity of Israel—began the Dispersion. The Jew face and form were thenceforward familiar wherever men went on land or sea. They were in all the Persian Empire in Esther's day. Under Alexander the Great and his successors, they wandered everywhere among the nations. All the cities of the Roman Empire swarmed with these children of Abraham. They were everywhere in Asia, Europe, and Africa. Their cosmopolitan character was seen at Pentecost of the crucifixion year.[1] Many, like Josephus, were granted the high privilege of Roman citizenship; and others, like Paul, were born into that heritage. The Dispersion covered four, five, six centuries before the Advent.

The *Babylonian* or Eastern Dispersion had precedence.[2] It dated from the Captivity, and grew into great volume

---

[1] "And there were dwelling at Jerusalem Jews, devout men, out of every nation under heaven."—Acts 2: 5. These are described, Chap. 2: 9-11, as Parthians, Medes, Elamites, and dwellers in Mesopotamia, Capadocia, Pontus, Asia, Phrygia, Pamphylia, Egyptians, Lybians, Romans, Cretes, and Arabians.

"James, a servant of God and of the Lord Jesus Christ, to the twelve tribes which are scattered abroad, greeting."—James 1: 1.

[2] "At Babylon where there were Jews in great numbers."—JOSEPHUS. *Antiq.*, 15: 2: 2.

"At the beginning of the Christian era, the Dispersion was divided into three sections, the *Babylonian*, the *Syrian*, the *Egyptian*. Precedence was given to the first."—SMITH. *New Test. Hist.*, 145.

"Babylon was at that time, and for some hundreds of years after, a chief seat of Jewish culture."—Ditto, 636.

"They were most strongly represented in the Eastern countries, Babylonia and Eastern Syria."—UHLHORN. *Confl. of Christ. with Heath.*, p. 83.

"From Babylon the Jew had spread through every region of the East, and wherever he went he became a zealous missionary of his faith."—CUNNINGHAM GEIKE. *The Life of Christ*, 98.

"Their great colonies in Babylon and Mesopotamia are another headquarters of the race."—*Lu. Mundi*, 152. New York, 1890.

and importance. Babylonian Jews had prosperity and influence, were wealthy and cultured; and they spread through all Persia, and Media, and Parthia.

The *Egyptian* Dispersion, with headquarters at Alexandria, occupying two of the city's five districts—governed by a magistrate of its own—was a million strong in Philo's day. Alexandrian Jews had equal civil rights with the Greeks; and the highest offices and dignities were open to them. They had a temple and priesthood of their own, and one of their synagogues—the Diapleuston —was so vast and magnificent, that it was said of it: "Whosoever has not seen it has not seen the glory of Israel." From Alexandria, the Jews spread to the southern boundary of Ethiopia, and westward to the Lybian Desert.[1]

The *Syrian* Dispersion had its headquarters at Antioch, and spread through all Syria, through Asia Minor, through Greece and the Mediterranean Isles. Josephus thought it

---

[1] "In Egypt they constituted more than one-eighth of the entire population. . . . . In Alexandria, they occupied two of its five wards and were scattered through the others."—UHLHORN, *Confl. of Christ. with Heath.*, p. 83.

"Before the dawn of the Christian era they had increased to a million," (in Alexandria)—FARRAR. *Early Days of Christ.*, p. 162.

"They are an eighth part (one million) of the population of Alexandria."—*Lux Mundi*, 152. New York, 1890.

"Egypt and other parts of Africa had a vast Jewish population."— CUNNINGHAM GEIKE. *The Life of Christ*, 98.

"For as the Jewish nation is widely dispersed over all the habitable earth among its inhabitants, so is it very much intermingled with Syria by reason of its neighborhood, and had the greatest multitudes in Antioch."—JOSEPHUS. *Wars*, 7:4:3.

"Not less numerous were they in Antioch. . . . . From there they spread over all of Asia Minor and found their way into Greece."— UHLHORN. *Confl. of Christ. with Heath.*, p. 83.

"Three centuries or more before the Christian era, Judaism was already strong enough in Egypt and Syria to claim political attention as an important element in society."—HUIDEKOPER. *Judaism at Rome*, 41.

numerically the greatest. It was powerful and flourishing in Christ's day.

The Dispersion did not, perhaps, reach Rome till about 63 B. C., when Pompey carried many Jewish captives thither, and colonized them beyond the Tiber. The number grew, and in brief years was represented in the highest circles, among rich and titled bankers, and even in the palace of the Cæsars.[1]

The Dispersed mingled with all races and nations, and yet kept separate from them. They were solitary in society—isolated—a distinct race—unlike the rest of the world—never amalgamating with those among whom they lived. Association brings assimilation; but they did not assimilate. Other races under similar circumstances have disappeared, and inevitable disappearance seemed to await

---

[1] "In Rome under Augustus, the Jews numbered perhaps 40,000, in the time of Tiberius perhaps 80,000."—UHLHORN. *Confl. of Christ. with Heathenism*, 83.

"The number of Jews in Rome in the post-Augustan period may be reckoned as over 20,000. . . . So were the Jews also to be found in the palace of the Cæsars."—ADOLPH HARNACK. *Princeton Rev.*, 54*th year*, p. 253.

"Jews in Rome; for since the campaigns of Pompey and Gabrinius, they had been so numerous in the capital that they formed a great quarter on the other side of the river."—GEIKE. *The Life of Christ*, 203.

"The West was as full of Jews as the East."—*Ditto*, 98.

"To persecute the Jews at Rome would not have been an easy matter. They were sufficiently numerous to be formidable, and had overawed Cicero in the zenith of his fame. Besides this the Jewish religion was recognized, tolerated, licensed."—*Early Christianity*, FARRAR p. 41.

"Next in order is that odium of Jewish gold. . . . . You know what a band there is of them, with what concord it acts, how much it can accomplish in assemblies. I will lower my voice so that only the judges can hear. For there are not wanting some who would incite them against me, and against every prominent man."—CICERO. *Pro Flacco*, c. 28.

them; but they did not disappear. A subject race for centuries—under Babylonian, Persian, Grecian, Roman masters—their nationality was never lost; their race characteristics remained unaltered. They resisted the modifying influence of every social environment. They moved forward over changing centuries, but changed not.

Yet they clad themselves, with apparent ease, in the customs, usages, civilizations of all races of men, except simply as to religion. They were among all Gentile peoples religious aliens. They stood as monopolists of divine truth; clung to the customs of their fathers; would enter into no new religious conditions; and held all forms of worship, except their own, as idolatrous. Here they were the "Shibboleth" shouters in history—an *imperium in imperio*. That brought them trouble. There sprang up along all paths of the Dispersion irritation, restriction, conflict. They were at times antagonized and oppressed. They suffered from the contradictory moods of human nature. Local uprisings sometimes decimated their numbers. Haman plotted their total immolation. And Antiochus Epiphanes sought to extirpate both their faith and nationality. Yet their faith survived all misfortunes; their nationality outlived its enemies; and they multiplied in number.

The pre-Messianic Jews—the Dispersion proper—are not however, to be confounded with the Jews after the capture and burning of Jerusalem by the Romans; the former everywhere influential in society, though creating religious discontents; the latter ostracised, persecuted, oppressed. The Dispersed, for four centuries before Christ, were, with the Greeks and Romans, the chief makers of history. Mommsen makes Judaism the third factor in forming the Roman Empire.[a] The Dispersed now and then made rulers their debtors, and, in consequence, were

---

[a] *Hist. of Rome*, 5 : 14.

spared from exactions, and even granted exceptional privileges. Conspicuous among rulers making them notable grants are Cyrus the Great, Darius, Artaxerxes, Alexander the Great, Antiochus the Great, Julius Cæsar, Mark Antony, and Augustus Cæsar.[1] By special edicts they were granted liberty to live according to the customs of their fathers; were exempted from tribute every seventh year; from being taken before a magistrate on the Sabbath; and even from military services because they would neither fight or march on Sabbath days. The very edicts that

---

[1] "He (Alexander the Great,) granted the Jews, not only in Judea, but also in Media and Babylonia, the free enjoyment of their laws, and exemption from tribute during the Sabbatic year."—SMITH. *N. T. Hist.*, 16.

"Antiochus (the Great) granted them a great many privileges."—*Rollin*, 2: 135.

"Seleucus Nicator made the Jews citizens in the cities which he built in Asia and Syria."—JOSEPHUS. *Antiq.*, 12: 3: 1.

"The Jews were granted by the first Ptolemy great privileges in the new capital, (Alexandria); and these they retained to the time of the Roman Empire."—RAWLINSON. *Anc. Hist.*, 263.

"The privilege of the Jews had been secured to them under the Roman Empire by the generous edicts of Julius Cæsar and other Emperors."—FARRAR. *Early Christ.*, 163.

Julius Cæsar granted them exemption from tribute every seventh year, and to live "according to the customs of their forefathers."—JOSEPHUS. *Antiq.*, 14: 10: 2: 8.

Marc Antony and Dolabella, Consuls, granted them "freedom from going into the army;" and also "to use the customs of their fathers." JOSEPHUS. *Antiq.*, 14: 10: 12.

Augustus Cæsar ordained, "that the Jews have liberty to make use of their own customs."—JOSEPHUS. *Antiq.*, 16: 6: 2.

Claudius Cæsar decreed, "to permit the Jews, who are in all the world under us, to keep their own customs, without being hindered to do so."—JOSEPHUS. *Antiq.*, 19: 5: 3.

"To numbers and ubiquity, they add privilege in the shape of rights and immunities, begun by the policy of the successors of Alexander, but vigorously taken up and pushed by Rome as early as 139 B. C., greatly developed by Cæsar, around whose pyre at Rome they wept, and maintained by the almost constant policy of the Empire."—*Lux Mundi*, 152. New York, 1890.

secured these immunities are reporters of the religious friction that followed their steps. The relief was occasional and temporary. It deferred but did not prevent the catastrophe.

The Dispersed took with them everywhere the Sabbath, the Synagogue, and the Law. They built among all Polytheists an altar to the One God; reared his Tent of Meeting beside the fanes of heathen idolatry; and kept the seventh-day rest among all peoples who had lost it, or had never known it.[1] Paul found this trinity of Judaisms—the Day, the Book, the House—in nearly all the cities whither he went preaching the Gospel. And James reports them as everywhere known and used of old. "For

---

[1] Jerusalem, according to the Rabbins, had 480 synagogues. Acts 6: 9 reports synagogues of Libertines, Cyrenians, Alexandrians, Cilicians, and Asians.

"Alexandria contained several synagogues, one of which was very splendid."—PHILO. *App.* ii. 565.

"Their synagogue (at Alexandria) the famous Diapleuston, with its seventy gilded chairs, and its size so vast that the signal for the 'Amens' of the congregation, had to be given by a flag—was the greatest in the world."—FARRAR. *Early Christ.*, 162.

"The Jews....had built their synagogues in all the commercial cities of the Roman Empire."—NAST. *Com.*, Gen. Intro. ¶ 34.

"The synagogue....assembled the faithful on that day within its precincts, in every town and hamlet, in and out of Palestine, before and after the exile."—*The Inter. Cyc.*, Art. Sabbath.

"In Leontopolis (Egypt) they had a temple of their own....The existence of seven synagogues in Rome has been definitely established, and probably there were others."—UHLHORN. *Confl. of Christ. with Heath.*, 83.

"Greece....and Macedonia, where in the Apostle's time, we find in all the important cities....communities with synagogues or proseuchæ."—McCLINTOCK & STRONG. *Cycl.*, Art. Dispersion.

The Sabbath, like the Synagogue, was taken everywhere—into every land—into all cities. The testimony is voluminous. A single quotation is given.

"There is not any city of the Grecians, nor any of the barbarians, nor any nation whatsoever, whither our custom of resting on the seventh day has not come."—JOSEPHUS. *Apion*, 2: 40.

Moses of old time," he says, "hath in every city them that preach him, being read in the synagogue every Sabbath day." [a] The six centuries that came and went before Christ spread widely among all nations the Sabbath, the Synagogue, and the Law. These Judaisms were permanently in Babylon six hundred years before the Christian era; in Egypt and in Antioch three hundred years; and in Rome at least sixty-three years. From those centers they found their way into all the cities of the world. They represented the only religion that then interested itself in man's morality. And everywhere a breath of reform attended them.

Jewish peculiarities, during the Dispersion, may be summed up as Monotheism, Circumcision, Temple offerings and Sabbatism. Monotheism brought the Dispersed no reported trouble. Circumcision invited ridicule, but not persecution. And Temple offerings, not interfering with State tribute, provoked no antagonism. It was seventh-day Sabbatism, their chief distinguishing trait, that made their life and history troublous. They would not, on Sabbath days, litigate, go on a journey, march or fight as soldiers, or perform any kind of labor.[1] This septen-

---

[a] Acts 15: 21.

[1] It was chiefly Sabbath-keeping that brought them trouble. They would not fight in holy time. 1. *Macc.* 2: 32-8. JOSEPHUS. *Antiq.*, 14: 4: 2-3 and 12: 1: 1. Or they would repel but not attack an enemy. 1 *Macc.* 2: 41. JOSEPHUS. *Antiq.*, 18: 9: 2. *Wars*, 1: 7: 3. Jerusalem was often captured on Sabbath days, because of these Jewish customs—by Antiochus Epiphanes – by Pompey—by Titus. ROLLIN, 2: 194, 275. *The Inter Cyc.*, Art. Sabbath.

"Nor is it lawful for us to journey, either on the Sabbath day, or on a festival day."—JOSEPHUS. *Antiq.*, 13: 8: 4.

This Sabbatism brought perpetual conflict. Edicts of relief, by Romans, were many. JOSEPHUS quotes a number: Ordering that "no one compel the Jews to come before a judge on the Sabbath day." *Antiq.*, 16: 6: 2-4.; granting freedom "from going into the army on account of the superstition they are under," *Antiq.* 14: 10: 13 allowing them "to celebrate their Sabbaths," *Antiq.* 14: 10: 21

ary rest that so dominated them challenged either the world's recognition, or its opposition. It was confronted and opposed; not by a rival day of rest or worship, as first day, that nowhere appears; but by opposition to the institution itself. Antipathy to the Sabbatism of the seven-day week is everywhere; harmony with it, or with a competing day, nowhere. Persian masters, Greek masters, Roman masters reluctantly yielded their Jew vassals a seventh of days for rest—partial exemption from tribute—exemption from military service. The day is challenged and opposed by all Greek and Roman writers of the period who discuss the subject. Between the two Testaments, the Sabbath, throughout all the world, was an institution peculiarly Jewish. Gentile nations had no competing institution. It differentiated the Jew from all other peoples. He had it; they had not. He kept it; they satirized it. Sabbatic differences, not to be minimized, stand in history as the chief contention between the Jew and the Gentile.[1]

The Sabbath of the Dispersion was not a sad but a joyous day. It did not foster a self-torturing spirit; that

---

"that the Jews may be allowed to observe their Sabbaths," *Antiq.* 14: 10: 20; "that as many men and women of the Jews, as are willing so to do, may celebrate their Sabbaths," *Antiq.* 14; 10: 23; and "that....no one of them should be hindered from keeping the Sabbath-day, or be fined for so doing," *Antiq.* 14: 10: 25.

"Rights and immunities guarding their distinctive customs, such as their observance of the Sabbath."—*Lux Mundi.*, 152.

"On this account alone (their Sabbatism) the Romans found themselves compelled to exempt the Jews from all military service."—*Cycl. Brit.*, Art. Sabbath.

[1] "The cessation from labor every seventh day by the Jews struck foreigners as something strange, and provoked their ridicule."—*Bible Com.*, Art. Sabbath Forgotten.

"At the time of the exile the Sabbath was already an institution peculiarly Jewish, otherwise it could not have served as a mark of distinction from heathenism."—W. R. SMITH, LL. D., *Encyc. Brit.*, Art. Sabbath.

came later. The corrupting traditions of the elders were indeed beginning to rob it of some of its divine sweetness; but enough still remained to make it blessed among days. It wove a garment of glory in the loom of the passing years. To the pre-Messianic Jew, it must have had a sweetness that never flagged; a beauty that never ceased to attract; for at peril and sacrifice he kept up its weekly celebration through revolving centuries.[1] It was at once the romance and the tragedy of his life; a romance that grew not old or faded; a tragedy that reddened many fields of the Orient. His Sabbath mornings and evenings were fringed with a shout and a song. The day was made restful throughout by sacred readings and pleasing addresses. It covered the Dispersed, "in bondage among the Gentiles," with trailing garments of light. It entranced them with high and holy raptures as they chanted: "This is the day the Lord hath made; we will rejoice and be glad therein."

---

[1] "The Hebrews solemnize the Sabbath with mutual feasting."— PLUTARCH. *Sympos., lib. IV. qu.* 5.

"And she fasted all the days of her widowhood, save the eves of the Sabbaths and the Sabbaths."—*Judith,* 8: 6.

"She.... went down into the house in which she abode in the Sabbath days, and in her feast days."—*Judith,* 10: 2.

Introductory—Sabbath morning benediction—"Blessed art thou O Lord our God, king of the universe, who hath sanctified us by his laws, and hath made us partakers in his grace, and hath in his love and in his mercy, given us the Sabbath, as a remembrance of creation as the first day of holy convocations, and in memory of redemption from Egypt; for thou hast chosen us and sanctified us from all peoples, and hast given us thy holy Sabbath in love and in grace. Blessed art thou, O Lord, who sanctifieth the Sabbath."

Valedictory—Sabbath-evening Prayer.—"Blessed art thou, O Lord our God, king of the universe, who divided between holy and unholy, between light and darkness, between Israel and the peoples, between the Sabbath and the six-days of creation. Blessed art thou, O Lord, who divideth between holy and unholy."

Providential Outcome of the Judaic Sabbath.

One providential mission of ancient Judaism was to preserve the Sabbath in history, and at last rekindle its fires among the nations. Six centuries before Christ, the Gentiles had no seven-day week or Sabbatism. They had dropped out of their life. They were slowly lost. They were to be slowly recovered. The order of nature changes slowly; as continents emerging from the sea; as planets to be the seat of life. So of social institutions and customs. So of the seven-day week and its Sabbatism. The Dispersion, a seed sown for a future harvest, began their restoration. The Dispersed, to whom the institutions were divinely handed for safe-keeping and transmission, long kept them alive and renewed them in the world. They stand in history, between the two Testaments, as the restorers of the seven-day week and its Sabbatism. Judaism was the continuous stream into which the ancient institutions were gathered, and out of which the modern institutions have flowed and are flowing.

The Dispersed Jew was conspicuous as the Sabbath torch-light bearer. He marched across the nations and down the centuries with the Sabbath flag unfurled and held aloft. He began the mighty march at the Babylonian captivity—perhaps earlier at the captivity of Israel—began it from Jerusalem—began it in Babylon—began it in Nineveh. His moving columns occupied every city in the Persian Empire—in the Grecian Empire—in the Roman Empire. The Sabbath, always and everywhere was one of his essential belongings. He fought and won no battles of his own; planted no cities; conquered no territories; founded no Empires; but he built Synagogues, studied Moses, and kept the seventh-day rest. Uniting the energy of youth with the majesty of an immemorial antiquity, he kept steadily, persistently, everywhere, at this work through four, five, six centuries. He was the repairer of the breach; the restorer of the weekly cycle; the renewer of the Sabbath.

Great events move as pathfinders before humanity. The Dispersion, with its Sabbath flag waving in the breeze of every city for centuries, is one of the greatest events in pre-Christian history. It was at its apogee of splendor and influence about the time of the Advent, when the first Cæsars were granting all Jews special protection and privileges. It had made the spectacle of the seventh-day Sabbath world-wide and somewhat popular. Its providential work was done. It had accomplished three things.

First. The seven-day week and the seventh-day Sabbath were again *known* to the Gentiles—not recalled by them—but brought to them.[1] The far-off was brought nigh; and the Dispersed Jew was the providential bringer. On the Nile, the Euphrates, and the Tiber, as well as on the Sacred Jordan, the seven-day week and its Sabbath were known. The people everywhere saw the Sabbath light of Judaism. Seeds of Sabbatism were scattered widely among the nations.

Second. The Sabbath made converts *in the way of proselytes* to Judaism. Samaritans, an alien and various

---

[1] The Jewish Sabbath is a much reported day in pre-Christian history. Two samples out of multitudes are here given.

Agatharchides (a Greek writer about 300 B. C.,) as quoted by Josephus (Apion 1: 22) speaks of the "Jews . . . accustomed to rest every seventh day."

Diogenes (a Greek rhetorician about 15 A. D.) not only knew but kept the Jewish Sabbath. Suetonious (*Tiberius*, 32, Bohn's trans.) says of him: "Diogenes, the grammarian, who used to hold public disquisitions at Rhodes every Sabbath-day, once refused him (Tiberius) admittance upon his coming to hear him out of course, and sent him a message by a servant, postponing his admission until the next seventh day."

people, became Sabbatarians after the Jewish type.¹ And Judaism, in wide favor about the time of the Advent, was everywhere marching with the swing of conquest—was seeking expansion—was a vast and active propagandism. "Ye compass sea and land," said Jesus, "to make one proselyte."ᵃ Horace, about forty years before, had implied the same thing.

> "I'll force you, like the proselyting Jews,
> To be like us, a brother of the muse." b

Proselytes were made: perhaps among them Naaman, the Syrian, Cornelius the centurion, and the eunuch of Queen Candace.² The keepers of Pentecost in crucifixion year, are described as "Jews and proselytes." One of the seven deacons, elected in the Apostolic church, was "Nicolas a proselyte of Antioch." And Paul and Barnabas, at Antioch in Pisidia, were at one time followed by "Jews

---

a Matt. 22: 15.   b Lib. 1, Sat. 4, lines 142-3.

¹ 2. Kings, chap. 17. The Samaritans, in an official document about 170 B. C., said: "Our forefathers, upon certain frequent plagues, and as following a certain ancient superstition, had a custom of observing that day which by the Jews is called the Sabbath."—JOSEPHUS. *Antiq.*, 12: 5: 5.

² "The propagandists of Judaism in the Roman Empire."—*Judaism at Rome*, 27.

"The number of proselytes, gained over the world by this propaganda, was incredible."—GEIKE. *Life of Christ*, 98.

"Multitudes of early converts had been Jewish proselytes before they became Christian disciples."—FARRAR. *Life and Work of St. Paul*, 2: 120.

"The people of Damascus . . . Yet did they distrust their own wives, who were almost all of them addicted to the Jewish religion."—JOSEPHUS. *Wars*, 2: 20: 2.

"In various degrees, multitudes (of whom women doubtless formed a a considerable majority) adopted the customs and brought themselves into connection with the religion of the Jews."—*Lux Mundi*, 154. New York, 1890.

"The heathen also, contemptible as the Jews seemed to them, having become convinced of the profound truths of the Israelitish system, and of the emptiness and impotence of their own religion, yielded, in exceptional but by no means rare cases, to the better influences of Judaism."—KURTZ. *Ch. Hist*, 54.

and religious proselytes." Judaism was thus becoming the inheritance, not of Jews only, but of many Gentile Converts. The conquered became, religiously, conquerors. The seventh-day Sabbath won victories. The Greek and Jew races—the one now descending from lofty pinnacles of greatness—the other representing a vast Dispersion—were widely meeting in history: and many Greeks entered the Synagogue as proselytes; accepted the seven-day week; and kept the seventh-day Sabbath.[1] The Roman and Jew

---

[1] "Greeks knew the Jew and his Sabbath from the sixth century B. C. (Clearchus 400 B. C.) reports his master Aristotle, as telling about a Jew from Cœlosyria who communicated to him more knowledge than he received from him.—JOSEPHUS. *Apion*, 1: 22. Hermippus testifies that Pythagoras (540 B. C.) "transferred into his own philosophy" "doctrines of the Jews."—JOSEPHUS. *Apion*, 1: 22. Hecateus (300 B. C.) wrote a book about the Jews.—JOSEPHUS. *Apion*, 1: 22. Megasthenes (300 B. C.) testified that "all matters of natural science . . . were taught . . . in Syria by those called Jews." CLEMENT OF ALEXANDRIA. *Strom.*, 1: 72. Josephus further reports the following Greek writers as mentioning the Jews: Theophilus, Aristophanes, Mnases, Zoperion, Euhemerus, Hermogenes, Menander, Conon, Eupolemus, and Nicolas. Onomacritus (500 B. C.) evidently knew about Moses and Sinai when he wrote:

" So speaks the lore
Of ancient wisdom: so the man, who sprang
From the cradling waters, speaks; who took
The double tables of the law from God."
—Quoted from *Poets and Poetry of the Ancients*, 88.

Greek and Jew meeting in history, the Jew conquered—the Jew faith triumphed—Greek proselytes were many.

"They also made proselytes of a great many of the Greeks perpetually."—JOSEPHUS. *Wars*, 7: 3: 3.

"Jews believed in a Supreme Being who took interest in human morality. Many Greeks accepted this belief."—*Judaism at Rome*, 384.

"At length the Greeks became more acquainted with their Sacred Books, and conversions from Paganism to Judaism was not an uncommon occurrence. Synagogues, composed in great part of proselytes, existed in many of the Grecian cities, at the beginning of the Christian era."—ANTHON. *Man. Class. Lit.*, 541.

Greek proselytes were numerous enough among early Christian converts to complain "against the Hebrews because their widows were neglected in the daily ministration."—Acts 6: 1.

races—the civilization of the sword, and the civilization of religion—the one representing soldiers and statesmen, the other merchants and Sabbatarians—were also widely coming together in history: and Romans, not a few, bowed the knee to Jehovah; appeared in the synagogue as proselytes; and observed the Jewish Sabbath.[1] Thus the only era of propagandism, ever known to Judaism, was crowned with success. Proselytes were numerous. The Sabbath won disciples and widened its area.

Third. The seven-day week and its Sabbatism slowly but steadily spread among all Gentile peoples. They did not invent these divine institutions; did not even seek their return. They were paraded before them—brought to them—pressed upon their acceptance. At last—here

---

[1] Romans had the Jews and their Sabbath at Rome from 63 B. C.; and certainly knew them much earlier in history; perhaps about a century earlier. Cicero, (106-43 B. C.) as quoted by Augustine, (*De Civitate Dei* 6: 11) says: "The Jewish faith is now received over every land: the conquered have given laws to the conquerors."

"To-day is the thirtieth Sabbath; and would you be willing to oppress the Jews."—HORACE (65—8 B. C.) *Sat.* 1: 9.

"The seventh-day held sacred by the Jew."—OVID, (43 B. C.—18 A. D.) *De Art. Amand,* i., 76.

From the time that Jew and Roman met in history, the Jew faith made converts. So Seneca has already reported. Some other reports here follow:

"The seventh-day which is kept holy by the Jews is also a festival of the Roman women."—TIBULLUS. (About 18 B. C.)

Julia a (Roman) woman of great dignity, and one that had embraced the Jewish religion."—JOSEPHUS. *Antiq.*, 18: 3: 5.

"They (Jews at Rome) were accorded full freedom of worship, and were even successful in making converts."—McCLINTOCK & STRONG. *Cycl.*, Art. Dispersion.

"Roman ladies thronged the synagogues of the Jews, and many a Roman observed the Jewish Sabbath."—ULLHORN. *Confl. of Christ. with Heuth.*, 63.

"Their views were, before the Christian era, gaining rapid foothold at Rome."—*Judaism at Rome*, 1. See also JUVENAL, *Sat.* 14: 96-106.

and there—Gentile peoples began to receive them back; began to appreciate and use them. They were accepted as a more convenient arrangement of the days—by Greeks as better than the decade—by Romans as better than nundinæ. The initial changes cannot be named. The steps of change, from the beginning to the culmination, cannot be traced. But enough surface facts appear to show the going on of a deep and wide social and moral revolution. The leavening process was everywhere—in all lands—among all peoples—in all cities.[1] The idea of a new epoch was in the air. Not indeed till the beginning of the third Christian century—not till Christianity had changed Sabbatism from the Seventh to the First day— was the great revolution to be complete. But honor to whom honor. It was not the Christian, it was the Jew, who brought back and restored to the world the seven day week and its Sabbatism. Out of his mighty Dispersion— world-wide—centuries long—the Sabbath issued to be once more a world institution.

The world was divinely prepared for Christ and Christianity.[2] A world empire—the Roman—had removed

---

[1] "Every synagogue was, as it were, a mission station of Monotheism."—Dr. NAST. *Com. Gen. Intro.*, § 34.

"The clear, strong, deep religious faith of the Jews scattered everywhere, and everywhere, as we know, to an extraordinary extent leavening society."—*Lux Mundi*, 149.

"But not a few were attracted into the shadow of the synagogue, and the majority of those were women."—FARRAR. *The Life and Work of St. Paul*, 2 : 120.

"In Syria and portions of Asia Minor, and perhaps even to the eastward of these countries, they had, at the Christian era, largely displaced the ancient religions."—HUIDEKOPER. *Judaism in Rome*, 1.

[2] "At the birth of Christ the striking spectacle presented itself, in a degree unknown before or since, of the world united under one scepter. From the Euphrates to the Atlantic; from the mouths of the Rhine to the slopes of the Atlas, the Roman Emperor was the sole lord."—CUNNINGHAM GEIKE. *The Life of Christ*, 18.

impediments from the way, and made broad highways for intercourse, between the nations. A world language—the Grecian—had everywhere promoted and made possible international intercourse. Partition walls between civilized nations were broken down, and laws and customs, more or less common, united East and West, North and South. All these prepared the way of the Lord. But other providential preparations were more potent. The Dispersion was God's mightiest factor.[1] Judaism, a religious oasis in the world's desert, a protest against the impiety of the period, was the cradle of the Gospel. It built in all cities the Synagogue—the Tent of Meeting. It preached everywhere Mosaism—the Scriptures—the Book. It unfurled in every atmosphere the Sabbath flag—the Day. These were God's chief preparative forces. They gave new and divine shaping to world-history.

---

[1] They (Jews) "had been merely chosen servants to keep the truth alive, that the world might at last know it, and be saved."—*Ben Hur*, 20.

"Augustus got the fame in Rome of being the patron of the Jews, and in the provinces, even among the Jews themselves, of being the magnanimous protector of their religion. His tolerance, moreover, served an end which he did not contemplate. It secured the slow but certain conquest of the West, first by Judaism, the pioneer of a new and higher faith, and then by Christianity—the faith for which it had prepared the way."—GEIKE. *The Life of Christ*, 203.

"Notwithstanding Cyrus allowed all the Jews in his dominions to return to their own land, many of them did not return. This happened agreeable to God's purpose in permitting them to be carried away captive into Assyria and Babylonia; for he intended to make himself known among the heathen by reason of the knowledge of his being and perfections, which the Jews in their dispersion would communicate to them."—DR. MACKNIGHT. Quoted in *Meth. Quar.*, 1885, p. 438.

"The Dispersion of the chosen people was one of those three vast and world-wide events, in which the Christian cannot but see the hand of God so ordering the course of history as to prepare the world for a revelation of his Son."—FARRAR. *The Life and Work of St. Paul*, 2: 116.

They heralded and brought in Christ and Christianity. They are of the Jew. Sabbatism is of the Jew. It was a boon that the world needed, and which Judaism restored to the nations. The Jew, as God's ancient knight, walked the wide world four, five, six centuries to reorganize world Sabbatism—to usher in the new and better era.

JESUS AND THE SABBATH.

> "Oh day of days! Shall hearts set free
> No minstrel rapture find for thee?
> Thou art the Sun of other days;
> They shine by giving back thy rays."—

The Sabbath of the Gospels is the lingering Sabbath of Judaism under the interpretations of Jesus; his interpretations as seen in his life and teachings—as seen in what he did and what he said. The words and deeds of Jesus give us our ideal Sabbath—the Sabbath in its latest divine statement. What then is the attitude of Jesus towards the day?

WHAT HE DID.

He kept the Sabbath; kept it inviolate; kept it first and last. He honored it in every way and at all times. His high regard for it is an underlying fact of his entire ministry. The sacred day, in the record of his life and work, is always observed, revered, sanctified. All his reported places of resort on the Sabbath were places of worship. He began his public ministry at Nazareth by "entering into the synagogue on the Sabbath day, *as his custom was*, and standing up to read." He passed thence to Capernaum, "and taught them on the Sabbath day." As he began, so he continued, and so he ended. From this Sabbath-keeping custom there is no known departure. He was a Sabbatarian. As God, on the seventh day, after creation-work was ended, so Jesus in all his earthly ministry, was a Sabbatarian. He kept the day. He reinstituted it, if not by express law, by example. His acts are legislative. They are authoritative. His example is a living, walking, talking law, whose influence is potential and universal.

He wrought miracles of healing on the Sabbath. At least seven of his thirty-three recorded miracles were Sabbath work. He healed on Sabbath-days the man with an unclean spirit in the synagogue at Capernaum, Mark 1: 23-6; Simon's wife's mother, Mark 1: 29-31; the man with a withered hand, Matt. 12: 9-13; the man born blind, John 9: 14; the impotent man at Bethesda's pool, John 5: 9; the woman with a spirit of infirmity, Luke 13: 11-4; and the man with dropsy, Luke 14: 1-4.

Inspect these seven Sabbatic miracles. The cases were not urgent; all, excepting Simon's wife's mother, being chronic ailments that might easily have waited for secular time. They were not pressed upon the Divine Healer—not solicited by the patients, or by friends. The people about him did not believe in Sabbath healings; and it was only in secular, never in sacred time, that they came, or brought friends, to be healed. The miracles were spontaneous with Jesus; innovations on the usages of the epoch; a surprise to patients and on-lookers; and wrought with the greatest publicity. The Divine Worker, in his Sabbath miracles, seemed to invite attention—to court notoriety—to solicit a questioning of his work. Why this publicity? What did Jesus mean? What did he mean in making Sabbatic salve out of clay to anoint blind eyes? What did he mean in sending a healed man to carry his bed through Sabbatic streets? What did he mean—to take in a related idea—in justifying Sabbath corn-gathering by his disciples? Let his own words and deeds answer.

He justifies Sabbath miracles out of his own epoch; pointing the questioning Jews to themselves, on Sabbaths, pulling sheep and oxen out of ditches; and telling them, irresistibly, that a man, because better than a sheep or ox, is entitled to be healed on that day. He also justifies Sabbath miracles, and corn-pulling to appease hunger, by Old

Testament examples, as Sabbath Temple sacrifices—Sabbath circumcisions—and David appeasing hunger with forbidden shew-bread. This was his surface argument; and it completely vanquished the questioning Jews. But his real meaning lies deeper and goes farther. What is it?

He meant to recall holy time from oppressive strictness: to prune it of alien growths; to pry it out of traditional ruts. The Jews, as custodians of the Sabbath, had fastened upon it many human additions and corruptions. Jewish Sabbatism was all awry; a caricature on the Sabbath of the Decalogue; burdensome in multiplied and oppressive rites; destroying much of the blessedness and helpfulness of sacred rest. It would pull a sheep or an ox out of a ditch, but refuse healing to a paralyzed man; circumcise a child, but denounce sight-giving to a blind man; offer Temple sacrifices, but anathematize the straightening of a crooked human arm. This Phariseeism in the Jewish Sabbath, Jesus struck down, not the day itself. He antagonized, not the divine original, but only the human counterfeit. He made human traditions, not the sacred seventh of time, melt, like wax, before even bodily necessities. He granted relief from formalism, not from obligation; from misinterpretation, not from law; from burdensome rites, not from Sabbatic duty.

He meant, in a word, to restate and revive the Sabbath of the Decalogue. His restatement sets forth works of necessity and mercy as suitable Sabbath-furniture, as not merely allowable, but of the very essence of the day. No real Sabbatism, according to his restatement, can exclude miracles of healing—deeds of humanity—acts of charity. Humanities are masters of the day. It admits even of such necessary secular acts, as bed-carrying by the healed, salve-making to anoint blind eyes, and corn-pulling to appease hunger pangs. Jesus, in all this, did not abrogate, but refurnished, the Sabbath. He did not strike down, but renewed, the restful Sabbath of Eden and of Sinai. For his restated and restored duties and privileges presuppose the continuance and perpetuity of the day. He thus recognizes its enduring character and immutable obligation. Such is New Testament Sabbatism as interpreted by the deeds of Jesus.

What He Said.

Six of his conversations, or discourses, discuss the Sabbath. They give us by direct statement, his Sabbath views in four great watchwords.

A first watchword—"The Son of man is Lord even of the Sabbath day"—declares his own supremacy over the day. Jesus, in these words, refers to himself. He advances and asserts his own dignity and authority. He declares his lordship over holy time. He is lord of the Sabbath, because he instituted it—preserves and perpetuates it—keeps it in its endless on-going. This makes it a New Testament institution; a living, not a dying or dead institution; for Jesus "is not the God of the dead but of the living." His lordship over the day must affirm, among other things, his right to decide and order what is true Sabbath-keeping; to say what things should and what should not be done; and to make any needed readjustments of the day. It is thought by some that his lordship over the day was advanced to set forth that he meant to abrogate it, or at least to relax its claims and duties. It is not however of the nature of lordship to abolish—to destroy—to relax—but to continue—to improve—and to rule. His lordship over the day implies therefore that it was not to be destroyed, but to be continued and perpetuated in his Gospel kingdom.

A second watchword—"The Sabbath was made for man, and not man for the Sabbath"—sets forth holy time in its relations to man, positively and negatively—in the light of what it is, and in the light of what it is not. *Man was not made for the Sabbath.* This is its negative side. This is what it is not. Man, as to the earth, stands at the apex of all known creatures. All things—the globe itself, its revolving seasons, its mighty forces, its living and dead forms—were made for him, and exist for him, not he for them. It is so also as to the Sabbath. Judaism made man the slave of the Sabbath. This watchword of Christ is the proclamation of his freedom. The Sabbath, like marriage, like the atonement, was instituted for man's use and welfare. *It was made for man.* This is its positive side. This is what it is—what it is for. The Sabbath, in its exact self, as given at Creation, as renewed in the Decalogue, as now restated by Jesus, was made for man. It was made for man somehow as light is made for the eyes or sound for the ear.[1] It is a divine bequest to him of a septenary rest-day; a hallowed and blessed septenary rest-day. Like the atmosphere, the sunbeam, the rain-drop, it brings benedictions to high and low, to rich and poor, to grave and gay, to young and old. It was instituted for man's welfare, and meets deep and universal human needs. As he Sabbatizes he comes into the plans and purposes of God. It enriches the soul, improves the mind, and affords rest and comfort to the wearied body.

As the Sabbath was made for *man*, it was made for the Gentile as well as the Jew; and is a world-wide, a universal, institution. As it was made for *man*, it was made for the last even as for the first man; and is a time-long institution. This watchword of Jesus makes the Sabbath as broad as mankind, and co-extensive with the human period. It teaches the unity of mankind. It ranks

---

[1] "The Sabbath was made *for man* in the same high sense that the family was made for man—the two great and unchangeable institutions sacred to man from the ruins of Paradise."—DR. J. O. PECK. *Sabbath Essays.*

Sabbatism among world ideas. It is a bell that is ever helping to ring the death-knell of prejudice, exclusiveness, bigotry. World ideas were long lost. Jesus restored them. The Sabbath is one of his restored world ideas.

A third watchword—"My Father worketh hitherto, and I work"—reminds us that divine work goes on unceasingly with God as a Sabbatarian. His Sabbath-cycle, his seventh-day rest, the now of all time, is occupied by him in upholding and governing all things that he created in the beginning, and in redeeming man. This divine work, sending rain on the good and the evil, sunlight on the just and the unjust, and giving a measure of the spirit to all, is ever going on; on our Sabbath as on our workdays; in our sacred as in our secular time. The work of Jesus on Jewish Sabbaths was after this divine pattern. It was work done for others; miracles of healing, building up broken human forms; doing good to the souls and bodies of men. This example of the Father and of Jesus—the Divine Workers hitherto—justifies all work done on the Sabbath for others—for their betterment. Work not for self, but for others—for their helping and improvement—is real Sabbatism—the Sabbatism of the Father—the Sabbatism of Jesus. Self-seeking work occupies us so constantly that it tires us—makes the brow sweat, the loins ache, the hands and feet weary. This is "*thy* work." It is the work that is forbidden on the Sabbath. Work for others is change and recreation. It is divine work. It is restful. "Take my yoke upon you," says Jesus,—my self-sacrificing for the good of others—"and ye shall find rest to your souls." This work is ever to go on. This Sabbatism is imperishable.

A fourth watchword—"Wherefore it is lawful to do well on the Sabbath day"—justifies all well-doing in sacred time. What wonderful words! How broad and forceful in meaning! "It is lawful"—not merely allowable as an exception, but right, as of the very nature of the institution—"to do well on the Sabbath day." To do well—no limitation or restriction is placed upon the utterance—is suitable Sabbath furniture. Works of necessity and mercy are of the very essence of Sabbath-keeping. Jesus, here as in the Fourth Commandment, lifts Sabbath-keeping from the low plain of mere formalities to the lofty level of the humanities. He fits all well-doing into the institution. He prescribes this as among its high duties and privileges, and so transmits the day on into the future. For prescription of duty and of privilege is not a warrant of death, but of continuance and of perpetuity.

Two Added Words.

To direct discourses on the Sabbath, six in number, Jesus adds a direct allusion to future Sabbatism. He had prevision of the future. He foresaw about forty years later in history, the destruction of Jerusalem, the demolition of the Temple, the slaughter and the world-wide oppression of the Jews; and he said to his disciples of that period, "Pray ye that your flight be not in the winter, neither on the Sabbath day." The Sabbath was thus before him as a belonging of the future. It was not to perish. It was to survive his earthly day, and still live on.

To direct discourses on the Sabbath, six in number, Jesus also adds an indirect allusion to the Sabbath law. He is not the law destroyer, but the law fulfiller. He puts himself in this light in his inimitable sermon on the mount. He did not come to destroy, but to fulfill the law —the moral law—its admirable summary in the Ten Commandments. Of that code he is the fulfiller, not the destroyer. He did not abrogate or weaken it, or any part of it. He did not abrogate or weaken the Fourth Commandment. He did not recall it, as if worn out and useless; nor secularize it, as if too binding. He fulfilled it. He obeyed it. He restated and reinstituted it by example and teaching. There is no repeal, no weakening, but re-enthronement, transmission, perpetuity. Moral elements continue to exist without re-enactment.

This is now the attitude of Jesus towards the Sabbath, as seen in his life and teachings, in what he did and what he said. The sketch is full and fair. Nothing is omitted; nothing overstated. How any thinker ever held and taught that Jesus meant either to abrogate the Sabbath or relax its claims, is among things unaccountable. He no more abrogated or weakened the Sabbath law, than he did the eternal laws of right—of truth—of purity—of love. It, even as they, belongs to imperishable and changeless verities.

The Risen Jesus and the Sabbath.

Change of Day.

> "Hail to the day when He by whom was given
> New life to man—he tomb asunder riven—
> Arose! that day his Church has still confessed
> At once Creation's and Redemption's feasts,—
> Sign of a world called forth, a world forgiven."

Sabbatism entered the Christian Era as an element of strife. Two practices, giving birth to two theories, started in the beginning, and ran parallel in history; one using the first-day of the week alone; the other using also the seventh-day. Seventh-day at last dropped out; and First-day alone remained for Sabbatism. A momentous question thus confronts us. Was the day *divinely* changed? Is there a fairly authorized ending of one series of Sabbaths? Is there a fairly authorized beginning of a new series of Sabbaths?

A Change of Day Possible.

Inherent sanctity belongs equally to all time, or is equally absent from all time. All days, as to intrinsic excellencies, or holy uses, are essentially alike. There is nothing in any one day, in itself, to differentiate it from others, to make it exceptionally sacred; to invest it with Sabbatism. This is self-evident. The day itself, any particular day of twenty-four hours, is not therefore of the essence of the institution. It is an accident. It is of the nature of mere forms. History and Philosophy alike so teach. An observance of the same twenty-four hour day, by the whole world population, is, from the nature of things, unattainable. It is impossible because the world turns over. Antipodal people can't observe the same holy time; nor can the people of differing longitudes. The Sabbath in Chicago is an hour later, in San Francisco three hours later, than in Philadelphia. New difficulties arise from varying national calendars. For, while God builds days, months, years, and appoints the septenary period closing with Sabbatism, he commits to man the framing of calendars and the construction of chronologies. And so different nations, by difference in their methods of reckoning time, had, and have, no agreeing day. The day among the Jews was from sunset to sunset; among the Babylonians from sunrise to sunrise; and among the Romans from midnight to midnight. A single unit of twenty-four hours for sacred time, to be used by all the nations throughout the world, is simply impossible. Sabbatism is therefore separable from any particular twenty-four hour day, even as worship is separable from temples and altars.

The portion of the weekly period—a period coeval with man and Eden—to be kept as sacred time is settled beyond all controversy. It is a seventh of days—one day in seven. This proportion of time is of the very essence of the institution. It is forever unchangeable, because it is suited to human nature as it is—meets abiding human needs. One day in seven is to be Sabbatic—is to be kept holy. But the day itself is immaterial. It is changeable and may be changed. It is of the nature of a by-law, alterable at the will of the Sabbath Maker. All that is needed to make any day in the weekly period Sabbatic, is that it be divinely appointed, and so have in it Sabbatic elements. God created the Sabbath; and he alone can change the day. The setting apart of one day in seven for sacred uses—the selection and arrangement of the day—are of God, not of man. The original seventh-day Sabbath was not of man's choosing, but of God's ordering. It was the

Maker of days who made the last day of the weekly period differ from others; equipped it with holiness and blessing; and assigned it as the day of rest and worship. The seventh-day thus set up by God can by him alone be taken down, or changed. Sabbatism is transferable from it to any other day in the week—as from the seventh to the first—only by the Lord of the Sabbath. The change requires an equal authority with that appearing in the original institution of the day. No mere man—no body of men—has the right to make such a transferrence. The next day after the Sabbath—First day—could be in no just sense a world-wide day of rest and worship till divinely set apart as such. God—Christ—alone has this authority. If the day is changed it must be by his ordering.

Great emphasis is placed by many on the want of an express command authorizing a change in the day. But in this they ask for something wholly unwarranted. The Old Testament, as the book of beginnings, more usually makes known the authoritative will of God by abrupt command; but the New Testament, as the book of transition and continuance, by example and use. A direct command to substitute baptism for circumcision, the Lord's Supper for the Passover, and the church for the synagogue, will be sought for in vain. No direct command can be found for women at the Lord's table. Christianity, in a word, though turning on the pivot of our Lord's resurrection, did not displace Judaism by direct command, or even immediately, but by growth—growth away from the old—growth towards the new. Indeed all the institutions and customs peculiar to the New Testament were gradually formed; they came, not by revolution, but by evolution. Example and use, without the formality of a precept, have been thus employed to declare God's will. So the change of the day for Sabbatism. All that is needed is to show that the risen Christ substituted the first for the seventh day by example—by exclusive approval and use. If First day was by Him exclusively used and approved, as the day for religious meetings and worship, then it is to be accepted as the Sabbath of his institution.

A Change of Day Probable.

Our Lord rose from the grave on First day. Wide and sound scholarship so interprets the Gospel narrative; always has so interpreted it; so interprets it to-day. Of late, however, some dissent is made by Seventh-day Sabbatarians. They impeach First day as the Christ-resurrection day, and clearly because it gives a death blow to seventh-day Sabbatism.

The four Evangelists, with trifling verbal differences, teach, in precise and careful statements, that Christ was crucified and buried on "preparation day," the day before the Jewish Sabbath, our Friday; that he lay in the sepulcher over the Jewish Sabbath, our Saturday; and that he rose on the morning of the day following the morning of the first day of the week, our Sabbath.[1] The Gospel nar-

---

[1] "The day of Preparation was the day preceding the Sabbath; that is Friday.—Nast's *Com. on Matt.* 27 : 62.

"While there was a regular 'preparation' for the Sabbath, there is no mention of any 'preparation' for the festivals. It seems to be essentially connected with the Sabbath itself."—*Dr. Smith's New Test. Hist.*, 343.

"And thus the Redeemer was left pale, but victorious—to sleep through the Sabbath."—Geike. *The Life of Christ*, 791.

"'The first day of the week.' The day which is observed by Christians as the Sabbath. The Jews observed the seventh day of the week, or our Saturday. During that day our Savior was in the grave. As he rose on the morning of the first day, it has always been observed in commemoration of so great an event."—*Barnes' Notes, Matt.* 28: 1.

"On the day of the preparation, at the third hour, He received the sentence from Pilate, the Father permitting that to happen; at the sixth hour He was crucified; at the ninth hour He gave up the ghost; and before sunset He was buried. During the Sabbath He continued under the earth..... At the dawn of the Lord's day he arose from the dead..... The day of the preparation, then, comprises the passion; the Sabbath embraces the burial; the Lord's day contains the resurrection."—Ignatius. *Epistle to the Trallians*, Longer Form. *Ante-Nicene Fathers*, 1 : 70.

rative, as harmonized, has no other fairly possible interpretation.[1] Its testimony to the resurrection on First day—the point in contention—is very complete and quite harmonious. The resurrection and the visit of the women to the sepulcher are associated as occurring about the same time. Now the visit of the women, according to all four Evangelists, was at an early hour on the morning of First day. Matthew says, "as it began to dawn." Mark says, "Early in the morning .... at the rising of the sun." Luke says, "very early in the morning." And John says, "Early, when it was yet dark." This clearly locates the visit of the women. It was not in the *evening*, when the sun was setting and the stars beginning to appear; when, in Jewish reckoning, the old day died and the new day

---

[1] TIME OF BURIAL HARMONIZED.—THE DAY.

MATTHEW.	MARK.	LUKE.	JOHN.
"The day of the preparation."—27:62.	"It was the preparation."—15:42. "And laid him in a sepulcher."—15:46.	"And laid it in a sepulcher..... And that day was the preparation."—15:41-2.	"There laid they Jesus therefore, because of the Jews' preparation day."—John 19:42. See also 20:31.

RELATION OF BURIAL DAY TO THE SABBATH.

MATTHEW.	MARK.	LUKE.	JOHN.
"Now the next day that followed the day of the preparation."—27:62.	"It was the preparation, that is the day before the Sabbath."—15:42.	"That day was the preparation, and the Sabbath drew on."—23:54.	"That the bodies should not remain on the cross on the Sabbath day, for that Sabbath day was a high day."—20:31.

TIME OF WOMEN'S VISIT HARMONIZED—ITS RELATION TO THE SABBATH.

MATTHEW.	MARK.	LUKE.	JOHN.
"In the end of the Sabbath."—28:1.	"When the Sabbath was past."—16:1.	"They rested the Sabbath day according to the Scriptures."—23:56.	No record.

ITS RELATIONS TO FIRST DAY.

MATTHEW.	MARK.	LUKE.	JOHN.
"As it began to dawn toward the first day of the week."—28:1.	"Very early in the morning the first day of the week... At the rising of the sun."—16:2. "Now when Jesus was risen on the first day of the week."—16:9.	"Upon the first day of the week very early in the morning."—24:1.	"The first day of the week..... When it was yet dark."—20:1.

was born. But it was in the *morning,* at the hour of dawn, at the time of day-break; when *apparent* night was fleeing, and *apparent* day advancing.[1] All four Evangelists say so. There is no break anywhere in their testimony. Their speech is explicit, clear, plain, and cannot fairly be misunderstood. They set forth, beyond fair challenge, the time of the visit of the women—and so of the resurrection—as at an early hour on the morning of First day. All ripe scholarship so consents, and so teaches.

Three of the Evangelists report the visit of the women —and so the time of the resurrection—in its relations to the Jewish Sabbath. The fourth Evangelist, John, is silent. Luke says of the women, "They rested the Sabbath day, according to the commandment," and then starts their visit "on the first day of the week." Mark begins their visit "on the first day of the week," "when the Sabbath was past." But Matthew's Greek text has an element of uncertainty. It is the only element of uncertainty in the whole Gospel narrative. It may be translated—and by some versionists is translated—"late in the Sabbath"; and this, it is claimed by Seventh-day Sabbatarians, locates both the visit and the resurrection on the Sabbath day. This claim is violent and uncritical. It makes Matthew self-contradictory; for, with the very next stroke of his pen, he begins the visit as "at dawn towards the first day of the week." It also makes Matthew contradict

---

[1] "At the early dawn of the first day of the week, our Sunday, a number of women started, according to the four Evangelists, for the sepulcher of the Lord."—NAST's *Com.* Matt. 28:2.

"The true-hearted women had resolved to reach the grave by sunrise. .... The grey dawn had hardly shown itself when they were afoot on their errand."—GEIKE. *The Life of Christ,* 794.

"Our Lord was crucified on a Friday and rose again on a Sunday." —*Encycl. Brit.* Art. Irenæus.

all the other Evangelists, who report the visit as beginning after the Sabbath was past—in an early morning hour of First day. The claim made is the dogmatism of partial inquiry. It makes Scripture contradict Scripture—Evangelist battle with Evangelist. Sound criticism is obliged to translate ὀψὲ in Matthew as, not "*late in*," but "*after*," the Sabbath; an allowable rendering as shown by eminent scholars.[1] This is a sound canon of criticism. It makes the doubtful, not contradict, but harmonize with the plain. It harmonizes Matthew with himself, and with all the other Evangelists. When Matthew is so interpreted, there is entire harmony among all the Evangelists. The first three report the visit as after the Sabbath; and then all four, without a break,

---

The critics explain Matthew:

[1] "The Greek expression would justify the translation *after the* Sabbath."—*Nast's Com.*, Matt. 28: 1.

"Hence by, *late in the Sabbath*, we are not to suppose Saturday evening to be intended . . . but *far on in the Saturday night*, after midnight, *toward daybreak* on Sunday."—MEYER. *Com.* Matt. 28: 1.

"It is not the accurate Jewish division of time, according to which the Sabbath ended at six on Saturday evening, but the ordinary reckoning of the day, which extends from sunrise to sunrise, and adds the night to the preceding day."—LANGE. *Com.* Matt. 28: 1.

"Verse 1. *In the end of the Sabbath.* ὀψὲ δε σαββάτων. *After the end of the week*: this is the translation given by several eminent critics; and in this way the word ὀψε is used by the most eminent Greek writers. Thucydides, lib. iv, chap. 93, τῆς ἡμέρας ὀψε ἠν—the day was *ended*. Plutarch, ὀψε των βασιλεως χθονων—*after* the times of the king. Philostratus, ὀψε των Τροικων—*after* the Trojan war. . . . The transaction mentioned here evidently took place early on the morning of the *third* day after our Lord's crucifixion; what is called our Sunday morning, or first day of the week."—*Clarke's Com.* Matt. 28 : 1.

The critics report Matthew:

"Sabbath being over, and the first day of the week beginning to dawn."—CAMPBELL.

"Being, 'early,' that is, about break of day, on the first day of the week, (corresponding to our Sunday)."—*Cottage Bible.*

"'*In the end of the Sabbath, as it began to dawn.*'—After the Sabbath, as it grew toward daylight—'toward the first day of the week.'"—JAMIESON-FAUSSET-BROWN. *Com.* Matt. 28 : 1.

locate it in an early morning hour "on the first day of the week." This is decisive and final. It is all that fair reason could wish or demand. It should bind our faith and conduct. The Christ resurrection is clearly set forth in the Gospels as a First day event. So all the Evangelists teach. The *consensus* of scholarship here approaches the absolute.

But the statement in Matthew,[a] that Christ should be "three days and three nights in the heart of the earth," and that in John[b] "in three days I will rear it up," seem to conflict with the actual time that, in the accepted theory, he lay in the sepulcher—some thirty-six hours. The difficulty is but seeming not real.[1] Time computations em-

---

[a] Matt. 12: 40.   [b] John 2: 19.

[1] "One hour more is reckoned as a day, and one day more as a year."—*Jerusalem Talmud.*.

"A day and night together make up an *okkah*, or νυχθήμεραν, and any part of such a period is counted as a whole."—*Jerusalem Talmud.*

"The phrase is doubtless equivalent to the Greek νυχθήμεραν, a day and night of twenty-four hours. But the Hebrew form, *three days and three nights*, was likewise used generally and indefinitely for *three days* simply; as is obvious from I. Samuel 30: 1, 12, and the circumstances there narrated."—DR. ROBINSON.

"It is of great importance to observe that the Easterns reckoned any part of the day of 24 hours for a whole day, and, say a thing was done after three or seven days, &c., if it was done on the third or seventh day from that last mentioned. . . . So that to say a thing happened *after* three days and three nights was the same as to say, it happened in three days, or on the third day."—DODDRIDGE.

"The *time* of the resurrection is stated by St. Mark, as 'early on the first day of the week,' which began from the sunset of the evening before . . . The portion, however brief, of this day (according to Jewish reckoning) that Jesus remained in the Tomb is reckoned as one day, like the brief interval between his burial and Friday's sunset, and thus he remained *three days* in the earth."—*Dr. Smith's N. T. Hist.* p. 349.

"First day. The portion however brief, of this day . . . that Jesus remained in the tomb is reckoned as one day, like the brief interval between his burial and the Friday's sunset; and thus he remained three days in the earth."—WM. SMITH, LL. D. *Butler's Bible Work*, N. T., 559.

brace as full days beginning and ending fractional days. Birthday, though the birth be in one of its latest hours, is always counted as a day in the life-period. The day that money is loaned in a bank is counted as a full day in the note, though the money change hands at a very late hour. This is a wide custom among mankind. It was, and is, the custom in the East. It prevailed in all Bible times. In the Bible a fractional beginning day, or ending day, always counts as a full day. This is what is done in the case of the crucified and risen Christ. He died about three o'clock in the afternoon on crucifixion day, and was buried before the day ended. This counts as a day. He lay in the sepulcher all the Jewish Sabbath. This is the second day. He arose about day-break on First-day morning. This counts as the third day. This is the accepted theory; and it is the clear meaning of the Gospel narrative. It is the only true theory. Our Lord certainly did not lay in the sepulcher seventy-two hours—three full twenty-four hour days. The Gospel narrative does not permit, but forbids, this idea. And contemporaneous history, sacred and profane, also forbids it. Paul testifies that he "rose again the third day"—sometime during the day—while it was yet going on—before its end was reached. And Josephus, a contemporary of the Apostles, and undoubtedly repeating what was current in his times, says, "he appeared to them alive again the third day"—before the day ended—they saw him alive again sometime during the third day. These are proofs that the third day was a fractional day. They refute and set aside the seventy-two hour theory. They establish the accepted theory. The time of the entombment fixes the resurrection as a first-day event. Mark calls it such. He says, "now when Jesus was risen the first day of the week." This is Gospel. When he went forth from the sepulcher, the Sabbath was fully past, the first day was well begun.[1]

It was reserved for the vanity and scepticism of this nineteenth century to challenge the Christ-resurrection as a first-day event. The challenge rests on insubstantial foundations, and has really nothing but quibbles to support it. If Christ did not rise on the first-day, we have to explain how that particular belief has entered into and colored all associated History, Art, Literature, and has been taught by an unbroken series of writers from the very beginning; and how the four Gospels, the Apostles, and the first Christians all asserted the fact of the resurrection, and always as a First-day event. We have also to explain how First-day has ever since been monumental of the event, and how First-day worship goes clear back to the event, and issued out of it. First-day, as the Christ-resurrection day, has thus, from the first, the support of continuous history, and of continuous institutional testimony. This proof is most unquestionable, is not liable to

---

[1] "He rose again the third day, according to the Scriptures."—I. Cor. 15: 4.

"And when Pilate, at the suggestion of the principal men among us, had condemned him to the cross, those that loved him at first did not forsake him; for he *appeared to them alive again the third day.*"— JOSEPHUS. *Antiq.* 18: 3: 3.

"Three days" and resurrection on "third day" are equally New Testament phrases in describing the event. "Build it in three days," Matt. 26: 61. "Buildest it in three days," Matt. 27: 40 and Mark 15: 29. "After three days I will build it again," Matt. 27: 63. "Within three days I will build another," Mark 14: 58. "After three days rise again." Mark 8: 31.

The event was to end sometime during the third day. "Be raised again the third day," Matt. 16: 21. "The third day he shall be raised again," Matt. 17: 23. "The third day he shall rise again," Matt. 20: 19, Mark 10: 34, Luke 18: 33. "He shall rise the third day," Mark 9: 31. "Be raised from the dead the third day," Luke 9: 22. "The third day I shall be perfected," Luke 13: 22. "The third day rise again," Luke 24: 7. "To rise from the dead the third day," Luke 24: 46. These Scriptures, explaining the former, suggest a fractional third day.

fraud, and is not diminished but strengthened by the lapse of time. Nothing, I apprehend, that a man does not himself see or hear, can be regarded as more certain. Seventh-day Sabbatarians discredit their scholarship when they attack the resurrection of Christ as a first-day event.[1]

Nations and races of men commemorate, by monumental shafts and institutions, great events in their history. Our Fourth of July is monumental of Revolutionary scenes and of American Independence, and our Decoration day, of the lives given to re-cement the Union. This instinct to plant monumental institutions has descended to us from our Maker. God was the first Monument builder. To commemorate Creation, a work worthy of himself, he kept and instituted the seventh-day Sabbath; and he gave it to man as a joyful token of his work as World-Builder. Creation has thus its monumental Sabbath, connecting the Sabbath-keeper with the Creator.

Our Lord's resurrection was a most momentous event; keystone in the mighty arch of Redemption; supreme day in the history of time and man. It was reported by

---

[1] "The *dawn* was purpling o'er the sky;
* * * * * * *
When He whom stone, and seal, and guard,
Had safely to the tomb consigned,
Triumphant rose, and buried Death
Deep in the grave he left behind."
—*From the Latin.*

"T'was on the Easter Sunday *morn*,
That from the blessed skies,
Came down the holy angels
To see the Lord arise."
—Mrs. Howitt.

"For He was crucified on the day before that of Saturn (the Jewish Sabbath); and on the day after Saturn, which is the day of the sun, having appeared to His Apostles and disciples, He taught them these things."—Justin Martyr. *First Apology*, About 139 A. D. Ante-Nicene Fathers, 1 : 186.

"The *time* of the resurrection is stated by St. Mark as 'early on the first day of the week,' which began from the sunset of the evening before."—*Dr. Smith's N. T. Hist.*, 349.

"According to all the four Evangelists, the resurrection of our Lord took place on the first day of the week after his crucifixion."—*Encycl. Brit.*, Art. Sunday.

angels; retold by the women; and is the loftiest Apostolic utterance. It is the closing story of the Gospels; the central theme of the Epistles; the immovable foundation of Christianity. Redemption, complete in the risen Christ, is a greater work than Creation.

> "'Twas great to speak the world from naught;
> 'Twas greater to redeem."

In the divine balances, where real values are weighed and ascertained, love is greater than power; redeeming love greater than creating power; self-sacrificing love, giving birth to a new spiritual creation, greater than omnipotent power, peopling space with new worlds and tenanting them with new forms of life. Shall power have its memorial, and love not? Creating power its weekly monument, and redeeming love not? Omnipotent power its Sabbatism, and self-sacrificing love not? Love, outranking power, is even more entitled to a monument—to a weekly remembrancer—to Sabbatism. The glory of the greater demands a New Testament Sabbath, even as the glory of the lesser had its Old Testament Sabbath. A new day for Sabbatism would make the institution a roll call for Redemption as well as for Creation.

Seventh-day Sabbatarians have no weekly monument of the Christ resurrection; no weekly monument of Redemption, but only of Creation; no weekly monument of Christ as Redeemer, but only of Jehovah as Creator. This, in Jews, who reject the divine Christ and his atonement, is consistent; but, in receivers of his divinity and atonement, an anomaly and absurdity. Is not Redemption entitled to a place in the monumental Sabbath? It could not have it in the *old* but only in a *new* day. Seventh-day was preoccupied. And to disciples, as the day when Christ lay in the sepulcher, it was, and would be, a day of gloom and sorrow; while First-day, when he rose, was a day of thrilling and unbounded joy. As our Lord selected and privileged First-day; as First-day, whose morning sun shone on the empty sepulcher, is the most wonderful and memorable day in the world's history; it is entitled to be the Sabbath of Christianity. It would have been strange if that unparalleled event had not made First-day the day of days—a holy day—a joyous and blessed day to disciples—the Sabbath of the new era.

Christianity, the greatest moral movement in history, began a new order of things. It was a new creation. It inaugurated new world ideas. It started a new epoch in history. It made a new era in time. It gave chronology a new date. Why not also the weekly calendar a new Sabbath? Without this the transition would have been incomplete. If all old forms disappeared, and all appearing forms were new, then the old seventh day, because a mere form, would die in the Christ sepulcher, and the new First-day rise thence to life.

Christianity, as a new religious movement, needed a stated day for worship, for instruction, and for the mutual encouragement of disciples. The day, as coming from the Lord of the seventh-day Sabbath, would certainly be a septenary day. It could not be seventh-day; for that was already engaged, and would give the new movement a too great Judaic tinge. After seventh-day, no other day in the weekly period would have equal claims with First day; the day of our Lord's resurrection; the day of marvels to the disciples. Its selection and use would, by its rousing memories, impart an inspiration to all workers in the new movement.

Change of Day Beginning.

It was not accident, but a divine purpose and arrangement, that brought Christ from the grave on First day, and that made after revelations of himself to the disciples —perhaps all of them—First day events. Ten post-resurrection appearings of Christ are recorded; six of the ten on First day; five on resurrection day itself; and one on next First day. Indeed all the recorded appearings of our risen but unascended Lord, whose dates are ascertainable, were on First day; and not one on Seventh day. This is very remarkable. The risen Jesus selected First days, never Seventh days, in revealing himself to the disciples.

Study resurrection day itself—$\mu\iota\alpha$ $\tau\tilde{\omega}\nu$ $\sigma\alpha\beta\beta\acute{\alpha}\tau\omega\nu$.[1]—The first day of the week. At its beginning, in its early morning, through its noontide hours, in its afternoon, and in its evening, Jesus was meeting with his disciples, and

---

[1] $M\iota\alpha$ $\sigma\alpha\beta\beta\acute{\alpha}\tau\omega\nu$—"one of the Sabbaths"—or "one (day) from the Sabbath"—is used eight times in the New Testament, and is always translated "the first day of the week." It is the first divine name for that day. The Jews had no names for the secular days of the week. They reckoned them numerically from the Sabbath. The ancient seven-day week was evidently created and measured by the Sabbath. Early Chaldeans designated the days of the week by ordinals. So too the Jews. Each day was counted from the Sabbath. The first Christians used this Jewish calendar. But counting the days from the Sabbath soon began to change. The secular days began to have names. First day was called by Justin Martyr Sunday; fourth day, by Clement of Alexandria, Ermou; and sixth day, by the same author, Aphrodites. Soon all the secular days had names—planetary names. I give here the divine name for First-day as used in the Greek Testament:

Matt. 28:1. $\epsilon\iota\varsigma$ $\mu\iota\alpha\nu$ $\sigma\alpha\beta\beta\acute{\alpha}\tau\omega\nu$. First day of the week.

Mark 16:2. $\pi\rho o\grave{\iota}$ $\tau\tilde{\eta}\varsigma$ $\mu\iota\alpha\varsigma$ $\sigma\alpha\beta\beta\acute{\alpha}\tau\omega\nu$. The first day of the week.

Mark 16:9. $\pi\rho o\grave{\iota}$ $\pi\rho\grave{\omega}\tau\eta$ $\sigma\alpha\beta\beta\acute{\alpha}\tau o\upsilon$ Early on the first day of the week.

Luke 24:1. $\tau\tilde{\eta}$ $\delta\grave{\epsilon}$ $\mu\iota\tilde{\alpha}$ $\tau\omega\nu$ $\sigma\alpha\beta\beta\acute{\alpha}\tau\omega\nu$. On the first day of the week.

John 20:1. $\tau\tilde{\eta}$ $\delta\epsilon$ $\mu\iota\alpha$ $\tau\tilde{\omega}\nu$ $\epsilon\alpha\beta\beta\acute{\alpha}\tau\omega\nu$. On the first day of the week.

John 20:10. $\tau\tilde{\eta}$ $\mu\iota\tilde{\alpha}$ $\tau\grave{o}\nu$ $\sigma\alpha\beta\beta\acute{\alpha}\tau\omega\nu$. The first day of the week.

Acts 20:7. $\tau\tilde{\eta}$ $\mu\iota\alpha$ $\tau\tilde{\omega}\nu$ $\sigma\alpha\beta\beta\acute{\alpha}\tau\omega\nu$. The first day of the week.

I. Cor. 16:2. $\kappa\alpha\tau\alpha$ $\mu\iota\alpha\nu$ $\sigma\alpha\beta\beta\acute{\alpha}\tau\omega\nu$. Upon the first day of the week.

"Our Lord Jesus Christ who rose from the dead on the first day of week ($\tau\tilde{\eta}$ $\mu\iota\alpha$ $\sigma\beta\beta\acute{\alpha}\tau\omega\nu$.)"—JUSTIN MARTYR. *Dial. with Trypho the Jew.*

filling their hearts with peace and joy. How blessed and restful to Mary—to the other women at the sepulcher—to Peter, newly forgiven—and to the two disciples on their way to Emmaus. And then its surprising and tender evening meeting! Read John's comforting statement: "Then the same day at evening, being the first day of the week, when the doors were shut where the disciples were assembled for fear of the Jews, came Jesus and stood in the midst, and said, 'Peace be unto you' . . . And . . . he breathed on them, and said unto them, 'Receive ye the Holy Ghost.'" What a meeting! What a time for tender memories! It was restful—blessed—hallowing—Sabbatic! And mark how the Evangelist particularly notes that it was "the first day of the week," as if he would intimate the divine choice of the day for Christian meetings.[1] The meeting must have extended well into the

---

[1] "The first Lord's day of the new creation."—*Suggestive Commentary*, Luke 24: 1.

Sunday the 17th of Nisan (April 8th). "The first Lord's day." "Easter Day."—Dr. *Smith's New Test. Hist.*, p. 348.

"'*The first day of the week.*' This.... means our Sunday, the Lord's day, the first day following the Jewish Sabbath."—RYLE. *Com.* John 20: 1.

"The first remarkable mention of the Lord's day is combined with the resurrection of our Lord."—BENGEL's *Gnomon*, on Matt. 28: 1.

"Our Lord rested in the grave on the Jewish Sabbath before he instituted by his resurrection the new Sabbath of holy joy and active benevolence—the Lord's Day."—SMITH. *New Test. Hist.*, 315.

"'*In the end of the* (Jewish) *Sabbath.*'—The Evangelist, without doubt, intended by the selection of this peculiar and significant expression to bring forward the fact, that the Christian Sunday had now caused the Sabbath to cease."—LANGE. *Com.*, Matt. 28: 1.

"'*The first day of the week.*' All the Evangelists at the commencement of their narratives of the resurrection mention that it was the first day of the week."—JACOBUS' *Notes*, John 20: 19.

John 20: 19. "This verse, compared with verse 1, may help to settle the question as to the time when the Christian Sabbath commences. 'They went early the *first* day,'—this verse says 'evening of the same day:' this was the evening of the Christian Sabbath."—*Cottage Bible*, 2: 1183.

night; for Luke brings to it the two disciples who ate their evening meal at Emmaus, six or seven miles away; and it was after they arrived and reported how the Lord had appeared to them, that Jesus entered with his gracious and inspiring words. This evidently late evening meeting could only be called a First-day meeting by Roman not by Jewish reckoning. The day throughout, down well into the night, was thus an interesting opening of the new Sabbath. The Jewish Sabbath, with Christ in the sepulcher, closed the old order of things; First day, with Christ risen and meeting the disciples, began the new.

The Passover Sabbath, in Jewish reckoning, was a date for numbering both the days and the Sabbaths up to Pentecost. It was so given by Moses.[a] It is so used in the Gospels.[1] The fiftieth day thereafter was Pentecost. "After

---

[a] Lev. 23: 15-21.

[1] The phrase "eight days," in its terminal period, is equivalent to "eighth day," which has a remarkable Old Testament use. Note these facts: Circumcision on eighth day, Lev. 17: 12; Mothers ceremonially clean on eighth day, Lev. 12: 1; first born of cattle given to the Lord on eighth day, Ex. 22: 3; high priest consecrated on eighth day, Lev. 9: 1; leper cleansing complete on eighth day, Lev. 22: 27; and defiled Nazarite clean on eighth day, Lev. 15: 14, 29. Eighth day is thus signalized in the Mosaic economy as having special value. It reports the ending of trial periods; and is a Hebraism for First-day from the date of the trial period. It seems to have been made prominent for some future divine purpose. Was it meant to indicate that First-day would yet become the completion of the weekly period, even the Sabbath itself?

If the day on which Christ rose from the dead is made the Sabbath of a new weekly period—the beginning of a new weekly calendar—the first of a new series of Sabbaths—then the week in the new era would close with the "eighth day"—the second Sabbath be on the "eighth day." "After eight days" is so used by the fourth Evangelist. And "eighth day" appears at once, and with this meaning, in the Church Fathers—contemporaries and immediate successors of the Apostles.

"We celebrate the *eighth* day with joy, on which too Jesus rose from the dead."—BARNABAS. C. 15.

"The *eighth* day on which our Lord sprang up."—IGNATIUS. *Magnesians*, C. 15, longer form.

eight days," and "after forty days," would be so many days after the Passover Sabbath, including it. "After eight days," on crucifixion year when the Passover fell on the Jewish Sabbath, would be, in Jewish reckoning, the second First day. Scholarship is a fair unit here. For the small Seventh-day Sabbatarian dissent, I have never seen even a show of reason. "Eight days after" the Sabbath of the Passover—the Sabbath in the sepulcher—would be the second First day.

The disciples lingered in Jerusalem after the Passover week was ended, and after the following Jewish Sabbath was over. They strangely lingered over the second First-day, and, not only lingered, but held a meeting some time during the day. Thomas, the doubter, was present. John is the reporter. He says: "And after eight days, again his disciples were within, and Thomas with them; then came Jesus . . . . and said, 'Peace be unto you.' Then saith he unto Thomas, ... 'be not faithless but believing.' And Thomas . . . . said, 'My Lord and my God.'" This meeting, if held elsewhere than in Jerusalem, is then even a more remarkable Gospel testimony to this First-day meeting. The risen Christ crowned the meeting with his presence and blessing. How hallowed the occasion! How restful and Sabbatic to Thomas; doubt gone; peace filling his heart! The Christ resurrection thus started from the very beginning a new weekly day of meeting. On two First days—not on Seventh-days—the disciples assemble, and Jesus meets with them. The old has evidently ended; the new begins. The Sabbath of the Jew has died in the sepulcher of the Savior, that the Sabbath of Christianity might be born with his resurrection.' (See notes on opposite page.)

If Jesus, the Sabbath-Maker—the Lord of the Sabbath—changes the day, the change is authoritative. Study the risen Jesus in his attitude so far towards Sabbatism. In no recorded instance did he ever meet with his disciples on any seventh day. He kept seventh-day *before* but in no known instance *after* his passion. All his recorded post-resurrection meetings with disciples, of ascertainable date, were on First-days. Ten are recorded; six of the ten on First-days—five on resurrection day itself—and one on next First-day. Five First-days elapsed between his resurrection and his ascension; and on two of the five he is known to have met with his disciples. This now begins

---

[1] "Jesus again appeared to them on the next Sunday, and Thomas was convinced."—*Farrar's Early Days of Christ.*, p. 436.

"The second appearance of Christ, on the first Sunday after the resurrection day, in the midst of the disciples."—LANGE. *Com.* John 20: 26.

"*After eight days.* This is the first record of Christian Sabbath observance."—*Jacobus' Notes.* John 20: 26.

"*After eight days.* It seems likely that this was precisely on that day se'nnight, on which Christ had appeared to them before; and from this we may learn that this was the *weekly meeting* of the Apostles; and though Thomas was not found at the *former* meeting, he was determined not to be absent from *this*."—*Clarke's Com.* John 20: 26.

"Here we have one of the incidental notices—more valuable than any formal statement, because they show how regularly the custom was established—of those meetings of the Christians on the Lord's Day for social converse and divine worship, which Pliny mentions as their only known institution."—*Dr. Smith's N. T. Hist.*, p. 536.

"Eight days later the Lord appeared to his assembled disciples again, Thomas being present, (John 20: 26). The Passover had lasted to the preceding Friday. On Saturday, the Jewish Sabbath, the disciples did not travel, and staid also the second Sunday at Jerusalem—a proof that this day had already become to them the Sabbath of the New Testament."—*Nast's Com.* Matt. 28: 1.

"A whole week elapsed before the next recorded appearance. On Sunday, known, henceforth, as 'the first day of the week,' in contrast to the Jewish Sabbath, the seventh; and as especially 'the Lord's day,' the Eleven having once more assembled. . . . Jesus, honoring his resurrection day, once more stood in the midst of them."—CUNNINGHAM GEIKE. *The Life of Christ*, 805.

the Scriptural proofs, that Christ fairly authorized the transference of Sabbatism from Seventh to First day. For his doings are interpreters of his mind and will. Their fair interpretation, so far, is that Seventh-day was divinely vacated, and First-day selected for meetings and worship. Christ thus changed the day, not by express law, but by example—by use—by approval. He dismissed the old; he inaugurated the new.[1] There was that in the Judaic Sabbath, which grew old and died in the sepulcher of Jesus—the day itself—and that which, surviving all time and change, belongs to things imperishable—the Sabbatic elements that passed over into First-day in the new era. Man, standing by the First-day Sabbath, is the exalted man of the ages; retaining, by transfer, Old Testament Sabbatism as monumental of Creation; and using also New Testament Sabbatism as monumental of Redemption.

---

[1] "In the interim we may suppose that he enacted by word what in his majesty he had sanctioned by act."—POPE. *Comp. of Christ. Theol.*, 3 : 291.

THE ASCENDED JESUS AND THE SABBATH.

THE APOSTOLIC AGE.

"O day of rest! how beautiful, how fair,
  How welcome to the weary and the old!
Day of the Lord! and truce to earthly care!
Day of the Lord, as all our days should be."
—LONGFELLOW.

As the Gospels close in resurrection effulgence and ascension glory, Apostolic Church History opens amid a blaze of Pentecostal light and power. Jesus ceases to be visible upon the stage. The Apostles appear to guide the forming customs of the church. The planting of Christianity begins.

The social and religious habits of nations and races of men are not born—a new community does not grow up out of an old one—in a day. Great social transformations require time as well as the chiseling influence of new ideas. From Judaism to Christianity stretched the chasm of a vast social and religious revolution: Judaism the bud; Christianity the flower and fruit: Judaism atmosphered in prophecy, circumcision, the passover, seventh-day rest, temple worship, and local ideas, all fleeing shadows; and Christianity atmosphered in the Gospel, baptism, the Lord's Supper, first-day rest, church worship, and world ideas, all abiding realities. The movement pivoted itself on the resurrection of our Lord; the old remaining in his sepulcher, the new rising with him; the old ages ending, the new beginning. So it started. It started off at once. But it was to be, and was, a growth; advancing from germ to fruit. It reached a notable stage at the fall of Jerusalem. Then the Temple, with its priests and altars, its clouds of ever-ascending incense, its bleating and lowing sacrificial victims, wholly disappeared. The magnificent ritual of Jewish worship ceased. Jewish nationality ended. Mosaism fell into decay. That great catastrophe was the emancipation of Christianity, that had started with the air of a Jewish sect, and was in danger of becoming tributary to Judaism. It would not now be too Judaistic, but its simple and pure self.

I am now to take my stand upon the breast of this mighty movement, and trace its divine Sabbatism. I am to discuss New Testament Sabbatism, under the Apostles: two days from the first running along together—indeed running side by side still—but First-day steadily superseding Seventh-day; the Old dropping out, and the New coming to the front. But back of the Apostles, the conspicuous workers of the hour, are two recorded special interventions of our ascended Lord, that still further report his mind and will respecting the day for Sabbatism in the Christian Era. These demand attention. The Apostles are preceptors. But Christ is still the Great Teacher. We listen, not yet to them, but wait for his voice.

PENTECOST.

Christ, ascending, appointed a future meeting for the disciples: to tarry at Jerusalem—to await the promise of the Father—to expect an enduement of divine power.[1] The Jewish Pentecost discloses this meeting—this Christ-appointed meeting—as held on that day. Now on what day was Pentecost in the Crucifixion year? On what day of the week?

That the Jewish Passover, as given by Moses, was regulated by observations of the moon's phases, is open to

---

[1] "But tarry ye in the city of Jerusalem until ye be endued with power from on high."—*Luke* 24 : 49.

"Commanded that they should not depart from Jerusalem, but wait for the promise of the Father, which, saith he, ye have heard of me."—*Acts* 1 : 4.

doubt. The Mosaic Passover Sabbath does not seem a movable Sabbath. The Hebrew *sacred* year, as arranged by Moses, seems always to have begun with a Seventh-day Sabbath. That would make the Passover Sabbath and the Seventh-day Sabbath always synchronize on the fifteenth day of the first month; and then Pentecost would always fall on Jewish First day. Some scholars adopt this view. They make every Pentecost fall on First day.[1]

But some historic evidences suggest that the later Passover Sabbath was a movable Sabbath—possibly a corruption after the Egyptian Dispersion.[2] Pentecost, then, would not always fall on First day. It would only fall

---

[1] "The Pentecost always occurred on the first day of the Jewish week."—POND. *Con. on the Bible*, 474.

"This (Lev. 23: 3-39,) describes Pentecost, which was to be celebrated on the first day of the week."—CRAFT. *Sabbath for Man*, 533.

"The first day of unleavened bread was always to fall upon a Sabbath; which I think is hinted in Lev. 23: 11. The wave sheaf was to be waved on the morrow after a Sabbath; but the wave sheaf was thus offered on the second day of unleavened bread; and consequently, if that day was the morrow after a Sabbath, then the day preceding, or first day of unleavened bread, was a Sabbath. . . . In the third month the Sabbaths will fall thus; the fourth day a Sabbath; and the day after this Sabbath was the day of Pentecost. . . . Accordingly, from the sixteenth of the first month to the fifth day of the third month, counting inclusively, are fifty days; and the fiftieth day falls regularly on the morrow or day after the Sabbath."—*Shuckford's Connection*, 2: 7-8. Woodward, Philada., 1824.

[2] "Petavius seems to think"—that the Hebrews used lunar months—"not till after the times of Alexander the Great, when they fell under the government of the Syro-Macedonian kings."—*Pet. Ration. Temp.*, 2: 1: 6.

"It can never be proved that the Hebrews used lunar months before the Babylonian captivity."—*Chronol. Pref. to the Reader.* See also SCALIGER. *Emend. Temp.*, 151.

"It is, I think, undeniable, that the Jews did admit the use of a new form of computing their year some time after the captivity, which differed in many points from this more ancient method, and which obliged them in time to make many rules for the translation of days and feasts."—*Shuckford's Connection*, 2: 18-9.

on First day in the years when the Passover Sabbath synchronized with the Seventh-day Sabbath. The many scholars who adopt this theory, teach with great unanimity, that the Passover Sabbath and the Seventh day Sabbath synchronized in crucifixion year, and that Pentecost in that year fell on First day.[1]

The New Testament records the entombment as covering the Jewish Sabbath, and puts the resurrection on First day. This locates Pentecost beyond fair controversy on First day. The evidence is thus complete. Pentecost in crucifixion year was on Jewish First day. It was on the seventh First day in the new era. The Gospels so teach.

The New Testament makes this statement: "And when the day of Pentecost was fully come, the disciples were all

---

[1] "Sunday, May 24, Day of Pentecost."—LEWIN.

"On that day (First day) it is believed, fell the day of Pentecost."—*Cot. Bible*, Acts 20: 7.

"On the day of Pentecost which in that year fell on the first day of week."—*Smith's Dict. of the Bible*. Art. Lord's Day.

"Moreover, it was when they were so assembled on the first day of the week that the Pentecostal outpouring of the Holy Spirit took place."—DR. J. H. MCILVAINE. *Pres. Rev.*, vol. 4, p. 263.

"When the day of Pentecost had dawned. It was the first day of the week."—FARRAR. *The Life and Work of St. Paul*, 2: 89.

"On the day of Pentecost, which in that year fell on the first day of the week."—McCLINTOCK & STRONG. *Cycl.*, Art. Lord's Day.

"On this day (the first day of the week) the Apostles were assembled, when the Holy Ghost came down so visibly upon them, to quicken them for the conversion of the world."—BUCK. *Theo. Dict.*, Art. Sab.

"Seven weeks were numbered from the 16th of Nisan, and the following day, the 6th of Sivan, was the day of Pentecost. Since in A. D. 30, the 16th of Nisan fell, as we have seen, on Saturday, the 7th of April, the day of Pentecost fell on Sunday, May 27th."—SMITH. *N. T. Hist.*, 380. Note.

"It (Pentecost) consequently occurred, in the year in which Christ died, on the first day of the week, or our Sunday. . . . This statement is sustained by the very ancient tradition of the Church that the first Christian Pentecost season occurred on Sunday."—LANGE. *Com.* Acts 2: 1-4.

with one accord in one place." Thus Peter, James, and John are already using First day for meetings and worship. They assemble on that day "with one accord in one place;" and not these three pillar Apostles alone, nor merely the Twelve; but as many as one hundred and twenty disciples. This meeting for religious purposes on a stated day—an evidently arranged and understood day —*a Christ-appointed day*—has essential Sabbatic elements. Christ honored the day and the assembled disciples with a wonderful baptism of the Spirit, a miraculous gift of tongues, and the greatest one-day religious revival known to history.[1] Thus First day—the day of our Lord's resurrection—was at the opening of the Gospel, characterized, instead of the Sabbath in the Mosaic ritual, by a Christ-appointed meeting of the disciples, and singular divine manifestations. These are remarkable First-day events. Adverse criticism cannot belittle them. The birth of the Christian Church, as well as the resurrection of Christ, crowns and honors the first day of the week. And so far this is the only day known for meetings between the risen and now ascended Christ and his disciples; no other day appears; the Seventh does not. This is a farther interpretation of the mind and will of Christ. It is a farther authoritative change of the day. Seventh-day Sabbatism is dropping out of sight; and First-day Sabbatism is appearing in New Testament history.

Pentecost seems thereafter an important *annual* in the New Testament Church. Paul, to Corinthian Christians, (Gentiles mainly,) writes about Pentecost as if the day was well-known to them.[a] And Luke reports Paul, at a time,

---

[a] I. Cor. 16: 8.

[1] "With his resurrection began his formal appointment of the First day, and, with the Pentecost, he finally ratified it."—POPE. *Com. on Christ.*, 3 : 291.

"The Pentecostal outpouring of the Spirit, seven weeks later. . . . cannot have failed to give an additional sacredness to the day (First day) in the eyes of the earliest converts."—*Cycl. Brit.*, Art. Sunday.

as hastening to be at Jerusalem at Pentecost.[b] It was certainly not as a Jew but as a Christian that he hasted to any Pentecost at Jerusalem.[1] Pentecost must have already become a notable Christian annual, a day for special Christian as well as Jewish gatherings; a day of delightful Christian as well as Jewish memories. The Christians at Jerusalem must have had a Pentecost of their own. History confirms this view. An annual Pentecost appears among post-Apostolic Christians, and it evidently arose as an Apostolic institution and custom. Thus one First-day—Pentecost—was conspicuous as an annual among Apostolic men. So far, religious meetings, since Christ's resurrection, are not at all of the Seventh but wholly of First-day.

"THE LORD'S DAY."

The last revelation the ascended Christ has visibly made of himself—perhaps the last to be made for all time—was made to John on the Isle of Patmos. John

---

[b] Acts 20: 16.

[1] Lewin, Howson, Smith—special writers about Paul—think that his five visits to Jerusalem were each at a Pentecost.—Acts 18: 21-2; 20: 16. I. Cor. 16: 8.

"From the latter date we can safely reckon back, through his two years' imprisonment at Cesarea, to the Pentecost of A. D. 58, as the date of his last arrival at Jerusalem."—SMITH. *N. T. Hist.*, 420.

"The two most ancient feasts of the Church were in honor of the Resurrection of Christ, and of the descent of the Holy Spirit."—*Waddington's Ch. Histo.*, 1: 44.

"We remember the higher and Christian meaning which he gave to the Jewish festival. It was no longer an Israelitish ceremony, but it was the Easter of the New Dispensation."—*Life and Epistles of St. Paul*, 2: 203.

"Nor was it only at this annual feast that they kept in memory the resurrection of their Lord; every Sunday likewise was a festival in memory of the same event; the Church never failed to meet for common prayer and praise on that day of the week; and it very soon acquired the name of the Lord's day, which it has since retained."—*Life and Epistles of St. Paul*, 1: 440.

was in the Spirit—ἐν τῇ κυριακῇ ἡμέρᾳ—"on the Lord's day." This Greek phrase occurs no where else in the New Testament, and nothing in the context explains its meaning here. But the familiarity with which it is used indicates that its meaning was well and widely known—needed no interpretation—would be everywhere understood. The explanation must be sought, and will be found, in John's own era—in patristic usage—in the writings of the earliest Church Fathers.[1]

It has passed into church history that the first day of the week is called the Lord's day. When did this usage begin? How far back can it be traced? It is of very ancient date. It appears, about the close of the second

---

[1] John's ἡ κυριακὴ ἡμέρα appears in complete form in early patristic writings, where it always means the first day of the week—the Christ resurrection-day. It was current in and near the Johannic period.

κυριακὴν ἡμέραν. The Lord's day.	Julius Africanus, About 220 A. D.
κυριακὴν ἐκείνην τὴν ἡμέραν. This Lord's day.	Clemens Alexandrinus. fl. 180–215 A. D.
τῇ τῆς κυριακῆς ἡμέρᾳ. On the Lord's day.	Irenæus. About 178 A. D. fl. about 160–200 A. D.
τὴν κυριακὴν ἁγίαν ἡμέραν. The Lord's holy day.	Dionysius of Corinth. About 170 A. D.

These are very ancient uses of the Greek phrase, some of them perhaps within fifty years of John's time. Its meaning is fixed—stereotyped—back that far. It had quite earlier currency, in defective form; the adjective κυριακή alone appearing; the noun to be supplied. Scholarship with unanimity supplies ἡμέρα-day.

κατὰ κυριακὴν δὲ κυρίου. But on the Lord's (day.)	"Teaching" From 100 to 140 A. D.
κατὰ κυριακὴν ζῶντες. Living according to the Lord's (day.)	Ignatius. fl. about 75–115 A. D.

This takes us back to within the Johannic period, and shows the phrase, complete or defective, to have been current from his day.

"Mr. Elliott, *Hor. Apoc.* 4: 367, note, points out that the Peshito renders οὐκ ἐστιν κυριακὸν δεῖπνον φαγεῖν, I. Cor. 11: 20. 'Not as befitting the day of the Lord ye eat and drink,' which is an interesting proof of the early use."—ALFORD. *Greek Test.*, Rev. 1: 10.

century, in Julius Africanus and Clement of Alexandria. It appears still earlier, probably within fifty years of St. John's time, in Dionysius of Corinth and in Irenæus, a friend of Polycarp, who was a disciple of St. John. These Church Fathers all use John's Greek phrase—his identical phrase—and, in their writings, it never means Easter, or Seventh day, or Judgment-day, but always First-day. The evidence here is very complete. Patristic usage back to within about fifty years of St. John's time, fixes the meaning of the Greek phrase in Rev. 1 : 10 as First-day—the Christ-resurrection day. Proofs of this go even farther back. A part of this Greek phrase—its essential part—appears still earlier; in the "Teaching of the Twelve Apostles;" and also in the writings of Ignatius a contemporary of St. John. These very primitive Christian documents mention the Lord's —— in such groups of words as fairly suggest that the word "day" should fill the blank. Scholarship with unanimity so fills it. Despite a little room to quibble, historic integrity necessitates this. Thus St. John's Greek phrase is seen in use among his contemporaries and immediate successors as a name for First-day. The general consent of Christian antiquity and of modern scholarship has referred the phrase to the weekly festival of our Lord's resurrection—has identified it with the first day of the week.

The Christ-resurrection day has now a second divine name. It was called at the very first μία τῶν σαββάτων—"the first day of the week." It is now called ἡ κυριακὴ ἡμέρα—"the Lord's day." And the day, with this new Scriptural name, seems to bring the Lord of the Sabbath very near. The day to John on Patmos was restful, blessed, Sabbatic. The narrative of events is suggestive of tender and holy First-day experiences. Christ, as at Pentecost, honored "the Lord's day" on Patmos, with wonderful divine manifestations. John was "in the Spirit," was "caught up to heaven," and was gifted with wonderful celestial visions. Such was the day on Patmos. It was shrined in rapturous Sabbatic elements.[1]

AUTHORITATIVE CHANGE OF THE DAY.

The whole reported attitude of our Lord, risen and ascended, towards Seventh-day, and towards First-day, is now before the reader. His attitude towards Seventh-day is, as reported, that of non-use. He is never known to have kept Seventh-day as Sabbath; to have appointed any meeting with disciples for Seventh-day; to have revealed himself to disciples on any Seventh-day; or to

---

[1] "The κυριακὴ ἡμέρα . . . is the first day of the week, the Sunday, which was celebrated as the day of the resurrection of the Lord."—MEYER. *Commentary*, Rev. 1: 10.

"On the Lord's day . . . the first day of the week . . . It is the day of the 'Lord,' the risen and glorified Lord."—SHAFF. *On Rev.*, p. 33.

"On the Lord's day, *i. e.*, on the first day of the week, kept by the Christian Church as the weekly festival of the Lord's resurrection."—ALFORD. *Greek Testament*, 4: 554.

"On the Lord's day—*i. e.*, the Christian Sabbath—the first day of the week; so called, because on that day our Lord arose from the dead."—*Cot. Bible*, Rev. 1: 10.

"*The Lord's day.* The first day of the week, observed as the Christian Sabbath, because on it Jesus Christ rose from the dead."—A. CLARKE *Com.*, Rev. 1: 10.

"As the resurrection of Christ is the great fact, so the day of its occurrence is the great day of Christianity. From the time of the Apostles its weekly return has been called by the name of the Lord's day."—*Smith's N. T. Hist.*, 348.

"The term 'Lord's day' was used generally by the early Christians to denote the first day of the week."—MOSES STUART on Rev. 1: 10.

"It (the Johannic vision) occurred like the Pentecost, on the first day of the week—'the Lord's day;' thus setting a new honor on the Sabbath of the Christian dispensation."—POND. *Con. on the Bible*, 609.

"The Lord's day—the oldest and best designation of the Christian Sabbath; first used by St. John, Rev. 1: 10."—SHAFF-HERZOG. *Encycl. of Rel. Knowl.*, Art. Lord's day.

have dispensed Pentecostal gifts to disciples on any Seventh-day. He was a keeper of Seventh-day as Sabbath *before* but in no known instance *after* his passion. These are plain Scriptural facts. Seventh-day is never set forth in any way as used and approved by our risen and ascended Lord for Sabbatism. He disappoints all expectations of Seventh-day Sabbatarians. If disuse vacates, then Seventh-day is vacated by the risen and ascended Lord of the Sabbath; is authoritatively set aside; ceases to be Sabbatic.

His attitude towards First-day is that of use and approval. He rose from the grave on First-day. He made five recorded revelations of himself to disciples on the initial First-day in the new era; and one of these was in a meeting held by disciples. He revealed himself in another meeting of disciples held on the second First-day. He appointed at his Ascension, a meeting to the disciples that is afterwards found to be a First-day meeting. He poured out upon disciples his own promised gift of the Spirit on that seventh First-day. He, by that meeting of his own appointment, and by that outpouring of the Spirit according to his promise, began the formal planting of Christianity on that eventful First-day. And his last recorded visible showing of himself to a disciple was on a First-day. These also are plain Scriptural facts. First-day is the only day known to be used by our risen and ascended Lord for Sabbatism. This exclusive use of First-day for clear Sabbatic purposes, by the Sabbath-Maker, is its sufficient and authoritative institution. How can a day so hallowed by our risen and ascended Lord, fail of reverent observance by his disciples? The Seventh-day Sabbatarian is certainly not following in the steps of the risen Christ. The First-day Sabbatarian is.

Now, if anything can be vacated by disuse, and if anything can be instituted by example and use, then our risen and ascended Lord has vacated Seventh-day meetings and worship, and has instituted First-day meetings and worship. What else can be made of the fact that all revelations of himself to disciples, of ascertainable date, were on First-day, and not one on Seventh-day? Or of the fact that all meetings of disciples, appointed or attended by him, and whose date is recorded, were on First-day, and not one on Seventh-day? These are plain and reported doings of our Lord. They are an authoritative change of the day; not by abrupt command; but by use and approval. And the change is by competent authority. It is Jesus, the risen and ascended One, who, by disuse, discontinued the Old, and, by use and approval, instituted the New day. His authority is beyond question. He is the Sabbath-Maker. He is the Lord of the Sabbath. As risen, and then as ascended, he is never known as a Seventh-day, but always as a First-day Sabbatarian.[1]

---

[1] Christianity has retained the institution as belonging to divine worship; but by the same authority which gave the original law has modified it. . . . The day of our Lord's resurrection, the first day of the week, became the Christian Sabbath, or the Lord's day."—POPE. *Com. of Christ.* **3**: 290.

SABBATH OF THE APOSTLES.

"Chime on ye bells! Again begin
And ring the Sabbath morning in;
The laborer's week-day work is done,
The rest begun,
Which Christ hath for his people won."
—*From the German of F. Sachse.*

Christianity issued out of Judaism, as, later, Protestantism arose out of Romanism, and Methodism out of Anglicanism. Its Apostles were all graduates of the Law, the Synagogue, the Seventh-day Sabbath; Jews in race, temperament, training; and some of them of a very stern Judaic character. As heirs to fifteen centuries of Judaic history and glory, they would, by prepossession, linger long and lovingly with Mosaism, the Synagogue, and the old-time Sabbath. Emerging Christian institutions were in peril of a too great Judaic tinge.[1] The fall of Jerusalem prevented that. The social reaction that then sent Judaism into long exhaustion and doom enured to Christian separation and independence.

Christianity made an invading and conquering march through Paganism; Pagan Assyria, Pagan Egypt, Pagan Greece, Pagan Rome; each having its philosophy and tradition, its idolatrous sacrifices and temple worship; and each using, as human substitutes and corruptions of the ancient divine Sabbath, *nundinæ*, or *decades*, with annual festivals. Over and through all it swept as a mighty and

---

[1] "It must not be forgotten that one of the most constant difficulties to which the early church was subjected, arose from a tendency in the Jewish converts, not only to retain, but to enforce some of the rites and observances of their own law."—*Brit. Quar.* 21 : 79.

resistless Gulf-Stream, scattering everywhere a new spiritual warmth, purity, and life. The old mythology was to go down before the on-coming Christian faith.

To absorb and assimilate in a new religious unity the Jewish convert and the Gentile convert—two distinct historic personalities—social incongruents and business rivals—antagonists by race and religious prejudices—this was the difficult and delicate problem to be solved.[1] How this important task was accomplished—the *old* displaced and the *new* brought forward by steadily unfolding steps — history tells. I am now to study and report the divine Sabbatic stream, as it flowed, under Apostolic supervision, through the organizing Christianity.

THE APOSTLES AND THE FIRST DAY.

The Gospels report the use of First-day meetings, by the Apostles, from the very beginning. They met on the evening of the first day in the new era; on next First-day; and then, with one hundred and twenty disciples, in the early morning of seventh First-day. Thus three First-day meetings are recorded as held by them in the first seven weeks after the Christ resurrection. The custom continued.

The Greek phrase, μὶα τῶν σαββάτων—"the first day of the week"—occurs eight times in the New Testament; six times in association with our Lord's resurrection; and twice by Apostolic use. These two uses now invite attention.

---

[1] The religions and the philosophies of the age were local. A world religion was deemed impossible.

"It is not easy to find the Father and Creator of all existence; and, when he is found, it is impossible to make him known to all."—PLATO.

"He must be void of understanding who can believe that Greeks and Barbarians in Asia, Europe, and Syria—all nations to the ends of the earth—can unite in one religious doctrine."—CELSUS.

Luke used the phrase. In reporting a meeting at Troas he says: "And on the first day of the week, when the disciples were come together to break bread, Paul preached unto them."[*] Here are Sabbatic elements: an appointed and understood day; a day for the ordinance of the Eucharist; a day for preaching and social worship. The day had been waited for. Paul abode seven days in Troas, "ready to depart on the morrow," after this First day meeting. His tarrying extended over Seventh-day, which is not mentioned as used. This First-day meeting at Troas has the air of a usual arrangement; of a well and widely known custom; of a stated meeting that could be waited for, and that brought Christians together. This is in proof that Sabbatism had changed its day. First-day was in use at Troas. Luke makes sacred, not the Seventh but the First day.[1]

Paul used the phrase. He thus wrote to Corinthian Christians: "Now concerning collections for the saints, as I have given orders to the churches in Galatia, so do ye.

---

[*] Acts 20: 7.

[1] "The whole aim of the narrative favors the reference to what is now known as Sunday."—McCLINTOCK & STRONG. *Cycl.*, Art. Lord's Day.

"The disciples in Troas met weekly on the first day of the week for exhortation and the breaking of bread."—*Encycl. Brit.*, Art. Sunday.

"This is a passage of the utmost importance, as showing that the observance was customary."—*Life and Epistles of St. Paul*, 2: 206.

"Is it not clear to demonstration that Paul, wishing to meet the Church at Troas, waited there seven days till they met; that they did not meet until the first day of the week; and that, having fulfilled his purpose, Paul left them immediately after the Lord's day had closed?" —*British Quar.* 21: 79.

"To break bread. Evidently to celebrate the Lord's Supper. . . . So the Syriac understands it, 'to break the Eucharist,' *i. e.* the Eucharistic bread. It is probable that the Apostles and early Christians celebrated the Lord's Supper on every Lord's day. . . . . And upon the first day of the week. Showing thus that this day was observed as holy time."—*Barnes' Notes*, in loco.

Upon the first day of the week, let every one of you lay by him in store, that there be no gatherings when I come."[a] This Apostolic prescription for contributing gifts and offerings is clearly not for one First-day only, but for all First days; and not for one church only, but for many. It is established as a weekly custom in the churches of Corinth and Galatia. In those churches, therefore, First day was well-known, and was used for religious business—for sacred collections. All this is plain. And it suggests that First day was occupied by religious meetings; for seasons of worship are, in the Christian Church, the usual occasions for sacred gifts and offerings.[1]

---

[a] I. Cor. 16 : 2.

[1] "A plain indication that the day was already considered as a special one, and one more than others fitted for the performance of a religious duty."—ALFORD. *Greek N. T.* 2: 588.

"Already the day of the week on which Christ had risen had become noted as a suitable day for distinctively Christian work, and Christian worship."—ELLICOTT. *Commentary*, 2: 353.

"But no doubt it does show that to the Christian consciousness it was a holy day in whose consecration the appropriateness of such works of love was felt."—MEYER. *On Corinthians*, 2: 111.

"This weekly contribution was to be reserved for the 'Lord's day.' This renders it certain, by the way, that that day was already regarded by all Christians as a sacred day, and, as such, the proper day (as we find from Acts 20: 7) for public worship."—SCHAFF. *Paul's Epistles*, 231.

"This passage is important as the first in which there occurs a clear trace of a distinction put upon the first day of the week, as our Lord's resurrection day, yet we cannot find here any special observance of the day as Osiander does."—NEANDER. *On Corinthians*, 355.

"The passage certainly implies that this day of the resurrection of our Lord was for the Christians a holy day, out of which all other observances of the sort naturally developed themselves."—LANGE. *Com. in loco*.

"It is reasonable to think that the first day was specified as the proper time to make collections for the poor, because it was consecrated to religious duties."—NEVIN. *Pres. Encyc.*, Art. Sabbath.

"It appears from the whole that the first day of the week, which is the Christian Sabbath, was the day on which their principal religious meetings were held in Corinth and the churches of Galatia; and consequently in all other places where Christianity had prevailed."—*Clarke's Theology*, 170.

Some critics, as Stanley, Meyer, and Shaff, think the Greek text simply directs Christians to lay by of their weekly earnings, on each First-day, in their *own home*—not in the *assembled church*—and strictly translated such meaning may be made to appear. But this would have necessitated gatherings at the Apostle's coming, the very thing that he sought to prevent. The mere laying by of offerings, in many homes, does not fairly and fully meet the Apostolic requirement; and indeed nothing does short of an actual gift in the assembled church. Sacred gifts only become a reality when gathered. The Apostle desired the gathering to be done before his coming—to be done on First-days—to be done therefore in church assemblies. All this implies that the day was for Christians a special and holy day.

The new day for worship, brought forward after the Christ-resurrection, now stands complete. It has two New Testament names. Its first divine name is $\mu i\alpha\ \tau\tilde{\omega}\nu\ \sigma\alpha\beta\beta\acute{\alpha}\tau\omega\nu$—"the first day of the week"—resurrection day—memorable—Sabbatic. Its second divine name is $\dot{\eta}\ \kappa\nu\rho\iota\alpha\kappa\eta\ \pi\mu\acute{\epsilon}\rho\alpha$—"the Lord's day,"—bringing celestial visions to the man of Patmos—elevating—restful. It is the only day named in which the risen Christ was accustomed to meet with his disciples; in which he appointed to them a meeting; and on which he poured upon them Pentecostal gifts. It is the only day named and particularized for meetings of the disciples; for sacred collections; and for administering distinctive Christian ordinances, as baptism and the Lord's Supper. It is the Church's birth-day. It is the most notable day in the New Testament—the joy day of all disciples. If use institutes—if example teaches—then First-day stands out as the divinely appointed Sabbath of the new Christian brotherhood. The Apostles, after Christ, evidently recast Sabbatism in the mold of the new day. The institution, like a stream overleaping the bounds of an ancient and flowing into a new channel, swept out of the seventh into the first day.¹ Sabbatism entered the emerging Christian era, divinely clad in the drapery of First-day.

THE APOSTLES AND THE SEVENTH DAY.

The Greek σαββάτον is used *seventy* times in the New Testament: is *sixty* times translated *Sabbath ; nine* times *week ;* and *one* time *rest*. It is used *fifty-one* times before and in connection with our Lord's resurrection ; and *nineteen* times after. Of its *nineteen* post-resurrection uses, *eight* are translated week, and report the day changed. Four out of its remaining eleven uses are wholly indifferent to the question of change ; as a Sabbath-day's journey ;ª as two statements that Moses was read on the Sabbath-day ;ᵇ and as the farther statement that a rest (or Sabbatism) remaineth for the people of God.ᶜ This leaves but seven Apostolic uses and interpretations of the word to be considered.

ª Acts 1 : 12. ᵇ Acts 13 : 27 ; 15 : 21. ᶜ Heb. 4 : 9.

¹ "The primitive Christians were unanimous in setting apart the first day of the week, as being that on which our Savior rose from the dead, for the solemn celebration of public worship. This pious custom was derived from the example of the Church of Jerusalem on the express appointment of the Apostles."—*Waddington's Ch. Hist.*, 1 : 44.

"This change of the Sabbath from the seventh to the first day of the week was made not only for a sufficient reason, but also by competent authority. It is a simple historical fact that Christians of the apostolic age ceased to observe the seventh, and did observe the first day of the week as the day for religious worship." HODGE. *Sys. Theol.*, 3 : 330.

"It may, I think, unquestionably be taken for a fact, that the first day of the week, *i. e.* the day on which our blessed Savior triumphantly burst the bonds of death and arose from the grave, was expressly appointed by the Apostles themselves, during their continuance at Jerusalem, for the holding of their general solemn assemblies of the Christians for the purposes of religious worship."—*Mosheim's Commentaries.*—Murdock's trans., 1 : 149.

Luke, in *five* different places, tells of Paul and fellow-helpers using the seventh day.[1] They entered into synagogues on that day, and preached. Now if the New Tesment anywhere rehabilitates the old seventh day as Sabbath, it must be here. Is there here then a fair warrant of continuance? Did Apostolic use reinstitute? Is it a sufficient authorization for a transferrence of the seventh-day Sabbath out of Judaism into Christianity? *It is not.* Four important considerations require this negative reply. First: Paul and his co-laborers used the synagogue as well as the Seventh-day. But Apostolic use did not reinstitute and continue the synagogue; why then the Seventh day as Sabbath? Second: They used Seventh-day, even as the synagogue, for more convenient access to the Jews; not however as Jews, to promote Judaism; but as Christians to make Christian converts. Such use was a convenience, but not a reinstitution. Third: The only named use they made of the day was for *preaching*. They are never known to have used it for baptism, for the eucharist, for any distinctive Christian ordinances. These were celebrated on First never on Seventh-day. The day, as used by them, is not *Christianized*. Fourth: They were incompetent to reinstitute the old day, or to change to a new day. They were themselves under marching orders. They were to do whatsoever Christ had commanded them. Christ alone is Lord of the Sabbath. He alone, not Paul, nor Peter, nor John, nor all of them, could continue the

---

[1] "They .... went into the synagogue on the Sabbath day and sat down."—*Acts* 13:14.

"And the next Sabbath day came almost the whole city together to hear the Word of God."—*Acts* 13:44.

"And on the Sabbath we went out of the city by a river side .. and spoke unto the women which resorted thither."—*Acts* 16:13.

"And Paul ... three Sabbath days reasoned with them out of the Scriptures."—*Acts* 17:2.

"And he reasoned in the synagogue every Sabbath."—*Acts* 18:4.

old or change to a new day. The risen Christ never reinstituted Seventh-day worship; and he did, by use, institute First-day worship. So then these five Sabbatic texts report Apostolic use that did not, and could not, reinstitute and continue the seventh-day as Sabbath. The New Testament gives no support whatever to seventh-day Sabbatism in the Christian system.

Two post-resurrection Sabbath texts yet remain. In one of the two Paul interprets the Jewish seventh day. To Colossian Christians, he wrote: "Let no man judge you in meat, or in drink, or in respect of a holy day, or of the new moons, or of the Sabbath days, which are a shadow of things to come, but the body is of Christ."[a]

"Sabbath days—Greek σαββάτων—are *seventh* days. The Greek word in the New Testament, *always* means seventh day. There is no reason why it should be an exception here. The supposition that Jewish feast days are meant is violent and uncritical. In the New Testament, feast days are never called Sabbaths, nor are Sabbaths ever called feast days. The Greek word translated "holy day" is used twenty-seven times in the New Testament, and is elsewhere always translated "feast-days." It should be so translated here, and is so translated in the Revised Version. The use in the text of two different words with the same meaning is not probable. "Sabbath days" then do not mean feast days; and they do mean *seventh* days. Paul now gives two interpretations of Seventh-day in its relations to Sabbatism.

He first interprets *Seventh*-day as *no longer Sabbatic*—as vacated by divine Sabbatism. He distinguishes it from "*things*"—"things to come"—essences—abiding realities—that he declares to be of the very body of Christ. And he classes it with "*shadows*"—perishable forms—decaying

---
[a] Col. 2 : 16.

husks—that merged and disappeared in Gospel realities. "Sabbath-days," he says, that is Seventh-days for Sabbaths, "are shadows"—"shadows of things to come." Paul like Christ, and directed by the risen Christ's example, is here an innovator on Judaic Sabbatism. He faces and abandons all the traditions of his early life. He proclaims the emancipation of Christians, not from Sabbatism, but from its old day. He does not abrogate or in any way relax Sabbatism. He could not do that. None but the Lord of the Sabbath could do that. But he interprets the seventh day as no longer Sabbatic. Shadows were gone; all around him were abiding realities. Seventh-day was an exhausted and disused form; and living forces, ever at work, had already replaced it with the new and abiding First-day. According to Paul, then, Sabbatic elements were no longer in the seventh-day; they had been transferred. Christ himself, by use and example, had transferred them to the first day. The Jewish rubric, as to seventh-day Sabbath-keeping, was no longer binding.[1]

He, secondly, interprets the keeping of "Sabbath-days," that is of Seventh-days for Sabbaths, as *optional*. "Let no man judge you," from his pen, has this force and meaning. It grants freedom in the use of the things named—in the use, among other things, of Seventh-days for Sabbaths. But it is "shadows," not "things"—mere forms, not eternal verities—that are made optional. Food-eating, taking meat and drink, is a human need; we cannot live without it; but modes and times of eating and drinking are of the nature of mere forms—indifferent—optional. Periodic rest days, festal days, devotional days, are an abiding human need; we cannot reach our best without them; but the new moons, feast days, and Seventh-day Sabbaths of a worn out economy, were but mere forms—

---

[1] "Paul had quite distinctly laid down from the first days of Gentile Christianity, that the Jewish Sabbath was no longer binding on Christians."—W. R. SMITH., LL. D. *Encyc. Brit.*, Art. Sabbath.

indifferent—optional. Paul here teaches the abrogation of the entire Jewish calendar of new moons, feast days, and seventh-days for Sabbatism; not of the things; but of the forms. The bondage of ceremonies had ceased. Divine Sabbatism was no longer in the Seventh-day. Still its use, because a mere form, was optional. It was not, and it is not, wrong to be devotional on Seventh-day.

Thus Paul's Sabbatic word to Colossian Christians reports the ancient Sabbatic day as divinely abandoned. It was entangled among the ceremonial customs of Judaism, and, like the whole ritual of Mosaism, had lost its divine significance. The day remained but a shrivelled and shadowy form, from which the substance had fled to take up its abode in First-day. The Seventh-day Sabbath, after our Lord's resurrection, was but the moon lingering in the sky after the rising of the sun, but only to pale and disappear in the increasing glory of the new day.

Transfer of Sabbatic Name.

Sabbatic elements, as thus seen, were divinely transferred from Seventh to First day. Was the name also transferred? Is First-day entitled to be called Sabbath? Has this name of the day any New Testament usage and warrant? It would seem clear and plain that the old divine name should go with the substance. It certainly should not remain with the mere form—the husk—the vacated day. If all essential Sabbatic elements belong, in the new era, to First-day; if First-day is made the head of the week, even the Sabbath itself; then it should have the name also.

The Christ-resurrection day is given, in the Greek text, as μία τῶν σαββάτων—literal translation, *one of the Sabbaths*—Hebraic reckoning, *one* (day) *from the Sabbath*. This means—it can only mean—"the first day of the week." Yet the Greek text has a Sabbatic basis and fragrance that the English translation has not. This "first day of the week," in the eight times that it occurs in the New Testament, is, in the Greek text, associated with the Sabbatic word, as it is not in our translation. This is something to be considered. These eight post-resurrection Scriptures, in the beginning and right along, always associate the old name with the new day. They, in a manner, put the Sabbatic name upon the day; not fully indeed; but suggestively. Perhaps even this statement does not exhaust the meaning of the Greek original. It would seem as if the Inspiring Spirit, in leading five New Testament writers—Matthew, Mark, Luke, John, and Paul—to use this Greek Sabbatic phrase for First-day, meant to shadow and suggest the ultimate transfer of the Sabbatic name from the seventh to the first day.

The New Testament post-resurrection uses of the Greek σαββάτον—nineteen in number—have all been considered but one. That one now invites attention. Luke makes this record; "The Gentiles besought that these words might be preached to them εἰς τό μεταξυ σάββατον—" on the between Sabbath."[a] Sound criticism, if no difficulties from without were in the way, would at once make this "between Sabbath" mean the newly appearing Christian day of convocation—the week's first day—the Christ-resurrection day. That would recognize a transfer of the name as well as the substance of Sabbatism from the seventh to the first day.

But scholars, because they do not find the Sabbatic name elsewhere in the New Testament transferred to First-day, nor for a long period after in Church history, do not accept a transfer of the name here. Hence they put a mistranslation of the Greek phrase in the English text, and hide the literal translation in the margin. This, to say the very best of it, is not heroic treatment. Like all

---
[a] Acts 13: 42.

error it brings with it the entailment of vast confusion. Some scholars make the "between Sabbath" mean "all week days;" though Sabbatism is always and essentially differentiated from secular or week days. Others make it mean "two weekly fast-days" then (I doubt this) supposed to be observed in the customs of the church, though New Testament Sabbatism never in any case means fast days. Others still make it mean the "next Sabbath;" though that directly and flatly contradicts the Greek μεταξυ —" between." Versionists and commentators are alike in inextricable confusion. Is there any way out of it?[1]

The fall of Jerusalem—the ruin of the Temple and the Priesthood—dealt a staggering blow to Judaism. Over a million of Jews perished in the siege. The catastrophe entailed other calamities incomparably vaster. It started against the Jews new bitterness and fiercer hatreds; and from Rome as a center they were thereafter regarded as social outcasts. They were expelled from Rome under Tiberius, then under Claudius, and their religion put

---

[1] "On the next following Sabbath."—MEYER.

"Either on the next Sabbath, or in the interval."—SMITH. *N. T. Hist.*, 444.

"On the ensuing week or Sabbath."—ADAM CLARKE.

"In the intermediate time, before the next Sabbath."—BARNES.

"The next Sabbath . . . or some intermediate days of meeting during the week."—CONYBEARE & HOWSON. *Life and Epis. of St. Paul*, 1: 178.

"Mean 'the next Sabbath day' not 'the following week.' This last rendering would hardly suit εις which fixes a definite meaning."—ALFORD.

"When they departed from them, they sought from them that these words might be spoken to them on another Sabbath."—Syriac Version.

"As they were going out, they entreated that these words should be preached to them in the course of the week, or the next Sabbath."—Many Ancient Versions.

"This request may have been for preaching on those days (2nd and 5th) of the week, observed more or less by the church of that time."—*Pres. Quar.*, 6: 713.

under ban.[1] Defeated peoples, whose history is written by their conquerers, are not only pushed to the wall, but are usually misrepresented—maligned—abused. That is what happened to the Jews. Roman writers of the period, as Persius, Juvenal, Appian, Martial, and Tacitus treated them as social outcasts.[2] They suffered odium such as has never fallen to the lot of any other people; were slandered and put in the pillory of ridicule; were caricatured at festivals and on the stage. Their Sabbath was singled out for special derision; was held up to scorn; was assaulted with debasing sarcasms. Violent antipathy

---

[1] "The others of that race, (Jews,) or proselytes to their views, he (Tiberius) removed from the city (Rome) under the pain of perpetual servitude, if they did not obey."—SUETONIUS. *Tiberius*, c. 36.

"The Roman Senate, in A. D. 18, drove the Jews out of Rome, prohibited under severe penalties any adherence to Jewish teaching, and searched homes for its converts."—*Judaism at Rome*, 7.

See also: Tacitus, *An.*, 2: 85; and Seneca, *Epist.*, 108: 22.

"Claudius had commanded all the Jews to depart from Rome."—Acts, 18: 2.

"Claudius banished from Rome all the Jews who were continually making disturbances at the instigation of one Chrestus."—SUETONIUS. *Claud.*, c. 25.

[2] Roman writers are prejudiced reporters in all things concerning the conquered, oppressed, persecuted Jews. Dion Cassius started the historic falsity, still copied by so many scholars—that the week came to the Romans from the Egyptians—because his prejudice would not allow him to trace it to the Jews. Tacitus copies the grossest tales against them; discolors and falsifies; treats them as Gibbon does Christians, with little humanity. Here are two or three specimens of Roman spleen:

> "Thou mutterest prayers, nor dost refuse,
> The feasts and Sabbaths of the curtailed Jews."
> PERSIUS. *Sat.* 5: 184.

"The rest of their institutions are awkward, impure, and got ground by their pravity. . . . The lewdest nation upon earth."—TACITUS. *Hist.*, 5: 5.

"While the East was under the dominion of the Assyrians, the Medes and the Persians, the Jews were of all slaves the most despicable. . . . This most profligate nation."—TACITUS. *Hist.*, 5: 8.

and ridicule sent the day and its name into long odium and decay.[1]

Now if Paul, who preached and broke bread at Troas on First-day, and prescribed First-day collections to the Churches of Corinth and Galatia, had already, in his brief stay at Antioch in Pisidia, organized a First-day meeting for the Christian ordinances and for the instruction of disciples, then it would have been very natural for some Gentile converts, pleased with an address delivered by him on the Sabbath, to ask for its repetition in the First-day meeting—εἰς τό μεταξὺ σαββάτου—" on the between Sabbath." Judaism was evidently in favor at Antioch. Gentiles attending the synagogue. This may be the reason why First-day is here called Sabbath, and not elsewhere in the New Testament. And the increased odium soon to fall upon the Sabbath may tell why this name for First-day does not again appear for some time in church history. This is our theory. It has reasonable support. First-day, as seen, had appeared right along as the day for disciples' meetings—for prayer and preaching —for the Christian ordinances—as the Sabbath, therefore,

---

[1] The Sabbath was a popular theme of Roman satire on the stage. One actor would say: "How long do you desire to live." Another would reply: "As long as a Jewish Sabbath shirt."

"They bring a camel wrapped in dark clothes upon the scene, and they say to one another, 'Why is this beast in mourning?' and they answer, 'Those Jews observe the Sabbatical year, and, for want of vegetables, they have eaten all his thorns; he now mourns the loss of his main support.'"—SMITH. *Dict. Gr. and Rom. Antiq.*, Art. Atellenæ Fabulæ.

"They bring their *mimos* (an actor of ludicrous and indelicate representations) upon their boards, with his head shaved, and one asks the other, 'Why is his head shaved?' and is answered: 'These Jews are Sabbath observers, and what they earn the whole week they eat up on the Sabbath; and when they have no wood with which to cook, they chop up their bedsteads and use them as fuel; and in consequence they sleep on the bare floor, and when their bodies are covered with dust, they oint them with oil; hence oil is dear, and the poor fellow here had to shave his head.'"—Ditto.

of the new era. It had not indeed the name, which still went with the old day. It had however the substance. It had also in its first New Testament name a reminder of the old name. And it has now an actual but exceptional transfer of the name. This fairly explains the Greek text; accepts its literal translation; and puts the old name upon the new day. The title of First-day to be called Sabbath has this New Testament usage and warrant.

Apostolic Sabbatism Summarized.

The New Testament story of Sabbatism is now told. Jesus, after his passion, was a First-day Sabbatarian. He rose on First-day. He met his disciples on First-days. He appointed to them a First-day meeting. He began Church planting on First-day. He revealed himself to John on Patmos on First-day. He thus stands of record as a First-day Sabbatarian. And, after his resurrection, he is never of record as a Seventh-day Sabbatarian. He is never recorded as meeting his disciples on Seventh-day; or as appointing to meet them on Seventh-day; or as, in any way, using Seventh-day. The old day is not once named—lies neglected—dying in silence and disuse. Thus the risen Sabbath-Maker authoritatively set aside Seventh-day; displaced it by disuse; abrogated it by disapproval. He translated and transferred Sabbatism. He moved it out of Seventh into First-day. He authorized, in the new era, a Sabbath that is monumental of his empty grave. First-day, not Seventh, has the seal of his high authority. It is the only known Sabbath of Jesus risen.

The New Testament Church, in the beginning, was exclusively Judaic, embracing but Jews and Jewish proselytes. The Jew Christian, earliest convert and worker, began with two Sabbaths; retained the old Seventh-day; and used the new First-day. This is the usual statement; and, in a sense, it is historically correct. Yet it does not appear that the Apostles ever used Seventh-day for *Christian* worship.[1] They are five times recorded as using the day; but only for *preaching;* never for anything else. They are never recorded as using it for any distinctive Christian ordinances; for baptism; for the Lord's Supper. The day, though used, was not Christianized. And it was a Jew Christian who classed it with mere forms, and reported it as vacated by Sabbatism. To the Jew, the Christian Sabbath, from the beginning, was First-day. It was a Christianized Jew who on First-days met and communed with our risen Lord; who, on Pentecostal First-day, prayed, preached, and baptized; who on First day preached and broke bread at Troas; who on First-day had celestial visions on Patmos; and who directed Christians at Corinth and throughout Galatia to make First-day collections. His rejection of Seventh and use of First-day for Sabbatic purposes is a wide and strong New Testament fact. Apostolic precept and example sanction the change of day. First-day was dedicated as holy time in Apostolic customs and practice.

The Gentile Christian, a later convert and worker, has but little prominence in New Testament history. There are, here and there, but the merest glimpses of his Sabbatism. He nowhere appears as a keeper of Seventh-day. Christian churches in Gentile lands are never connected with Seventh but only with First-day worship. The Seven Churches of Asia are connected with a notice of the Lord's

---

[1] "There is no trace whatever in Scripture of Christians, as such, convening for purposes of worship on the Jewish Sabbath."—*British Quar.*, 21:79.

"From the time of our Lord's resurrection, there is no recognition of a Seventh-day Sabbath in the Christian Church, especially among the Gentiles, though there are many proofs of the first day of the week being occupied in religious worship."—Cottage Bible. *Com.*, Acts 20:7.

"When Saturday was kept holy day, it was not as a Sabbath, but as a preparation for the Christian Sabbath."—ARCHBISHOP USSHER.

day. The Churches in Corinth and throughout Galatia are connected with a notice of First-day. And the Church at Troas had a First-day meeting and bread-breaking. Thus the New Testament Gentile Christian is not known to have ever used Seventh but only First-day. His exclusive use of First-day for meetings—for preaching and praying—for the Eucharist—for sacred collections—is a firm and strong New Testament fact.[1]

The New Testament, after the Christ-resurrection, gives no directory ritual for Seventh-day meetings; and it does give fragments of a directory ritual for First-day meetings. First-day meetings have Christ's dedication and use; Seventh-day meetings have not. First-day meetings have Apostolic dedication and use for the administration of baptism and the Eucharist; Seventh-day meetings have not. First-day meetings have also Apostolic dedication and use for sacred collections; Seventh-day meetings have

---

[1] "That Sunday was observed by the Apostles, however, as the day of Christ's resurrection, is certain."—*Shaff's Hist. of the Apos. Ch.*, 551.

"The first day of the week was, therefore, peculiarly honored in Apostolic times, and we know that it has been observed as the Christian Sabbath ever since."—Cottage Bible. *Com.* on Acts 20: 7.

"The divinely inspired Apostles, by their practice and by their precepts, marked the first day of the week as a day for meeting together to break bread, for communicating and receiving instruction, for laying up offerings in store for charitable purposes, for occupation in holy thought and prayer."—McCLINTOCK & STRONG. *Cycl.*, Art Lord's Day.

"But from the time of his resurrection, the day of the week on which it occurred, and which according to the reckoning then received was the first, began to be observed by his disciples as the day of assemblies for public worship, the celebration of the sacraments, Christian communion, and other sacred purposes."—DR. J. H. McILVAINE, in *Pres. Rev.*, 14: 262.

"The homiletical as well as the Eucharistic services were at first held daily. At a later period at least every Sunday. For very soon alongside of the Sabbath, and, among Gentile Christians instead of it, the first day of the week, as the day of Christ's resurrection, began to be observed as a festival."—*Kurtz's Ch. Hist.*, 1: 63.

APOSTOLIC SABBATISM SUMMARIZED.

not. First-day for Sabbatism is never challenged; Seventh-day for Sabbatism is challenged and set aside. First-day has thus the furniture and equipments for Sabbatism; Seventh-day has not. It will rigorously follow that our Lord's resurrection, and his post-resurrection example, transferred Sabbatism from Seventh to First-day; abrogated and set aside Seventh-day; instituted and put into its vacated place a youthful competitor. The Apostles obeyed these marching orders; reporting Sabbatism as no longer in Seventh-day; and using First-day alone for distinctive Christian training and ordinances. This is the plain teaching and custom till Apostolic times and writings end.

Sabbatism and the Apostolical Fathers.

> "Blest day of God! Most calm, most bright,
> The first, the best of days,
> The laborer's rest, the saint's delight,
> The day of prayer and praise."
> —HERBERT.

From celestial elevations, where divine breathings invest New Testament institutions with authority, the transition to uninspired thinkers and workers is great. The extraordinary divine agency upon teachers, in giving instruction and establishing customs, ended when the Apostles disappeared; the ordinary alone remained. Authority ceased. Inspiration's divine strains died away. The Church Fathers are but reporters and interpreters of what they received from the Apostles. We consult them simply to ascertain the Sabbatism that came to them. They are not authorities. They are but witnesses.

The earliest Fathers, as Barnabas, Polycarp, Ignatius, Clement of Rome, Papias, and Hermas, are called Apostolical, because contemporaries of the Apostles, and having probably conversed with some of them. Their literary remains illustrate the period from the death of Peter and Paul to a little beyond that of John—from the fall of Jerusalem to about A. D. 120. Polycarp, Papias, and Hermas say nothing about Sabbatism. The rest do. Their sayings follow:

APOSTOLICAL FATHERS AS WITNESSES.

"The Epistle to Diognetus," an anonymous Greek letter worthy of St. Paul, does not name First-day. But it arraigns the Jewish Sabbath as "a superstition," as "utterly ridiculous," and, like Paul, associates it with the passing shadows of the old dispensation. The writer, a lusty defender of Christianity, evidently did not use Seventh-day as his day of rest and worship.[1]

Clement of Rome, usually supposed to be the companion of St. Paul, does not mention either the Jewish Sabbath, or the Lord's day. But his "First Epistle to the Corinthians," written while St. John was yet living—not earlier than 68 A. D. nor later than 97 A. D.—and put on a level at first with canonical writings—speaks of "the stated times," and "the appointed times," commanded by our Lord for worship. Now our risen Lord, by example and use, is recorded as instituting First-day worship; and he is nowhere recorded as instituting Seventh-day worship. This testimony of Clement therefore sets forth, by indirection, First-day worship as of divine order.[2]

"The Epistle of Barnabas" dated by scholarship as of the first or very early in the second century, is mentioned by Clement of Alexandria, Origen, Eusebius, and Jerome. It was read in the early churches as Scripture. It was written to Jews, and to convince them that Judaism was abolished. It contrasts Seventh-day with First-day,

---

[1] "As to their scrupulosity concerning meats, and their superstition as respects the Sabbaths, and their boasting about circumcision, and their fancies about fasting and new moons, which are utterly ridiculous and unworthy of notice, I do not think that you require to learn anything of me."—*Epis. to Diognetus, Ante-Nicene Fathers*, 1: 26.

"No one will be disappointed with the Epistle to Diognetus. It is precious, not for its eloquence only, but also for its freedom from puerilities and superstition. . . . After proving the vanity of idols and the emptiness of Judaic ceremonialism, he shows that Christianity is but a new form of life in the midst of the old life."—FARRAR. *Lives of the Fathers*, 1:5.

[2] "It behooves us to do all things in order—πάντα τάξει ποιειν—which the Lord has commanded us to perform at stated times. He has enjoined offerings and services to be performed—προσφορει και λειτουργιαι—and that not thoughtlessly or negligently, but at the appointed times and hours—ὡριόμενοι καιροι καιώροι."—*I. Cor.* 1: 40.

calling them in the caption, "The False and the True Sabbath." It then reports this custom or practice of Christians: "We keep the eighth day with joy, on which also Jesus rose from the dead." Barnabas, in this, represents the old Seventh-day as divinely set aside, and our Lord's resurrection day—"the eighth day"—as its successor and substitute. Seventh-day Sabbatarians seek to neutralize the force of this testimony, by representing Barnabas as not a clear thinker. He was not. But his testimony here is plain enough. It directly reports First-day, not Seventh-day, as used in Christian worship.[1]

Ignatius, Bishop of Antioch, was martyred not later than 115 A. D., more likely in 107 A. D. Seven epistles, enumerated by Eusebius and Jerome, were attributed to him among the early Christians. Later, fifteen were ascribed to him, eight of which are certainly spurious. The seven genuine Epistles have also some questionable features. The Greek text is in shorter and longer forms; the shorter regarded as purer; the longer as more doubtful. "The Epistle to the Magnesians," one of the seven enumerated in antiquity, and now classed as genuine, utterly repudiates Judaism, as inconsistent with a profession of Christ, and

---

[1] "Αγομεν την ἡμέραν την ὀγδὐην εις ευφροσυνην εν ἡ και ὁ 'Ιησους ἀνέστη εκ νεκρον."—*Bar. Ep. i,* 15:

"We keep the eighth day with joy, on which also Jesus rose from the dead."—*Ante-Nicene Fathers,* vol. 1, p. 147.

"Barnabas here bears testimony to the observance of the Lord's day in early times."—HEFELE.

"It (the Epistle of Barnabas) has many good ideas and valuable testimonies, such as that in favor of the Christian Sabbath. But it goes to extremes in opposition to Judaism."—*Shaff's Hist. of the Christ. Ch.* ₰ 121.

"The letter extant under his (Barnabas) name is chiefly an argument addressed to the Jews showing that the Mosaic law had been abolished by Christ and a pure spiritual service substituted instead of their ceremonial rites and sacrifices.—*Manual of Classical Lit.*—ANTHON—pp. 542-3.

as at an end; and this, in the teaching of the times, carries with it the Judaic Seventh-day as Sabbath.[1] It farther represents Christians as "no longer observing the Sabbath, but living in the observance of the Lord's ———, on which also our life has sprung up again."[2]

What word is to be supplied here? "Day" say the many ripe scholars; "life" say the few Seventh-day Sabbatarians. They are uncritical. First: the blank is to be filled with a word that contrasts with "the Sabbath," as used immediately preceding in the sentence; with "day" therefore, not with "life." Second: it is to be filled with something "on which our life sprang up again," with our Lord's resurrection day therefore—the first day of the week. Third: the longer form, which though untrustworthy, may be used to illustrate and interpret the shorter form, fills the blank with the word "day"—"the Lord's Day"—"the queen and chief of all days."

---

[1] "It is absurd to profess Christ Jesus, and to Judaize."—*Shorter Form*.

"It is absurd to speak of Jesus Christ with the tongue, and to cherish in the mind a Judaism which has now come to an end."—*Longer Form. Epistle to the Magnesians*, 10, *Ante-Nicene Fathers*, 1 : 63.

[2] "Ει ούν οι εν παλαοις πραγμασιν αναστροφεντες, εις καινότητα ελπίδος ηλήθον-μηκετι σαββατιζοντες,αλλά κατά κυριακὴν (ζωὴν) ζωντες—ἐν ᾗ ἡ ζωὴ ἡμων ἀνέτειλεν δἰ αυτου, καὶ τοῦ Θανάτου αυτοῦ. (κατα κυριακην ζωντες is the true reading as corrected by Harnack and Zahn.)

SHORTER FORM: "If, therefore, those who were brought up in the ancient order of things, have come to the possession of a new hope, no longer observing the Sabbath, but living in the observance of the Lord's (day), on which also our life has sprung up again by him and by his death."

LONGER FORM: "If then those who were conversant with the ancient Scriptures came to newness of hope. . . . . Let us therefore no longer keep the Sabbath after the Jewish manner. . . . . But let every one of you keep the Sabbath after a spiritual manner. . . . And after the observance of the Sabbath, let every friend of Christ's keep the Lord's day as a festival, the resurrection day, the queen and chief of all the days" (of the week.) "To the end for the eighth day on which our life both sprang up again, and the victory over death was obtained in Christ."—*Ante-Nicene Fathers*, 1 : 62.

This testimony of Ignatius is very complete. He reports Seventh-day as not used by Christians. His words are full and plain. Destructive criticism cannot assail them. Christians, "no longer observed the Sabbath"—Seventh-day. He then tells what they did observe: "the Lord's (day), on which our life sprang up again." Thus Ignatius, perhaps a hearer of St. John, a bishop according to Chrysostom by the laying on of Apostolic hands, reports Sabbatism as changed from the seventh to First-day. The Judaic Seventh-day had disappeared; First-day had taken its place.

I place in this period "The Teaching of the Twelve Apostles," the manuscript of which was found by Archbishop Bryennios in 1883. It is in New Testament Greek. Its exact date is unknown. Luthardt thinks it may be as early as 100 A. D.; Hitchcock and Brown, American translators, as early as 120 A. D.; and Delitsch, Harnack, and Hilgenfeld, as early as 140 A. D. It is mentioned by Eusebius and Athanasius. Clement of Alexandria ranked it as Scripture. It is an important document. It says, in chapter fourteenth: "But on the Lord's——do ye assemble, and break bread, and give thanks, after confessing your transgressions, in order that your sacrifices may be pure." [1]

---

[1] Κατὰ κυριακὴν δὲ Κυρίου συναχθέντες κλάσατε άρτον καὶ ευχαριστήσατε προσεξομολγησάμενοι τα παραπτώματα ὑμῶν ὅπως καθαρὰ ἡ θυσιαχμῶνη.—Chap. 14.

[1] Translation: "On the Lord's day ye shall gather yourselves together, to break the bread and say thanks, after ye have confessed your misdeeds," etc.—PROF. HARNACK of Giessen.

"But on the Lord's day do ye assemble, and break bread, and give thanks, after confessing your transgressions, in order that your sacrifices may be pure."—HITCHCOCK AND BROWN.

Note by Hitchcock and Brown, the American translators: "The Lord's day is the day for worship and for the Eucharist. No mention is made of the seventh day of the week."

Even Seventh-day Sabbatarians have to confess that the Eucharist was, at this period, a belonging of First-day. *The Outlook*, July, 1884, p. 18, says: "We are willing that the 'Teaching' should indicate that Sunday was observed as an Eucharist day, when the document was written."

All ripe scholars fill this blank with the word "day;" but the few Seventh-day Sabbatarians with the word "table." One can hardly think them serious and sincere. The suggestion discredits their critical genius. It ranks among absurdities. The very atmosphere and wording of the chapter fill the blank with the word "day." It treats of worship; prescribes duties in social or public worship; and public worship implies, not a "table," but a "day." One prescribed duty—bread-breaking—the Eucharist—is never mentioned in the New Testament or among primitive Christians, as conducted at a "table," but on a "day;" and it is never known then as of the Seventh but only of First-day. This chapter on worship,—on the day of worship—is in harmony with the New Testament custom. No mention is made of Seventh-day for worship and for the Eucharist. The Lord's day, the first day of the week, appears, and not Seventh-day.

Yet the Greek σαββάτου is in the "Teaching;" but not as a day of worship; simply as a basis for reckoning the days of the week. The writer of the "Teaching" must have been a Jew. He employs σαββάτου—the Jewish basis for the weekly calendar—from which to count the week's seven days, but for no religious uses whatever. Sabbatic elements, according to "The Teaching," were no longer in the Seventh but wholly in the First-day.[1]

One other witness belongs to this period; not an Apostolical Father or document; but an outsider, the younger Pliny, Proconsul of Bithynia and Pontus. Christians under the Emperor Trajan were persecuted. Pliny conducted the persecution in his province. About 112 A. D., he wrote to the Emperor that "the main of the fault" of the persecuted Christians, according to their testimony, was this: "That they were wont, on a stated day, to meet to-

---

[1] νηστευουσι γαρ δευτερᾳ σαββάτων και πέμπτῃ. Chap. 8. Translation by Hitchcock and Brown: "For they fast on the second day of the week and on the fifth."

gether before it was light, and sing a hymn to Christ, as to a god, alternately. * * * After which it was their custom to depart, and to meet again at a common but innocent meal."[1] Pliny's "stated day" was certainly not Jewish Seventh-day, whose name was then widely known; and, in that case, would have been used. It was as certainly some new periodic day, whose name was not yet familiar among outsiders. Its early morning meeting is suggestive of the early morning meeting on the day of Pentecost. The "common but innocent meal," at a later meeting, is suggestive of the bread-breaking at Troas, on First-day—of the bread-breaking in the "Teaching" on the Lord's (day)—of the Eucharist that is never known, in the New Testament or in early church history, to have been of the Seventh but only of First-day. It is a fair historic certainty that Pliny's "stated day" was the first day of the week—the appearing day among Christians for worship and for bread-breaking.

THE TESTIMONY SUMMED UP.

Apostolical Fathers—contemporaries of some of the Apostles—have now spoken on the Sabbatism of their period—Sabbatism as it came immediately to them from the Apostles. All have spoken. None have been overlooked. The testimony is all in.

There is nothing for Seventh-day as the day for Christian worship; absolutely nothing; and much against it. The Epistolarian to Diognetus characterizes Jewish Sabbatism as a "superstition." Barnabas reports it disused. Ignatius ends it with Judaism, Christians no longer observing the day. And the "Teaching" separates the day altogether

---

[1] "They assured me that the main of their fault, or of their mistake, was this, that they were wont, on a stated day, to meet together before it was light, and to sing a hymn to Christ as to a god, alternately . . . after which it was their custom to depart, and to meet again at a common but innocent meal."—PLINY. *First Epistle.*

from religious worship, and makes it simply the basis for reckoning the days of the week. The whole Sabbatic strife of the period was about the old day—the friction of its displacement—contentions about its disuse. It is not in testimony, but known from other sources, that some Jewish Christians continued to keep Seventh as well as First-day. Time was needed for them to move entirely out from the old into the new day.[1] They are classed as Heretics. Reverence for Seventh-day was stronger in the East, weaker in the West. But the day is never associated with Christian worship and ordinances; is steadily associated with decaying Judaism; is sharply opposed; and has at best but a permissive existence and limited use. It is wholly Judaistic; not in any sense Christian.

There is nothing against First-day as the day for Christian meetings; absolutely nothing; and everything for it. Christians are set forth by Barnabas, as keepers of the "eighth day," the Christ-resurrection day; by Ignatius, as observing the Lord's (day), the day on which our life sprang up again; by the "Teaching," as assembling and breaking bread on the Lord's (day); and by Pliny, as holding meetings in the early morning and later on a "stated day." Thus First-day, in the literary remains of the period, was steadily associated in joy and triumph with our Lord's resurrection; had an enjoined existence; had an unrestricted use. It opened, like Pentecost, with an early morning meeting; had a later meeting; had bread-

---

[1] "Those Churches, however, which were composed of Jewish Christians, though they admitted with the rest the festival of Sunday, yet retained also that of the Sabbath."—*Neander's Hist. of the Christ. Rel. and Ch.*, Vol. 1, p. 296.

The Jewish Christians as already remarked, adhered to the Old Testament Sabbath, especially in Palestine; but with it they celebrated also the first day of the week in memory of the Savior's resurrection, and that too, it would appear, from the very day of the resurrection onward, which they looked upon as sanctioned for such purpose by Christ himself."—*Shaff's Hist. of the Apos. Church*, p. 552.

breaking; and sought the instruction of disciples. This looks, and was, a rest day—a septenary rest-day—a holy and blessed day. It has essential Sabbatic elements. And the Sabbatic strife of the period was not at all about the new day. No one objected to it—challenged it—opposed it. The reasons for its use were evidently so controlling that it occupied its place without friction—without criticism or comment—as a matter of course. It evidently came to the Apostolical Fathers, as a Christ-institution, sanctioned by Apostolic use.

Thus, as we emerge from Scripture, we find, not Seventh but First-day, employed for Sabbatic uses. Church history harmonizes with New Testament teaching. Their voice is one. Seventh-day is stript of Sabbatism; and, not without friction, is pushed aside. First-day is invested with Sabbatism, and is in unchallenged and unlimited use. This is history—the testimony of the Apostolical Fathers—no dissent whatever appearing. The credentials of First-day to Sabbatism are complete.

Sabbatism and the Church Fathers.

> "The Sundays of man's life,
> Threaded together on Time's string,
> Make bracelets to adorn the wife
> Of the eternal, glorious King."
> —HERBERT.

I step still farther away from the Apostles—from inspiration—from divine authority. I descend the stream of history. I pass from contemporaries to successors of the Apostles; to second century Church Fathers; to writers from 120 A. D. to about 200 A. D. From the Apostles, as special organs of the Holy Ghost, we reach the succeeding Church Fathers by many steps downward, like the descending traveler who passes from the pure fountain to where the streams begin to grow troubled and muddy. Our new witnesses represent the Christian sentiment of antiquity nearest to New Testament times. They lived near the date of Apostolic customs and institutions. They are competent witnesses of the Sabbatism they received from the Apostles and that was in use in their day.

What Second Century Fathers Say.

Justin Martyr, called the philosopher, was eminent among the most illustrious personages of his day. Eusebius says that he overshadowed all the great men who illuminated the second century.[a] He was conversant with the Apostolical Fathers. His First Apology, appearing about 139 A. D., discusses Sabbatism. He names and describes the day in use among primitive Christians for

---

[a] Hist. Eccl., 4: 11.

worship. It was not Seventh but First-day. He calls it by a new name—Sunday.[1] Christians, he says, assembled on Sundays; had sacred readings, instructions, and exhortations; celebrated the Eucharist with prayer and thanksgiving; and gathered a collection for the poor. This Sunday meeting has Luke's First-day bread-breaking at Troas, and Paul's First-day collections for the saints. Justin's Sunday was First-day. He characterizes it as the day on which "our Savior rose from the dead." Thus the Christian day for meeting and worship in 139 A. D. was First-day.

Justin, in his "Dialogue with Trypho the Jew," makes the contention cover three Judaisms; circumcision, Sabbaths, and feasts. He declares that Christians, *as Christians*, did not keep these three Judaisms, or any of them. Trypho replies that they did not.[2] Justin then sets forth that

---

[1] Τὴν δε του ἡλίου ἡμέραν κοινῇ τὴν συνέλευσιν ποιούμεθα, ἐπειδὴ πρώτη εστιν ἡμέρα, εν ἡ ὁ Θεος το σκότος, και τὴν ὑλην τρέψος κοσμον εποίησε, και ὁ Ιησοῦς Χριστὸς ὁ ἡμετερος Σωτὴρ τῃ αὐτῇ τῃ ἡμερᾳ εκ νεκρων ἀνέστη.—JUSTIN. *Apol.*, 1: 67.

"On the day of the Sun—Sunday—we all assemble in common, since that is the first day on which God, having changed darkness and chaos, made the world, and on the same day our Savior Jesus Christ arose from the dead."—*Ante-Nicene Fathers*, 1: 186.

"It is the mission of Justin to be a star in the West, leading its Wise Men to the cradle of Bethlehem."—*Ante-Nicene Fathers*, 1: 159.

[2] Trypho, the Jew, to Justin: "Be circumcised, then observe what ordinances have been enacted with respect to the Sabbath, and the feasts and the new moons."—*Ante-Nicene Fathers*, 1: 199.

Justin to Trypho: "Is there any other matter, my friend, in which we are blamed than this, that we live not after the law, and are not circumcised.....and do not observe Sabbaths, as you do?" Trypho to Justin: "You observe no festivals, or Sabbaths, and do not have the rite of circumcision."—*Ditto.*

Trypho to Justin: "But if some one.... recognizes that this man is Christ, and has believed in and obeys him, wishes, however, to observe these (Judaisms), will he be saved?" Justin to Trypho: "In my opinion, Trypho, he will." Trypho to Justin: "Why then have you said, 'In my opinion such an one will be saved,' unless there are some who affirm that such will not be saved?" Justin to Trypho: "There are such people, Trypho."

"Vindicating (as Justin, for instance, does in his Dialogue with Trypho the Jew) the neglect of Sabbath keeping by Gentile Christians."—*The Inter. Cycl.*, Art. Sabbath.

Christians were divided as to whether keepers of the three Judaisms could be real Christians—could be saved. Some thought they could not. As for himself he thought they might be, if they did not depend on the Judaisms, and did depend on Christ. "We," (Christians) he says, "do not observe Sabbaths." Justin thus opposes Seventh-day for Sabbath keeping.

This testimony of Justin is clear and final. Christians, as Christians, did not in 139 A. D. keep Seventh-day as Sabbath; and they did keep First-day—"the chief and first of days." Seventh-day Sabbatarians never go to Justin for comfort. He calls the Christian day of worship Sunday—First-day—the Christ resurrection day.

Dionysius, Bishop of Corinth, was the author of eight epistles, all now lost, except some brief fragments preserved by Eusebius. One fragment speaks of the Lord's day and its uses. It is an extract from a letter written to Soter, Bishop of Rome. Dionysius says: "To-day we have passed the Lord's holy day, in which we have read your Epistle."[1] The Greek phrase used by John on Patmos, is here used in full. It now, and frequently appears in patristic writings; and always with the meaning First-day—our Lord's resurrection day. The Soter letter was read on the Lord's day. It was the custom of the period to read Christian letters in First-day meetings.

Irenæus, a disciple of Polycarp, who was a disciple of St. John,[a] was called by Theodoret, "the light of the Western World." Like Justin, he held the Sabbath to be wholly Jewish; beginning with Moses; and not surviving Judaism. He meant in this the Judaic day—seventh day

---

[a] Euseb. H. E., 5: 20.

[1] "Greek text: τῆν σημεραν οὖν κυριακὴν ἁγίαν ἡμέραν διηγάγομεν, ἐν ᾗ ἀνέγνομεν ὑμῶντὴν ἐπιστολήν."—EUSEB. *Eccl. Hist.*, B. 4, c. 23.

Translation: "We have passed (kept) the Lord's holy day and perused your epistle, in the reading of which we find admonition."

—not Sabbatism itself; for he characterized the Decalogue as permanent, and as receiving in Christ, "extension and increase, not abrogation."[1] The temporary Judaic Sabbath, as he interprets it, had no longer divine significance. Like circumcision it had ceased.

Among the primitive Christians the *weekly* celebration of the Christ resurrection on First-day was never challenged; but its *yearly* celebration was. This is called the Easter controversy. The contention was, whether Easter should always be celebrated on First-day, or on the third day after the 14th of the Hebrew month Nisan. Irenæus, though seeking to be a peacemaker, advocated its celebration on First-day alone.[2] The churches of Gaul, chiefly through

---

[1] "God gave circumcision . . . . as a sign. . . . . This same does Ezekiel the prophet say with regard to the Sabbath. Sec. 1. . . . . . The laws of bondage . . . . were one by one promulgated to the people by Moses. . . . These things, therefore, which were given for bondage and for a sign to them, He canceled by the new covenant of liberty."—*Against Heretics*, sec. 5.

"The Lord did speak in His own person to all alike the words of the Decalogue: and therefore . . . do they remain permanently with us, receiving, by means of His advent in the flesh, extension and increase, but not abrogation."—*Ante-Nicene Fathers*, 1 : 480-2.

[2] "The mystery of the Lord's resurrection may not be celebrated on any other day than the Lord's day, and on this alone should we observe the breaking off of the Paschal feast."—EUSEB. 5 : 23 : 2.

[3] "This (custom) of not bending the knee on Sunday is a symbol of the resurrection, through which we have been set free, by the grace of Christ, from sins and from death which has been put to death under him. Now this custom took its rise from Apostolic times, as the blessed Irenæus, the martyr and Bishop of Lyons, declares in his treatise 'On Easter,' in which he makes mention of Pentecost also; upon which (feast) we do not bend the knee, because it is of equal significance with the Lord's day, for the reason already alleged concerning it."—*Lost Writings. 7th Fragment. Ante-Nicene Fathers*, 1 : 569.

"For Irenæus, Bishop of Lyons, who was a contemporary of the disciple of the Apostle Polycarp, Bishop of Smyrna, and martyr, and for this reason held in just estimation, wrote to an Alexandrian to the effect that it is right with respect to the feast of the resurrection, that we should celebrate it upon the first day of the week."—*50th Fragment.* Introductory note by Syriac editor. *Ante-Nicene Fathers*, 1 : 576.

his influence, sent a letter to Victor, Bishop of Rome, declaring this as their conviction. The letter is preserved in Eusebius. Another fragment from his pen, preserved by an unknown writer, repeats the same view. And in another preserved fragment, he is reported as making Easter of equal significance with the Lord's day.

This testimony, though partly incidental, is clear, distinct, very complete. The Churches of the West did not keep Seventh-day. They did keep the Lord's day.

Melita, Bishop of Sardis, about 170 A. D., is said to have composed a treatise on the Lord's day. It is among lost writings. Its title is however preserved in Eusebius.[a]

The Ebionites, Judaizing Christians, who like the Nazarenes clung to the Jewish ritual and its Sabbath, appeared, according to Hegesippus, in 108 A. D., some say as early as 66 A. D. Eusebius[b] reports them as half Jewish in observing the Sabbath, and half Christian in keeping the Lord's day. Theodoret describes them in like manner. He says: "They keep the Sabbath according to the Jewish law, and sanctify the Lord's day in like manner as we do." Thus Sabbath-keeping stands as Judaistic; keeping the Lord's day as Christian. Even the most Judaistic Christians, so Judaistic as to be accounted heretics, kept the Lord's day.[1]

Bardesanes, a Christian Gnostic, wrote a treatise on Fate, and addressed it to the Emperor, Marcus Aurelius Antoninus. He says: "What then shall we says respecting the new race of ourselves, who are Christians, whom in every country and in every region, the Messiah established at his coming; for lo! wherever we be, all of us are

---

[a] Euseb. H. E. 4: 26.   [b] Euseb. H E. 3: 27.

[1] "The Jewish Christians ceased to observe the Sabbath after the destruction of Jerusalem. The Ebionites and Nazarenes kept up the habit even longer."—SHAFF-HERZOG. *Encycl. of Knowl.*, Art. Sunday.

called by the one name of the Messiah, Christians; and upon one day, which is the first day of the week, we assemble ourselves together, and on the appointed days we abstain from food."[a]

Clement of Alexandria, a somewhat mystical writer, yet distinguished in Attic and also in Christian scholarship, was a disciple of Plato and afterwards of Jesus. His writings are prominent among the Christian remains of antiquity. Justin, Irenæus, and Clement are notable among the earlier founders of Christian literature. Clement discusses the transfer of Sabbatism from the Seventh to the Primal day. He names them as "the seventh and the eighth . . . the latter properly the Sabbath, and the seventh a day of work . . . the seven became six, and the eight seven . . . . seven glorifies eight."[1] These abbreviated steps in his argument show his real thought. He argues the transferrence of Sabbatism from the Hebrew seventh to the Hebrew eighth, that is to the first day in the weekly cycle. The Lord's day drops from his pen as an institution well and widely known. He names it with our Lord's resurrection, and thus identifies it as First-day.[2]

---

[a] *Spicilegium Syriacum.* Cureton's Translation.

[1] "That He (the Creator) gave us the seventh day as a day of rest, on account of the trouble that there is in life. . . . . The seventh day, therefore, is proclaimed a rest—abstraction from ills—preparing for the Primal day, our true rest . . . . since the discourse has turned on the seventh and the eighth. For the eighth may possibly turn out to be the seventh, and the seventh manifestly the sixth; and the latter properly the Sabbath, and the seventh a day of work. . . . The seven become six, and the eight seven. . . . Seven glorifies eight."—STROM. 6 : 16. *Ante-Nicene Fathers*, 2 : 512.

[2] "And the Lord's day, Plato prophetically speaks of in the tenth book of the *Republic.*"—STROM. 5 : 14. *Ante-Nicene Fathers*, 2 : 469.

"He, in fulfillment of the precept, according to the Gospel, keeps the Lord's day, when he abandons an evil disposition, and assumes that of the Gnostic, glorifying the Lord's resurrection in himself."—STROM. 7 : 12. *Ante-Nicene Fathers*, 2 : 545.

Minucius Felix, first to array Christianity in a Latin dress, has graces of style that make him a worthy disciple of Cicero. He wrote "Octavius," in which treatise Octavius and Cæcilius discuss Christianity and heathenism. One of the disputants says of Christians: "On a solemn day, persons of both sexes and of every age assemble at a feast with all their children, sisters, and mothers."[a] Bread-breaking among primitive Christians was always on First-day.

Tertullian, a Carthaginian—in temper sharp and vehement—in genius versatile and brilliant—stands in history as the founder of Latin Christianity. His writings abound in allusions to Sabbatism. Like Justin and Clement, he argues with Jews—that their Sabbath was temporary—not even patriarchal—dating only from Moses—disappearing in Christ.[1] He distinguishes Christians from Jews as to their respective days of worship; Christians keeping First-day; Jews, Seventh-day.[2] The *weekly* day of

---

[a] *Ante-Nicene Fathers*, 3: 178.

[1] "'Ye observe days, and months, and times, and years'—the Sabbaths, I suppose, and 'the preparation,' and the fasts, and the 'high days.' For the cessation of even these, no less than of circumcision, was appointed by the Creator's decrees."—*Against Marcion. Ante-Nicene Fathers*, 3: 436.

"Of *Jewish* ceremonies and *legal* solemnities: for these the Apostle unteaches."—*On Fasting*, 14. *Ante-Nicene Fathers*, 4: 112.

"The observance of the Sabbath is demonstrated to have been temporary."—*An Answer to the Jews. Ante-Nicene Fathers*, 3: 155.

[2] "We make Sunday a day of festivity. . . . The Jewish feasts are the Sabbath and 'the Purification.'"—*Ad Nationes*, 13. *Ante-Nicene Fathers*, 3: 123.

"Wherefore . . . . you who reproach us with the sun and Sunday should consider your proximity to us. We are not far off from your Saturn (the Jewish Sabbath) and your days of rest."

"By us to whom Sabbaths are strange."—*On Idolatry*, 14. *Ante-Nicene Fathers*, 3: 70.

"We neither accord with the Jews in their peculiarities in regard to food, nor in their sacred days."—*Apology*, 21. *Ante-Nicene Fathers*, 3: 34.

the Christ-resurrection, called by him "Sunday," "eighth day" and "the Lord's day," he emphasizes as the day for Christian meetings and worship; and its *annual* day as superior to all heathen festivals. The Lord's day, as he reports it still farther, was a day so joyful that Christians in worship did not kneel; and they put off their business and rested.[2] This testimony covers all grounds. At the close of the second Christian century Seventh-day worship was exclusively Judaic, and Christian worship belongs in all reports to First-day.[1]

The Testimony and the Times.

Second century Church Fathers have now been interrogated on the Sabbatism of their times; and none who speak on the subject have been omitted. Their testimony is a unit. Seventh-day worship is nowhere reported as Christian; but always as Judaic—as worn out—as set aside. An exception to this broad statement does not anywhere appear. First-day worship is everywhere reported as Christian; as in common use; and it is invariably traced to the Christ-resurrection. To this there is no

---

[1] "To the heathens each festive day occurs but once annually: you have a festive day every eighth day. Call out the individual solemnities of the nations, and set them out in a row, they will not be able to make up a Pentecost."—*On Idolatry*, 14. *Ante-Nicene Fathers*, 3: 70.

"We take also, in the congregation before daybreak, and from the hand of none but the presidents, the sacrament of the Eucharist, which the Lord hath commanded to be eaten by all alike."—Tertullian. *The Chaplet*, 3. *Ante-Nicene Fathers*, 3: 94.

[2] "We count fasting or kneeling in worship on the Lord's day to be unlawful."—*The Chaplet*, 3. *Ante-Nicene Fathers*, 3: 94.

"Not the Lord's day, not Pentecost even, if they had known them, would they have shared with us; for they would fear lest they should seem to be Christians."—Tertullian. *On Idolatry*, 14. *Ante-Nicene Fathers*, 3: 70.

"We however, (just as we have received,) only on the day of the Lord's resurrection ought to guard not only against kneeling, but every posture and office of solicitude; deferring even our business lest we give place to the devil."—*On Prayer*, 23. *Ante-Nicene Fathers*, 3: 689.

dissent. The witnesses all speak as one man. They do not ordain the day. They do not defend it. They simply report it. They keep it. They raise no doubt of their obligation to keep it. Always and everywhere, they report First-day as connecting them with Christian teachings and ordinances.[1]

Sunday, as a name for First day, emerged in patristic literature in this century—about 139 A. D. Justin first used it. It is a purely human name for the day; but it has nothing to do with the sun worship cult. Some writers indeed assume that Sunday was a heathen name for First-day before Justin used it, and regard its adoption as the emptying of the whole heathen cult upon Christianity. This is not sober sense. It is a historic falsehood. The name is of Christian birth and original. It is not found anywhere in use back of Justin. Keeping the day of the sun, *as a weekly festival*, was unknown before Christianity. The week, at the Advent, was exclusively Judaic—then Christian. Sun-worship, till brought in contact with Judaism, or Christianity, knew nothing of the weekly period, or of a weekly day of worship. Roman festivals were not weekly events; nor were Grecian; nor were Egyptian; nor were Syrian; till Judaism and Christianity made them such. Sunday, then, as a human name for First-day, has very little to do with heathenism.

---

[1] "The first day of the week was everywhere set apart for this purpose" (worship).—*Encycl. Brit.*, Art. Sabbath.

"The first day of the week was adopted by the early Christians as a day of worship. . . . Sunday was emphatically the weekly festival of the resurrection of Christ. . . . In the second century its observance was universal."—*Shaff-Herzog Encyc. of Knowl.*, Art. Sunday.

"The change in the Sabbath from the seventh to the first day falls in with the changes that were introduced in the external organization of the Church of God at the introduction of Christianity. Everything was changed by the example and authority of the divine Author of the Christian Dispensation."—NEVIN. *Pres. Encyc.*, Art. Sabbath.

New institutions may be affected by the scenery, the community, the times; and always receive some tinge from antagonizing and competing institutions. Action and reaction is a law among social and moral forces, as well as in mechanics. Christianity was tinged by Judaism and also by Paganism. And First-day worship would necessarily receive some new shapings from competing days of rest and devotion. But he must be a very minute philosopher who characterizes Christianity as a child of Paganism, because its sacred day has the name Sunday.

Chronology, one of the eyes of history, arranges the dates of events. Man, its builder, began very crudely. A common era, its essential basis, was not selected for long ages. The ante-diluvians had no common era. They reckoned by generations. And post-diluvians long had no common era. Accadians, Assyrians, Babylonians, Egyptians, Hebrews, all reckoned by generations.

The *year* goes back to immemorial times, and, among the earliest peoples, had twelve months. The months had no names. They were numbered—were designated by ordinals. Names came later, and, when first used, the ordinals were added in the way of explanation, showing that the names were of later origin.[a]

The *week* had a like history. It was created and measured by the Sabbath. Its days had no names. The Accadian week days had not. The early Assyrian week days had not. The Hebrew week days had not. They were numbered—were designated by ordinals. Each day was counted from the Sabbath. This weekly calendar continued down to the planting of Christianity. The first Christians used it. They, like the Jews, counted the days of the week from the Sabbath. But names for the days were an invention of the period. *Saturn*, as a name for

---
[a] Gen. 7: 11; 8: 13. *Origin of Laws* 1: 229.

seventh day, first appears in Tibullus, a Roman poet, about 18 B. C.;[a] *Sunday*, as a name for first day, in Justin, about 139 A. D.; *Ermou* (Wednesday) for fourth day, and *Aphrodites* (Friday) for sixth day, in Clement of Alexandria, about 200 A. D. Soon planetary names were put upon all the days of the week.

Now when the week came to be in prevailing use at Rome—about 200 A. D.[1]—it was not the Jewish but the Christian week; not the week that turns upon Seventh day, but the week that turns upon First day. This is a most remarkable fact. It attests that First day, as a day of rest and worship, had long been molding society. New ideas and customs make slow social transformations. Graceful ice forms, incrusting a window, are born of a winter night, and are as short lived. Social changes do not so swiftly come and go. Their evolution is slower,

---

[a] TIBULLUS. *Eleg.*, 1 : 3 : 18.

[1] "Week . . . was not introduced at Rome till after the reign of Theodosius."—*Encyc. Brit.*, Art. Calendar.

"The division (hebdomadal) was introduced among the Romans, it is said, not far from the beginning of the third century."—ANTHON. *Class. Man. Lit.*, 61.

"From the beginning of the third century, the Egyptian week, (erroneously following Dion Cassius), of which the seven days were consecrated to the planets, became common amongst the Romans."— GEISLER. *Eccl. Hist.*, 121, Note 30.

"Among the western nations, especially the Roman, the institution of *Sabbatism* was introduced by the Jews in the early days of the Empire, along with the institution of the seven-days week."—SCHRADER. *The Cunei. Ins. and the Old Test.*, 21.

"Before the death of Hadrian, A. D. 138, the hebdomadal division . . . had, in matters of common life, almost universally superseded in Greece, and even in Italy, the national division of the lunar month." —MCCLINTOCK & STRONG. *Cycl.*, Art. Lord's Day.

It was not the Judaic but the Christian week—not the Judaic Seventh-day but the Christian First-day—that prevailed at Rome about 200 A. D. Tertullian shows this; Christians abstaining from work on First-day (*On Prayer*, 23); and non-Christians also resting on First-day (*Ad Nationes*, 13).

like the tardy modifying of organic forms under the action of physical causes. In four centuries, two before and two after the Advent, Greeks and Egyptians passed from *decades*, and Romans from *nundinæ, Calends, Nones,* and *Ides,* to the *week* and its *Sabbatism*—to the *Christian* week and its *First day* Sabbatism. Unchristianized Romans, in Tertullian's time, were using the weekly calendar, with First-day as a partial or total rest day.[a] This incipient completion of the mighty social revolution is historic proof that First day had long been making a deep impression, throughout the Roman Empire, as a day of rest and devotion.

The planting of Christianity is the greatest chapter in the social progress of man. The Jews began the work; advanced it far on its way; then grew stationary; looked back, and clung to the past. The past never returns. Primitive Christians took up the work where the Jews laid it down; caught its fuller spirit; rolled the stone from the door of progress; kept their faces to the future, and their march was onward. Jews and Christians together rearranged the nations, and revolutionized the world.

The workers together in this great providential movement—Jews and Christians—had scarcely met in history till they began to separate. Sabbatism was a chief factor in making and widening the breach between them; not First-day Sabbatism, however, for no scrap of history shows any division here, even the Judaizing Nazarenes and Ebionites keeping First as well as Seventh-day; but Seventh-day Sabbatism that seems to have called out discussion and antagonism from the very beginning. The New Testament reports Judaizing teachers—disturbing the Church—resisted by Paul and Barnabas. And early Church Fathers had dialectic conflicts with Jews; Justin with Trypho; Tertullian against Jews; and Origen in his day. Early patristic writings were *apologetic* towards Gentiles, but *antagonistic* towards Jews. The keeping of seventh-day as Sabbath was a chief battle-field. The controversy steadily shows that Seventh-day worship was a pure Judaism—was in no sense Christian—and had but a limited existence and use. There is not a shred of testimony anywhere showing that Seventh day meetings among the Church Fathers of the first two centuries were any part of the Christian movement. All the Church Fathers, who speak on the subject, oppose them. Like Paul, they represent Seventh day as no longer Sabbatic. It had ceased as a divine institution.

The Constantine edict in 321 A. D., putting special honor on First-day by making it a day of *rest from labor*, applied to all Roman citizens—Pagans as well as Christians—and its only exception to universal use and obligation was in the rural districts where perhaps Pagans were still in the majority. The edict was a reporter as well as a creator of social customs. It made First-day a day of rest from labor, because it was already really and widely such.[1] Social revolutions are not born of edicts, but of ideas; do not spring up in a night, but are growths. The breath of the new rest day must have been long breathing upon society, before it molded and prepared the nations for the Constantine edict. The edict accepted Sunday rest as an already existing fact, and made it legal—did that and nothing more. It conformed to

---

[1] "The Greeks and the barbarians have this in common, that they accompany their sacred rites by a festal remission of labor."—*Strabo*, x: 3: 9.

"This practice (of resting from labor on the Lord's day) is naturally and even necessarily connected with the religious observance of the Lord's day as a day of worship and religious gladness."—*Cycl. Brit.*, Art. Sabbath.

"So long as the Christians were oppressed they could not keep the day as one of rest from labor as they desired, and as they did after the union of Church and State."—SHAFF-HERZOG. *Encycl. Rel. Knowl.* Art. Sunday.

and confirmed a widely prevailing custom. It is evidence therefore that Christians had long used First-day as a day of rest from labor.

Remission of ordinary business evidently belonged to the day, more or less, from the beginning. Thus we have glimpses of meetings held in all parts of the day; early morning meetings; day meetings; evening meetings; suggesting, when taken together, a day of no work. Tertullian farther lifts the veil, and shows Sunday a day of rest both to Christians and pagans; Christians deferring "work lest they should give place to the Devil;" and even Pagans making the day one of partial or of entire rest. Indeed it was only the keeping of Sunday as a day of rest from the beginning, that made the Constantine edict possible within three centuries from the resurrection of our Lord.

I write a closing word on the change of day—summarizing the facts that report the change. Sabbatism was moved out of Seventh into First day. It was moved by the Lord of the Sabbath himself; rising from the dead on First not on Seventh day; appearing to disciples always on First never on Seventh days; appointing a First not a Seventh day meeting to disciples; initiating his Gospel on First not on Seventh day; and making the last known visible revelation of himself on First not on Seventh day. By these acts He transferred Sabbatism. In his resurrection, and in his post-resurrection example, He ended the old series of Sabbaths—He began the new series of Sabbaths. His disuse and disapproval of the old day displaced it; His use and approval of the new day instituted it. If our risen Lord—our risen and ascended Lord—the Lord of the Sabbath—had authority to change the day, then the day is changed. His post-resurrection life and doings give no support whatever to Seventh day Sabbatism. They establish First-day Sabbatism. The risen One translated and transferred holy time.

The Apostles were not Sabbath-Makers. They could neither translate nor transfer Sabbatism. They were under marching orders. They were to shape the forming customs of the Church according to the teachings and the example of our risen Lord. In doing this, they steadily recognized the Divine transferrence of Sabbatism from Seventh to First day. *Five* times they are reported as using Seventh day. But they only used it as a convenience; to better reach assembled Jews; merely for preaching; never for any Christian ordinance. The day was not Christianized. And their only known teaching about the day reports it vacated of Sabbatism—a shrivelled form—a disused husk. Thus they report Seventh day as divinely set aside from Sabbatic uses,—as having no longer divine significance. *Six* times they are reported as using First day. They used it for prayer and preaching. They used it *alone* for sacred collections. They used it *alone* for the Christian ordinances—for baptism—for the Lord's Supper. The day was Christianized. It appears as part and parcel of Apostolic and so of Scriptural Christianity. Thus Apostolic history and writings report the ancient order of Sabbaths ended; and the new order of Sabbaths begun.

Church Fathers—Apostolic *contemporaries* and *successors*—report the day for Christian meetings and worship that came to them that was in use in their times—as never Seventh but always First-day. All the writers of the period who discuss Sabbatism say this. Their testimony is a unit. There is nowhere a dissenting voice. History corroborates them. Mighty social changes were widely establishing the custom of First-day rest; giving it prevalence at Rome at the end of the second century; and making it a law of the Roman Empire a century later. First-day is, by all testimony, the Sabbath of the Christian era.

THE SABBATH IN HISTORY.

> "That stream upon whose bosom we have passed,
> Floating at ease, while nations have effaced
> Nations, and death has gathered to his folds
> Long lines of mighty kings."

The Sabbath Sun that shines down upon this nineteenth Christian century is of immemorial antiquity. It is of to-day; it was of yesterday. It unites the present with the oldest times—with mythical ages—with the creation epoch. It has reached us "across the ages from afar." The channel in which it flows is centuries deep. History knows the institution as an old-time fact; older than pyramids; older than death's reign over man. It has run, as a silver thread, through all historic time, moving as steadily as the swift chariot of Phœbus has sped through the sky. Our earth has wrinkles; the Sabbath, like Time, has none.

The Sabbath from the beginning has walked a highway all its own. It is a historic unit. Its various epochs and eras form but one grand providential drama. There is nowhere visible in its divine history the gulf of a great revolution. Time, the mighty innovater, has wrought in it no material change. As we turn its pages backward to the beginning, the initial Sabbath has all the stateliness and completeness of the Sabbath of to-day. This is not said of the day as man has kept it; a blurred picture of the day as God appoints it; but it is said of the day as it stands inscribed in history—in the Decalogue—in the older Genesis record—in the still older inscriptions of Accad. Naturalists, who regard all institutions as a growth, meet an insoluble problem in the historic Sabbath; carried along now on quiet anon on turbulent streams; exhibiting blemishes indeed on its human side; but showing also a side so natural and so divine that it has essential identity back to the very beginning. This is an enigma to all their theories.[1]

Its Immemorial Antiquity.

As the Sabbath dates back beyond Sinai to the very sources of history; as it has descended to us in a continuous and unbroken stream; it is impossible to contemplate it without feelings of profound reverence. It rises before us as antedating and as surviving the oldest things before which we stand with bowed and reverent head. It has witnessed the rise and the fall of empires, kingdoms, thrones, and dynasties; the appearing and the disappearing of arts, sciences and literatures; and the coming and going in history of civilizations, and religions—the civilizations and religions of Assyria, Egypt, India, Greece, Rome. Gone are the best and most enduring works of early men; their builded temples and palaces; the creations of their genius and their power. Gone are the workers themselves; kings, prophets, priests, statesmen, teachers, singers, shouters, bronzed warriors and weary toilers. They are but moldering ruins—decaying sepulchers. Nothing but echoes of them remains. But the Sabbath stands, changeless, in the vast theater where they came and went, like some conspicuous mountain peak, firm as the earth beneath,

---

[1] "The use of the Sabbath, as it began, will end only with the world itself."—BISHOP HORSLEY. *Sermons*, 444.

"The Sabbath was believed to prevail in all its strictness from eternity, throughout the universe."—GEIKE. *The Life of Christ*, 450.

"From Genesis down to Revelation, I find the day published, republished, endorsed, sanctioned, and never repealed."—BISHOP RYLE, in *A word for Sunday*.

"Antiquity has bequeathed the Sabbath to modern nations; and the fact that this institution has subsisted in spite of the changes that have taken place in the domain of politics and religion, testifies to its intrinsic value and its absolute necessity."—HAEGLER. *Der Sonlag*.

and pure as the stars above. It is without a parallel in the institutions and creations of men; bright as the bow of promise that spanned and beautified the clouds above Noah; lovely as the fabled goddess beneath whose steps fragrant flowers are ever springing; and flowing ever the same beneath and above all changes that sweep over the face of Time and Nature. It is an abiding factor in the world's best history and life; and, amid social and moral factors and forces, stands so incomparably bright, so vital and enduring, so potent and pervasive, that it seems in itself a symbol as well as an institution of the immutable God.

Keeping the Sabbath is observing the Divine Meeting Day for mankind; and Sabbath worshipers are an unbroken line back to the beginning. Stand aside, and see the unending column pass by; floating its Sabbath banners; singing its Sabbath songs. Adam and Eve head the procession. Abel, Enoch and other antediluvian worthies move in the ranks. Noah renews the march. Accadians appear in the moving column. Job joins it in the land of Uz; Abraham, Isaac and Jacob in the land of Canaan. One can almost hear the bleating of their flocks and the lowing of their herds as they sweep by. Moses re-formed the procession, and started that mighty column of Judaism that eventually rekindled Sabbath campfires in all the world. Jesus changed the day, and initiated the march of the Christian hosts. Apostles head the new movement. Martyrs come and go. Reformers drift by. The procession is unending. It is a vast spectacle. We gaze upon it with awe, wonder, reverence.

As the Sabbath dates back beyond Sinai to the very sources of history; as it connects the man who stood in Eden with the sin-scarred man of to-day; it must be of

God, not of man; a divine arrangement, not a human contrivance. No creation of man has spanned such an arch of time. What is of man is short-lived. The Sabbath, if a human invention, would long since have perished. Its survival, amid the wide wreckage of human works, is proof that it unrolled itself from the bosom, not of man, but of God; and that it has been under oversight and keeping other than of man. It did not spring from the earth, but came down from the skies. It is well descended. It is of celestial birth and origin. It was born of the divine example and appointment. This is its genesis. And its history, like its origin, declares it divine. For its safe keeping in the changing centuries can be traced only to providential oversight and watchcare. Whence this earth and yon heavens? Whence man? The supernaturalist points to God. Whence the Sabbath? The supernaturalist still points to God. His theory gives the institution an adequate authorship. The day brings us forever into the presence of God.

As the Sabbath dates back beyond Sinai to the very sources of history; as it is of God's appointment, not of man's invention; and as it has never been abrogated, annulled, repealed; it will follow that it is binding upon all men in all time. It belongs, like the atonement, to world ideas and institutions. It cannot be limited to any one nation, locality, age; but relates to all peoples, countries, times. It is as binding upon the Gentile as upon the Jew; upon the sceptic as upon the believer; upon the sinner as upon the saint. Instituted by the same divine fiat that gave Adam birth, it is as obligatory upon every one of his descendants as upon himself. It is this that makes its keeping a universal and unchangeable duty. If it were of man—a product of the human invention—it would be wholly wanting in authority. But as it is of

God—a law of nature—its obligation is universal and immutable; it reports an immutable duty.

There must forever be something awful and solemn in the thought that Sabbath keeping is binding on us; that we must account for our use of holy time; that Sabbath-breakers must meet and answer the Sabbath-Maker. Anti-Christian demonstrations are, to-day, widely taking the form of Sabbath-breaking; greed robbing God of his reserved day, robbing toilers of needed rest, opening stores and saloons, and sending Sunday papers, steamboats, and railway trains to whirl through the day; and pleasure-seeking turning the day into a carnival, and flaring through it with parades, theatres, picnics, excursions, and ball games. This is a terrible record; yet we are accustomed to look on it with indifference; and many amuse themselves with the idea that it does no harm. It is all done on the presumption that it will escape the divine notice, and so go unpunished. But what does inexorable History say? An inevitable fate awaits all Sabbath-breaking. It works out its own punishment—physiological deterioration—thought degeneracy—moral depravation. It tinctures daily life; achieves irreparable ruin; and makes the social fabric a festering mass of rottenness. Man's sinful personality asserts itself. Population loses its finer fiber, and grows debauched. Corruption of classes of men is by insidious agencies that modify the men themselves—making them lower and worse men. Sabbath-breakers meet God in history, and go down—down to the lower levels. In the presence of this cancer in American life—indifferentism is not allowable. Patriotism forbids it. Christianity forbids it. Hence this appeal to better thinking citizens to cease from all kinds of Sabbath desecration.

God's Trinity of Reforming Agencies.

The Bible, a special divine revelation, has as its lieutenants, the Sabbath and the Church; a trinity of the mightiest forces that have left traces upon human society. The Bible, the Sabbath, the Church! The Book, the Day, the Tent of meeting! What honor they have put upon man! What dignity! What happiness! They have starry names. In their train appear the best forms of civil law and social order—the humane agencies that regenerate and uplift society—and the highest and noblest types of manhood and womanhood. They gave birth to Christianity, and were not born of it; to Judaism, and were not born of it; to the ancient patriarchal religion, and were not born of it. Their forms change, but their essences are eternal. The Bible, the Sabbath, the Church, like the rain, the sunbeam, and the atmosphere, are God's most precious gifts—are for all alike—are potent workers for human betterment. They make life purer, sweeter, happier. They are the organizing forces in all movements that build the best things for man.[1] All men and women who shut them out of their thoughts remain at their worst, commit the irreparable mistake, make life a failure.

The Day is a need of the Sabbath and the Church—indeed the lungs of the Book and the Tent of Meeting. They are all inter-dependent. The stream of Sabbatism—sweeping as a mighty tide through Time and History—is kept pure only as it flows out of the Bible and through

---

[1] "Christianity has given us the Sabbath, the Jubilee of the world, whose light dawns welcome alike into the closet of the philosopher, into the garret of toil, and into prison cells; and everywhere suggests, even to the vile, the dignity of being."—EMERSON.

"The Church of God, the Book of God, and the Day of God, are a sacred trinity on earth, the chief pillars of Christian society and national prosperity. Without them Europe and America would soon relapse into heathenism and barbarity."—PHILIP SHAFF.

"Of all divine institutions, the most divine is that which secures a day of rest for man. I hold it to be the most valuable blessing ever conceded to man. It is the corner-stone of civilization, and its fracture might even affect the health of the people."—*D'Israeli in British Parliament.*

the Church. It was so in Judaism. It is so in Christianity. The Sabbath, so ordered, gathers the tribes of Israel in temples to meditate on divine things; kindles fires of devotion on sacred altars; and furnishes high opportunity for song, and prayer, and divine teaching. Tender and sweet are the memories of Sabbath worship—the hush of breathless stillness—hearts beating in rapture—unspoken aspirations—souls mounting heavenward—the Lord himself coming near and feasting his saints! Such Sabbath-keeping is simple duty—something that we ought to do—because God commands it—and because it is best for us. Keeping the Sabbath makes God known, benefits the worshiper, promotes good morals, and regenerates society. And decline in Sabbath keeping is a sure token of religious decay, of waning morals, and of deteriorating character in the individual—the community—the nation.

'Tis strange that the Day, a strong bulwark against immorality and worldliness, a balance wheel of religious institutions, a necessity of Christianity, should have pronounced and bitter enemies. Yet there are many who not only rob God of the day, but speak big words against it. They oppose it because it does not suit their notions; or because its holy rest is to them a weariness; or because the Lord of the Sabbath is not their Lord. They array against it their most active forces; seize and occupy its outworks; attack its walls and towers. Innovation follows innovation. Holy time is in peril. And the danger is not wholly from the attacking parties—Atheists, Liberal Leagues, Secularists, Seventh-day Sabbatarians—but also from the apathy of Sabbath defenders. The citadel of the Sabbath, if not betrayed from within, can never be successfully stormed from without. The massing of forces against the Day is not so alarming as the indifference of Sabbath-keepers within. They seem unmoved spectators of the conflict, except as to a solitary sentinel here and there upon the watch towers. This, not the attacks of outside foes—not the hurling of their combined forces against the bulwarks—is the chief danger. This awakens alarm. The defenders are not cowards—not traitors—but asleep—indifferent—insensible to the danger. O if they could only be awaked—startled from indifference—made to see the peril! Rouse ye, Sabbath-keepers! Man the walls. Guard the gates. Sally forth and attack the besiegers. Let the cause take no default from your indifference. Hand the day on to posterity better, on its human side, than when it came to you.

The Sabbath, walking the highways of history for six thousand years, sweeping between the eternities, assailed by puny man!—the actor of an hour!—a bubble upon the ocean of being! Its abolition is impossible. The utmost the assailants can do is to lower the human interpretations of the day—to diminish its human uses—to lure individuals and communities from its Tent of blessings. They can wreck themselves and others but not the divine Sabbath. It is an important and an imperishable factor in the drama of the world. And in the long run woe ever betides the man, community, nation, that assails the day. Their deed works irreparable ruin, not to the Sabbath, but to themselves—strewing the shores of time with social and moral wrecks. The Sabbath of God standeth forever. It has "no variableness, neither shadow of turning." It is not a vanishing form. Time mutilates it not as it does inscriptions on tombs and monuments. It is indestructible. Its name is written in God's Book of Life.[1] It is an Ark of God forever riding safely above all the tides of human passion; sweeping steadily through time within

---

[1] "The Word and Power of the invisible, the unchangeable, and eternal God of the Sabbath, are our all-sufficient security that the institution is to be universal in the world, and to endure forever."—GILFILLAN. *The Sabbath*, 605.

hearing of wails of defeat and peans of victory; and showing always and everywhere the identity of an imperishable life.

The Sabbath of the Bible stands as a prophet of an Eden to come, as well as a reminder of an Eden lost. It has not only come to us out of the distant past, but has the promise of an unending future. It was a heritage of man innocent; is a heritage of man redeemed; and will be a heritage of man glorified. As a law and need of our nature it is imperishable as the framework of the universe; imperishable as ourselves; imperishable as the Sabbatizing God. Sabbath-keeping will be eternal. The day of the Sabbath is to have no evening; is a broad sunrise and illuminant without any setting. Its unending future stands assured in the Bible. "There remaineth therefore a rest"—the keeping of a Sabbath—"to the people of God."[a] This fairly means the identity of the heavenly with the earthly Sabbath. It means that the heavenly is the continuance and perfection of the earthly. It preannounces a septenary Meeting Day for saints and angels in the Christ-preparing mansions. The worship begun on earth will be continued in heaven. Of this we have prophetic intimations. To each saint the Meeting Day will bring a communion life broader and deeper than his own—communion with all sainted ones—communion with the innumerable company of angels—communion with Jesus as the second Adam—communion with the all-loving Divine Father. There will not be wanting the high exhilaration of song, and sacred teaching, and worship. Amid such Sabbath scenes, all the best seeking of man will find its utmost realization. They all in that great

---

[a] Heb. 4: 9.

company will be satisfied. "Of that great Sabbath, God grant me (reader and writer) that Sabbath sight!"[1]

---

[1] "Oh! blissful world of the saints! where all is holy place, and all holy time, even one eternal Sabbath."—HARBAUGH. *Heavenly Home*, 330.

"There congregations ne'er break up,
And Sabbaths have no end."

"*Sabbathum Maximum non habens Vesperum.*"—The great Sabbath has no evening.—AUGUSTINE. *De Civitate Dei*, Ch. 30.

"As the full possession of providential blessings belongs only to the completeness of human obedience, it is probable that neither the natural results, nor the full knowledge of the Sabbath, have ever yet been enjoyed by the fallen race of mankind."—DR. CROLY. *Divine Origin and Obliga. of the Sab.*, 3.

THE SABBATH A NATURAL LAW.

"A Sabbath well spent brings a week of content,
And strength for the toils of the morrow;
But a Sabbath profaned, whatever seems gained,
Is a certain forerunner of sorrow."
—*A Motto of Matthew Hale.*

The adaptation of means to an end ranks among the higher tests of wisdom. The bird's wing was made for the atmosphere in which it flies; the fish's fin for the water in which it swims; and the ball for the socket joint in which it moves. So the Sabbath suits man. It is an adjustment to his nature—to his needs—to his better unfolding.[1] It is a necessity alike to his own well-being and to his usefulness in society. It is not a mere happening, nor an arbitrary appointment, but a natural law. "The Sabbath was made for man." It lifts him to the higher pinnacles and possibilities of his life. It is a key to unlock the richer treasures of his nature. It is forever a beneficent landmark in the flowing tides of time and history. At Sabbath gates we form friendships and start the purer longings that always help us and seem to have no ending.

There is in the incomprehensible nature of God something on which Sabbatism is founded. He Sabbatized on account of something in himself—some divine need—some divine need of rest. And he appointed Sabbatism to man on account of something in man—some human need—some human need of rest. The human worker needs a seventh-day rest, just as the divine Worker needed and

---

[1] "The same Infinite wisdom that made food for the body, air for the lungs, light for the eye, beauty for the taste, and truth for the mind, made the Sabbath for man as a moral and religious being. It is a necessity for his soul and body."—DR. J. O. PECK in *Sabbath Essays*.

took a seventh-day rest. This necessity in man is as changeless as the constitution of his nature. The Sabbath is not, therefore, an institution of a positive, limited, temporary character, but a natural and universal law—an immutable obligation. Its foundation, its ground-work, is laid deep in the bed rock of human need.[1] It is worthy of God, and suited to man. All this is shown in elaborate researches conducted by philologists, political economists, social reformers, philosophers, jurists, and statesmen.

Man and beast are so constituted as to need rest periods. Nightly rest in sleep does not sufficiently restore wasted energy; and God has provided further compensation in septenary rest days. These keep man and beast, neither of which can sustain incessant labor, from being overwrought. The wearied powers and wasted tissues are repaired and toned up. Strength is renewed; health preserved; life prolonged.[2] Were there no God—no im-

---

[1] "Eternal in the constitution of man is the necessity for the existence of a day of rest."—F. W. ROBERTSON.

"Proudhon has recently treated on it from the national economy point of view, and he has come to the conclusion that the proportion of the six days of work to the one of judicious rest is one of manifest wisdom and of great blessing to man."—*The Inter. Cyclo.*, Art. Sabbath.

"All men of whatsoever class, who must necessarily be occupied six days in the week, should abstain on the seventh, and in the course of life would assuredly be giving to their bodies the repose, and to their minds the change of ideas, suited to the day for which it was appointed by unerring wisdom."—J. R. FARRE, M. D. *Report of Sab. Com. of House of Commons*, (1832,) p. 119.

[2] "Although the night apparently equalizes the circulation, yet it does not sufficiently restore its balance for the attainment of a long life—hence one day in seven, by the bounty of Providence is thrown in as a day of compensation to perfect, by its repose, the animal system.—DR. J. R. FARRE. *Com. House of Commons*, (1832,) 116.

"Under the due observance of Sabbath, life would, on the average, be prolonged more than one-seventh of its whole period; that is *more* than 7 years in 50."—Dr. MUSSEY. *Of Ohio Medical College.*

mortality—no future state of rewards and punishments—man, as he is to-day, would still need the Sabbath. The weekly period of six day's work and one day's rest is founded in his very constitution.

The Sabbath a Physical Need.

The law of a weekly rest-day is written all over the *human body*, an elaborate, muscular, nervous machine, that cannot endure continuous strain, but needs halting and repairing seasons. Unremitting toil, no pause to hurrying hands and feet, would break down the strongest constitution, destroy health, and prematurely age men and women.[1] It would tame giant strength, extinguish mirth and laughter, and fill the world with weariness. The human machine would soon wear out. This imbruting power of continuous toil—this weariness attending incessant effort—is relieved by Sabbath rests. The Sabbath is a physical necessity. It descends with refreshing breezes to unfathomable depths in man. It liberates the toiler from unending labor. It breaks up time into sections; establishes regular breathing spaces; and ministers to bodily health and vigor. A septenary rest is beneficial even to the vegetable and mineral kingdoms. It is a greater need in the realm of animal life. Men and beasts of burden, it has been proven a thousand times, can do more and

---

[1] "Let us observe Sunday in the name of Hygiene, if not in the name of religion."—MICHEL CHERALIN. *French Political Economist.*

"It is unreasonable as inhuman to work beyond six days weekly."—HUMBOLDT.

"It is a law of God, established in our physical constitution, that demands rest as often as one day in seven. Any infringement upon that law weakens the constitution and lowers the Physical and moral tone of the being."—DR. HENRY FOSTER, of Clifton Springs.

"The Sabbatical appointment . . . . is to be numbered among the natural duties, if preservation of life be admitted to be a duty, and the premature destruction of it a suicidal act. This is simply said as a Physician, and without reference at all to the theological question."—DR. J. R. FARRE. *Com. House Commons,* 1832.

better work in six days out of seven, than by working continuously through the seven. Sabbath-keepers are fresher for the toils of secular days. Holy time well used is beneficent to the body. It is a central and chief conservator of health.[1]

---

[1] "A day of rest from bodily toil, both for man and beast, is not only desirable but indispensable."—*An Anti-Sab. Conv. in Boston*, 1840.

"Will men who labor six days in the week be more healthy, and live longer, other things being equal, than those who labor seven? Will they do more work, and do it in a better manner?"—The New Haven Med. Asso.—25 Physicians—unanimously voted "Aye."

A Committee of the Pennsylvania Legislature, in a report made in 1839, endorsed this statement: "That man and beast can do more and better work by resting one day in seven than by working the whole seven."

Bienconi, car proprietor in Ireland, owning 1,400 horses, would never employ them on the Sabbath. He began life as an organ-grinder, but prospered by reverent observance of the Day of Rest. He said: "I can work a horse 8 miles a day for six days in the week *much better* than I can 6 miles a day for seven days in the week. By not working on Sunday I save at least twelve per cent."—From LEAFLET. *How to get on.*

"The Sabbath must be observed as a day of rest. This I do not state as an opinion, but knowing that it has its foundation upon a law in man's nature as fixed as that he must take food or die."—DR. WILLARD PARKER.

"The observance of a weekly rest-day, is now very widely held to have a natural basis in the constitution of man. The persistency with which such an institution has been maintained for many ages among Jews, Christians, Mohammedans, and even some Pagan nations, supports this view."—*Johnston's Univer. Cyc.* Art. Sab.

"Of course I do not mean that a man will not produce more in a week by working seven days than by working six days. But I very much doubt whether, at the end of the year, he will have produced more by working seven days in a week than by working six days in a week. The natural difference between Campania and Spitzbergen is trifling when compared with the difference between a country inhabited by men full of bodily and mental vigor, and a country inhabited by men sunk in bodily and mental decrepitude. Therefore it is that we are not poorer, but richer, because we have through many ages rested from our labor one day in seven. The day is not lost. While industry is suspended, while the plow lies in the furrow, while the exchange is silent, while no smoke ascends from the factory, a process is going on quite as important to the wealth of the nation as the work which is performed on more busy days. Man, the machine of machines—the machine compared with which all the contrivances of the Watts and Arkwrights are worthless—is repairing and winding up, so that he returns to his labors on the Monday with clearer intellect, with livelier spirits, with renewed corporal vigor."—LORD MACAULAY.

Physical toilers have a deep and abiding interest in maintaining the Sabbath. What would they be without it? How would they resist the aggressive claims of greed? It is the poor man's day. It makes him happier by making him better—by repairing his wasted forces—by bringing him new equipments of resolution and strength. It is appointed for the rest and refreshment of men and women spent with toil. It blesses our toiling and careworn world.[1] O toiler of the hand, stand by the Sabbath; maintain its sacred character; and keep it running by the door of thy workshop and thy home. It enriches, not impoverishes. Sabbath-keeping and poverty do not usually live long together; for poverty gets turned out of doors. Sabbath rest is a prospering as well as a relieving angel in the path of toil.[2]

---

[1] "The observance of the Sabbath contributes to human happiness. Unremitting toil breaks down and humbles the strongest intellects."—MATTHEW HALE.

"Hail, Sabbath, thee I hail, the poor man's day."—GRAHAM.

"The best friend of the poor man is his weekly day of rest."—MOSES D. HOGE, D. D.

[2] "I am satisfied that the six days are the really true, fit, and adequate measure of time for work, whether as respects the physical strength of man, or his perseverance in uniform occupation. There is also something humane in the arrangement by which those animals that assist man in his work enjoy that rest along with him."—HUMBOLDT, in letter to a friend, 1850.

A mine boss at Stockton, Cal., says in a letter in *California Christian Advocate:* "When I close the mine on Sabbath regularly, I get a better class of workmen, moral and religious. They do as much work in six days as most others do in seven, take it month in and month out. Then there is no quarreling, no fighting, no drunkenness. The employes feel an interest in the work. *It is money in our pockets to shut down on Sabbaths.*"

"My neighbors said I would starve if I became a Christian, for I would not be allowed to do any work on Sundays; and that if I did really embrace Christianity they would never give me any more work. These statements startled me at first, and I scarcely knew what to do. But, after thinking over the matter, I concluded that God would take care of me if I sincerely tried to obey his will. I embraced these doctrines and became a Christian; and now what is the result? Why, with regard to keeping the Sabbath, I find that I now do more work in six days than I formerly did in seven; and, with regard to losing my business, I never had as much work in my life as I have had since I became a Christian."—LI YU MI. A converted Methodist blacksmith in China.

The Sabbath a Spiritual Need.

The law of a weekly rest is written all over the *human soul*, a celestial tenant in a perishable body, and wearing upon itself the impress and the image of God. The soul, like its divine Author, seems indeed tireless, incapable of weariness, susceptible of endless on-going; and yet, even as He, it needs rest-periods, a change of activities, the relief of other pursuits. This is a law of the soul. It needs rest-periods for feeding—for right training—for better unfolding. The Sabbath brings the needed weekly rest. And its sunlight is as much for the man clothed in rags as for the man wearing purple.

A desecration of the day sends men down to the lower spiritual levels. Sabbathless souls grow feeble, gaunt, shriveled; become secularized; forget their origin and end. A lusty and vigorous soul life, without rest-periods for feeding on soul food, is not known to history. The shores of time as they keep lengthening out, are everywhere strewn with soul-wrecks, many of them dashed to pieces on the rocks of Sabbath-breaking. Peril attends a desecration of the day. Selfishness is enthroned. Conscience is trodden under foot. Life's great forces are misused in seeking the special gratification of the lower and animal passions and appetites.[1]

---

[1] "Whenever a nation ceases to keep this (Sabbath) commandment, Christianity ceases to exist. There would then be an end to domestic life, to family ties; and civilization would soon be succeeded by barbarism."—Baron Augustine Cauchy, Member of French Institute.

"It is not to be doubted that, if the public teaching of religion on the Sabbath were once dropped among us, the generality of the people, whatever else might be done to obviate it, would, in seven years, relapse into as bad a state of barbarity as was ever in practice among the most of our Saxon or Danish ancestors."—Dean Prideaux.

"I am more and more sure by experience that the reason for the observance of the Sabbath lies deep in the everlasting necessities of human nature, and that, as long as man is man, the blessedness of keeping it not as a day of rest only, but as a day of spiritual rest, will never be annulled. . . . I certainly do feel by experience the eternal obligation, because of the eternal necessity, of the Sabbath. The soul withers without it; and thrives in proportion to the fidelity of its observance."—F. W. Robertson. *Life*, 248.

Sabbath-keeping sends men up to the higher spiritual levels. The educating power of the day cannot be told. It is the throne of religion. It is the treasure house of noble sentiments. It wears an imperial crown in the realm of spiritual forces. It is a star that outshines the sun, and never sets. It fills vast cathedrals with symphonies sweet and divine, checks secularizing tendencies, and gives heavenward uplifts. Prayers, sacred songs, pure teachings report and measure the impulses that it communicates to human improvement. It ministers to soul growth, creates the best civilization, and makes the purest types of men—philanthropists—missionaries—founders of schools and churches—promoters of all moral reforms. We are fanned and refreshed by the balmy breezes of holy day.

All who wish man to reach his best—to see the higher and better side of his nature called out—to see community in its purest forms—have a deep and abiding interest in maintaining the Sabbath. It is an Atlas on whose mighty shoulders rests our moral and spiritual well-being. The best in us is called out whenever the day is duly honored. O toiler in fields of human improvement, keep and maintain holy time. The soul needs it. It is a moral necessity. It is a balance wheel of the days, preserving and promoting all that is best in man. We cannot fight well the soul battles of the week without the rest and refreshment that come from the Sabbath pause.

The Sabbath an Intellectual Need.

The law of a weekly rest is also written all over the mind, our thinking selfhood; link between soul and body; partaker of both natures.

Body-like, the mind needs a seventh-day rest. Incessant mental strain breaks down the strongest intellect; or palsies its faculties; or rasps and wears it out. The brain, overtaxed with unremitting toil, loses its brightness and sinks into idiocy. Men of affairs, who carry business cares and perplexities into the Sabbath, are walking not far from the precipice of insanity—of suicide.[1] The brain forever plodding—the mind forever scheming—has no desirable outlook. Sabbath rest is needed to prevent utter impairment; to recruit wasted brain forces; to re-invigorate wearied mental energies; to re-kindle, in a word, the slumbering fires of brain and mind. The day is the gift of the God of love. It is fitted for mental rest and refreshment.

Soul-like also, the mind needs a seventh-day rest. The mind indeed thinks, as the heart beats, or as the lungs breathe, unconsciously and necessarily. But to select and dwell upon given trains of ideas is its high endowment; to change to new trains of thought; to revel in new mental visions. Sabbath rest brings such change—changed pursuits—changed companions—changed ideas. Sabbath keepers walk in a new world and under new skies. The currents of thought flow on, unconsciously, but in new channels. This not only prevents an unbalancing of the mental forces, but refreshes and strengthens them. It

---

[1] Sir Samuel Romilly, Solicitor General of England under Fox's administration, a severe worker seven days in the week, lost his reason, and suicided, Nov. 2, 1818. A little later, Lord Castlereagh, alike a seven-day worker, also suicided. Wilberforce, writing of this sad event to a friend, said: "If he had suffered his mind to enjoy such occasional remission—Sunday rests—it is highly probable that the strings of life would never have snapped from over-tension." *The Standard*, London, contrasting them with another Englishman of the day—Sir Robert Peel—said:

"Sir Robert does not work seven days in the week—full assurance that his work will not impair his health. Every Sunday finds him on his knees at public worship, with his family about him. We never knew a man to work seven days in the week, who did not kill himself, or kill his mind. We believe that the dull English Sunday, as it is stigmatized by fribbles and by fools, is the principal cause of the superior health and longevity of the English people."

repairs and tones up both brain and mind. It renews their health and vigor.[1] It dispenses light—intelligence—ideas. Thus the law of a seventh-day rest is written, by God's finger, upon all the tablets of the mind. The day is needed for mental building. It is a mental necessity. It recruits the mental frame, and keeps it in a happy equilibrium.

To many working people, a seventh-day rest is the only real home day; to get acquainted with their families; to train their children. It brings them special opportunity for mental culture. It brings such opportunity to all—to the individual—to community. O toiler after intellectual improvement, take good care of the weekly holy day. Preserve and perpetuate it in history. Keep it as a necessity in society. The day shows its training on all Sabbath keepers. They are not ignorant and barbarous. They are torch-bearers along the shores of time. Keeping

---

[1] "Brain as well as brawn needs the tonic of Sabbath rest."—*Sab. for Man*, 205.

"I never knew a man to escape failure in either body or mind, who worked seven days in the week."—SIR ROBERT PEEL.

"Those artists who wrought on Sunday were soon disqualified from working at all."—SIR DAVID WILKIE.

"My own experience is very strong as to the importance of the complete rest and change of thought once in the week."—DR. CARPENTER.

"To the studious especially, and whether younger or older, a Sabbath well spent—spent in happy exercises of the heart, devotional and domestic—a Sunday given to the soul, is the best of all means of refreshment to the intellect."—ISAAC TAYLOR.

"The Sabbath is God's best boon to the workingman, not only to the one that works with his hands, but also to the one that works with his brain."—BISHOP FELLOWS.

"Your petitioners, from their acquaintance with the laboring classes, and with the laws that regulate the human economy, are convinced that a seventh day of rest, instituted by God, and coeval with the creation of man, is essential to the bodily health and mental vigor of men in every station in life."—Memorial of 641 London Physicians to Parliament in 1853.

the day pays a high per cent. of interest in the way of intellectual improvement.[1]

Thus the Sabbath law is written upon man's whole nature forever—upon his body, soul, mind. It is written all over ourselves, our families, our helpers, our animals. It is too far-reaching, too beneficent in its results to be a contrivance of man. It is prescribed, not by physicians, moralists, political economists, or lawgivers—all wanting in the sufficient wisdom and authority—but by authority so divine and high as not to be contested, and with such sanctions as may well overawe us. It is a divine not a human institution. And it is founded by our Creator, not in the periodic revolutions of our solar system—not in the changes of the moon—but in the nature of man—in deep and abiding human needs. It is one of the natural laws —God's great thoughts by which he regulates and rules the world—that enswathe us, saturate us; fill the Empyrean above us, around us, beneath us; and color all that is within us. It is indestructible. No power can blot it from history. It stands on foundations as firm and enduring as the overarching skies. There it has stood while the centuries have piled up around it, and generations of men have swept by. The storms on the ocean touch but its surface; in its depths is eternal calm. So too in the Sabbath is the calm of the eternal God; it is but its surface that is ruffled with human passions.

---

[1] "It is needed by all the toiling millions of earth. To the laborer it is a boon of priceless value, and to the professional man, and the man of business, with nerve and brain strained to the utmost tension, it comes as a benediction indeed; to the Christian it is indispensable. All classes need the physical and moral recuperation it brings."—*Pastoral Address at Centennial Methodist Conference.*

"The longer I live, the more highly do I estimate the Christian Sabbath; and the more grateful do I feel towards those who impress its importance on community."—D. WEBSTER. *Harvey's Reminiscences,* 383.

SUNDAY AND THE STATE.

> "To-day on weary nations
> The heavenly manna falls
> To holy convocations
> The silver trumpet calls."
> WORDSWORTH.

My task approaches its ending. The Sabbath of the Bible—wonderful day!—is now before the reader. It needs a sequel. The Sabbath as Sunday—or Sunday and the State—invites a word. Some mere briefs on this theme—fragmentary paragraphs—simple suggestions of the larger and better things that might be said—will be given, also an appendix, and then this Sabbath pen be laid aside.

Society, like its constituent members, men and women, has a natural right to a seventh-day rest; just as it has a right to property, or to maintain justice, or to establish laws. The right is divine as well as natural. It springs from the right to live—to preserve its own life—to care for its own well-being. It has the right to adopt such measures as will secure its stability and safety.

The State—society organized for its own better ordering and safety—needs a seventh-day rest, even as its citizens need it. It is what its citizens are—what they put into it—what they make it. It partakes of their excellencies, and equally of their defects. As they are, so is it. As they are bettered by a seventh-day rest, the State shares in the betterment; and as they are injured by its desecration, the State shares in the damage. Whatever tends, therefore, to disturb a seventh-day rest, or to impair its efficiency, is a foe to the State.

The State a Keeper of Sunday.

As the State, even like its citizens, needs a seventh-day rest, it should itself keep Sunday. It is a moral person, and should observe rest periods. It is of conspicuous influence, and, among its duties and obligations, is that of setting a good example in keeping the weekly day of rest. All work on that day should be laid aside. Its whole machinery of government should be given pause—its military and naval movements—its affairs of state—its postal matters. The reason for this is that the law of a seventh-day rest is broadly written upon all its agents and employes. The Sunday of the State is not based upon the religious Sabbath, but upon the law in man's nature. A seventh-day resting State, like the Creator taking a seventh-day rest when creation-work was ended, would be conforming to a universal natural law; and it would be making itself a wholesome example of that law. But this is the ideal, not the real—the possible, not the actual—State. Our Government approaches, but does not attain, this ideal.[1]

Union of Church and State is happily un-American. Their divorce was pronounced by the founders of the Republic, and the decree incorporated in the organic law—in the First Amendment to the National Constitution.[2] That instrument inhibits Congress from "establishing religion," and also from prohibiting "the free exercise thereof." This certainly, inhibits it, among other things, from invading the Sabbath, the great day of

---

[1] "There is no religion without worship, and no worship without the Sabbath."—Montalembert.

"Where there is no Christian Sabbath, there is no Christian morality; and without this free institutions can not long be continued."—Justice McLean in *Sab. Asso. Reports.*

[2] National Constitution—First Amendment.—"Congress shall make no law respecting an establishment of religion, or *to prohibit the free exercise thereof.*"

religion—from organizing Sunday work. Sunday laws and regulations are not a function of Congress. They are reserved to the States. The States, not the Federal Government, have the Sunday realm under their control. Yet Congress, in direct violation of the National Constitution, has attempted, and has organized, Sunday work. Some attempts were failures. The House of Representative, May 12, and July 8, 1838, attempted to protract its Saturday sessions into Sunday morning. This was resisted by many members. The Speaker's casting vote defeated the motion to adjourn. Then many members declared that they would leave the House, and that no authority existed to compel their attendance on the Lord's day. The House, both days, had to adjourn. But Congress has succeeded in desecrating the great rest-day of religion, by authorizing the carrying and delivery of Sundry mails. Sunday delivery was authorized by Act of Congress, April 30, 1810.[1] This, at the time, was claimed to be unconstitutional. It was not, however, and has not been, tested in the Courts. But its unconstitutionality is obvious. It is not a prerogative of Congress to organize Sunday work. The Act, as to Sunday employes, interferes with their "free exercise" of religion; and Congress is by the Constitution inhibited from that. A beginning wrong makes possible and necessitates other wrongs. That initial infraction of the Constitution has issued in the whole Sunday mail system of the United States—its "expedited" Sunday mails—its Sunday carriers—all without warrant in the National Constitution. Our postal arrangements make Sunday widely a day of labor. The justification of

---

[1] Act of Congress, April 30, 1810.—"It shall be the duty of the postmaster at all reasonable hours, *on every day of the week*, to deliver, on demand, any letter, or paper, or packet, to the person entitled to, or authorized to receive, the same."

Sunday opening of mails: In United States 1 hour; in Great Britain 2 hours; in Switzerland 4 hours; in France all day.—*Sabbath for Man*, 500.

all this is in some supposed convenience, or necessity, in the way of business. Yet London and Toronto have no Sunday mails. No stagnation of business follows.

Our Federal Government, in its postal regulations, violates a great natural law, as well as the National Constitution. This is an infinitely more serious offense. It drives roughshod over the septenary law of rest—a law of nature—a universal and immutable institution. It violates this law in itself. It sets a bad example. And it additionally violates the natural rights of about eight hundred thousand employes to a seventh-day rest—makes them Sunday toilers—not by their own wish—but requiring them to work on Sunday, or forfeit their places. The tendency is to have the Sunday employes secularized—live without religion—with little thought of their origin and end—dropping into a grosser nature—dragging the State down with them. This is a wrong—a wrong to the Government—a wrong to the employes. A bad example is set. The measure is in every way harmful. And it is not needed in this age which is demanding reduced hours of daily labor. Six days' work and one day's rest is a physiological law out of which society should not pass.

THE STATE AND SUNDAY LAWS.

As the State, like its citizens, needs a seventh-day rest, it should not only keep the day itself, but it should make provision for its keeping throughout all its domain. The enforcement of Sunday as Sabbath—as a day for religion—is not of man but of God. But its enforcement as a natural law—as a day of rest from work—may be by man as well as by God—by society—by the State. The divine law of a seventh-day rest constrains man—society—nations. The State, in its own proper sphere, and in its own proper behoof, should unite in the constraining Act. It should frame and maintain a seventh-day rest by law. This is a legitimate function of the State, and just so far as such rest may help to make better citizens and more stable civil institutions.[1] It has divine sanction. The Jews, under God's supervision, interpreted and enforced the law of a seventh-day rest. It has also historic supports. All Christian nations have had Sunday laws; some stricter; some looser. Departures from this divine arrangement and from these historic models would be experimental and perilous. Abuse of law would issue in wider licentiousness. Sunday laws are both a need and a duty of the State. This is hardly debatable ground. And yet an irrepressible conflict forever rages between the friends and the foes of Sunday legislation; Seventh day Sabbatarians exceeding even sceptics and the dangerous classes in the fierceness of their assaults on Sunday laws. This contention is not for the enforcement of the *Sabbath*—requiring church attendance—prescribing and enforcing some particular form of religion—making citizens religious. It is for the enforcement of *Sunday*—stilling business—maintaining quiet—ruling out noisy parades—prohibiting the blare of marching bands. This Sunday is not the Sabbath—not at all a religious institution—not even based on religious grounds. It is based upon an immutable natural law—the human need of a seventh-day rest. This physiological necessity justifies Sunday legislation. So far as political action can settle anything this question is settled. Man, the citizen,

---

[1] "There is abundant justification of our Sabbath laws, regarding them as a mere civil institution, which they are; and he is no friend to the good order and welfare of society, who would break them down, or who himself sets an example of disobedience to them. They appeal to each citizen as a patriot, as an orderly member of the community, and as a well-wisher of his fellow-men, to uphold them with his influence, and to show respect for them by his conduct and example."— JUSTICE STRONG in *The Rights of the People to the Sunday Rest.*

"The civil as based on the religious Sabbath is an institution to which society has a natural right, precisely as it has to property."— MARK HOPKINS in *The Sab. and Free Institutions.*

has imperative need of Sunday rest; and the State should secure it to him.[1]

Its own well-being also obliges the State to establish and maintain a seventh-day rest from labor. Public as well as private virtues cluster about a quiet Sunday. It is an essential need of a free Commonwealth. The State needs healthy not infirm citizens; and sociologists call Sunday rest a Sanitarium to all six-day toilers. The hygiene of Moses, pivoted upon a seventh-day rest, has never been surpassed. The State needs intelligent not illiterate citizens; and Sunday rest is a school day of no mean moment to all six-day toilers. It needs moral not

---

[1] "The Sabbath, as a political institution, is of inestimable value, independently of its claims to divine authority."—ADAM SMITH, as quoted in *Memoirs of Sir John Sinclair.*

"The State as well as the individual is indebted to the Sabbath."—*Five Problems of State and Religion*, 45.

"Besides the notorious indecency and scandal of permitting any secular business to be publicly transacted on that day, in a country professing Christianity, and the corruption of morals that usually follows its profanation, the keeping of one day in seven holy, as a time of relaxation and refreshment, as well as for public worship, is of admirable service to the State, considered merely as a civil institution."—BLACKSTOCK. *Commentaries.* B. 4, C. 63.

"I wish to testify my belief, that the individual custom of our fathers, in remembering the Sabbath day to keep it holy, as the consecrator of their Christian religion, is the foundation of our political system, and the only hope of American freedom, progress, and glory."
—JOHN RANDOLPH TUCKER in *Rights of the People to Sunday Rest.*

"The first settlers of this country were a body of select men. They were profoundly impressed by the conviction that a weekly Sabbath was essential to the highest welfare of the communities which they established, and they therefore enacted laws to enforce a proper observance of that day. It was not more upon theological considerations than it was upon secular and social that they framed those laws, and enforced strict obedience to them. The Sabbath so observed, no one can doubt, contributed largely to the formation of that character which has stood us in so much stead in our own history, and which has been the admiration of the world."—HON. WM. STRONG. *Justice U. S. Supreme Court.*

vicious citizens; and Sunday rest is a very Bethesda for the moral purifying of all six-day toilers. Thus Sunday rest helps the Nation as well as the church, and is therefore entitled to National protection and support.

There is also a vital connection between a weekly rest day and free institutions. The area of representative and popular government is strangely coincident with the area of the stricter Sunday laws. It is not a mere happening that all nations, having a really stable popular government, are known as Sabbatarians—as the United States, England, Scotland, Canada, and Switzerland. Here is about the whole territory of popular freedom. Liberty and safety seem everywhere directly proportioned to firm Sunday laws.[1] A weekly rest is therefore an essential need in our

---

[1] "Every day's observation and experience confirms the opinion that the ordinances which require the observance of one day in seven, and the Christian faith which hallows it, are our chief security for all civil and religious liberty, for temporal blessings and spiritual hopes."—WM. L. SEWARD. *Letter to Sab. Conven.*, July 20, 1842.

"I am no fanatic, I hope, as to Sunday; but I look abroad over the map of popular freedom in the world, and it does not seem to me accidental that Switzerland, Scotland, England, and the United States, the countries which best observe Sunday, constitute almost the entire map of safe popular government."—JOSEPH COOK.

"What Sabbath observing nation, it has been asked, has ever been barbarous or ignorant? The lands of the Sabbath and of the Bible have always been the chosen abodes of knowledge and the lights of the earth. The Jews were in the possession of a literature when darkness covered all other people. Every nation that received the Gospel and the Christian Sabbath found them to be the elements of learning and civilization."—GILFILLAN. *The Sabbath*, 190.

"The religious character of an institution so ancient, so sacred, so lawful, and so necessary to the peace and comfort and the respectability of society, ought alone to suffice for its protection; but, that failing, surely the laws of the land made for its account ought to be as strictly enforced as the laws for the protection of person and property. Vice and crime are always progressive and cumulative. If the Sunday laws be neglected, the laws of person and property will soon share their fate, and be equally disregarded."—ATTORNEY-GENERAL BATES.

national life, The State, like the individual, is a debtor to Sunday rest, has important ends to gain from it; and it owes it to itself to maintain and preserve the day.

INVASIONS OF SUNDAY LAWS.

Sunday laws, in our Republic, are a function of the States, not of the Federal Government; are on the statute books of every State but one; and are political not religious measures. They have no religious intent. They but assure Sunday quiet; stilling the pulse of industry; and treating noisy demonstrations as a nuisance. This, with some earlier exceptions, has been, and is, our American Sunday. And it has been a potent factor in forming the American nation. The uplift and power of Sunday rest is under every American home; under the Sabbath-keeper's home; under the Sabbath-breaker's home. It has helped to make the American home what it is, and still has in its soil the seeds of a National Millennium. For Sunday rest is of value to the State even as to the church—to public morals even as to Christianity. But this time-honored Sunday of our fathers is now in peril. Our own, like every age, is witnessing invasion of Sunday laws.

Our Sunday laws are invaded and imperilled by *latitudinarian views*—by low and loose Sunday notions. They are characterized and denounced as a Judaistic superstition —as blue laws—as restricting personal liberty—as unfriendly to freedom of conscience. The assailants are many and various. They would strike down all Sunday laws. Some of them kindly allow God to make laws for the day, but not man. They stigmatize existing Sunday laws as Puritanical; or calumniate them that they may secure their repeal; or call for legislation so loose that it would be reactionary and revolutionary. They persistently cry: "Sunday is out of date; was made for another age and people; abridges human happiness; and its mission is at an end." This outcry is made chiefly by the vicious classes; by saloonists, libertines, Anarchists; promotors of all licentiousness; corrupters of social life; subverters of States. Its authors are not known as builders of schools and churches; as founders of stable institutions; as creators of desirable civilizations. Yet the outcry receives support—and in this is its danger—from other classes in society; from owners and managers of Sunday-breaking agencies; from the foes of Christianity; and from the small body of Seventh-day Sabbatarians. These loose and low Sunday ideas and policies are without support in reason—in history—in the field of human needs. They are confronted and opposed, not merely by the teachings of Revelation, but by the findings of all true science. Sociologists, physiologists, humanitarians, political economists, jurists, statesmen, and physicians, all unite in pronouncing a seventh-day rest a need of man—a need of man in society as well as of man the individual—a law of his nature—and enforced by the highest considerations, physical, intellectual, and moral. The proofs, as already given, are abundant, complete, convincing. This is the true Sunday theory, as opposed to the lower and loose views of the dangerous classes. It will win the day, which meets an abiding human need. It will prevail. The universality of its empire, like that of truth over error, is only a question of time. Happy are all they who fight its battles, and help it on to victory.

The looser and lower Sunday views, when weighed in the scales of time and history, are always found wanting. Sundayless communities are not happier for their destitution, and never attain to empire and influence. The stricter notions and observances of the day, judged by results, are approved. They have upon their brow the verdict of success. To stricter Sunday-keeping is largely due the wonderful progress of English-speaking peoples;

the like wonderful progress of the Protestant nations; and the diffusion of the clearest lights of science. It is the stricter Sunday-keeping peoples that, in modern history, are marching at the head of nations—grasping empires—wielding regal influence. Our own Republic is an example. Our stricter American Sunday is no experiment. It reaches down to us out of the past. It has stood the tests of time and history; has given tone and fiber to the people; and has been a potent factor in molding the hardy life and character of the Republic. All history, indeed, bids us have high rather than low Sunday views—strict rather than loose Sunday laws.

Our Sunday laws are invaded and imperilled by *social carousals;* turning the day into a holiday. Working people, it is claimed, need recreation in parks and pleasure grounds—excursions to rural districts—and so coaches, steamboats, and railway trains turn the day into a carnival. These social carousals, like drink-dens, beer-gardens, theatres, and concerts, are relentless Sunday foes, and rob the people of needed rest. This holiday Sunday is an exotic—an immigrant from abroad—a transplant from Europe. It is German rather than American; from the banks of the Rhine rather than from the banks of the Ohio. It comes from old-world usages now widely overrunning and threatening our purer American customs. It is foreigners chiefly who are leaders in Sunday parades, Sunday concerts, Sunday saloons and beer-gardens; trampling under foot our Sunday laws; defying the government that gives them protection. And, under the mantle of their lawlessness, connived at by municipal authorities, young America is engaging in Sunday picnics and base-ball games. The evil is still further multiplied by summer resorts and camp-meetings with open Sunday gates. These are not the weakest devices of the Devil. Idling and pleasure seeking in holy time bring no real rest. Sunday lawlessness is always a menace to the purer civil institutions—a wide and active demoralizer—a festering sore on the body politic. It takes into insatiate maws money, health and morals.[1]

Sunday, as a holiday, pulls down the State as well as the church—demoralizes the people as well as corrupts Christianity. The Republic is taking from it irreparable damage. Its fiber, especially in city centers, is growing coarser in direct proportion as its old-time Sunday sinks to the low level of a mere holiday. As it becomes a holiday, it is more and more a work day.[2] The French Sunday is a holiday; and it is widely a day of work. The German Sunday is a half holiday; and half the people there work seven days out of seven. It could not be otherwise. For the convenience of the pleasure seekers, the labor of other

---

[1] "It has been found that when the Sabbath is perverted to mere pleasure and recreation, more drunkenness keeps up the orgies of hell, more foul immoralities rot into society, more revelry and carousal, and fighting debase mankind, more crime riots, and more blood reddens the earth on that day that God commands to be kept holy, than on any other day of the week."—DR. J. O. PECK.

"The old despotic Stuarts were tolerable adepts in the art of kingcraft, and knew well what they were doing when they backed with their authority the Book of Sports. The many unthinking serfs, who, early in the reign of Charles the First, danced on Sabbath around the Maypole, were afterward the ready tools of despotism, and fought that England might be enslaved. The Ironsides, who, in the cause of religious liberty, bore them down, were staunch Sabbatarians."—HUGH MILLER. *First Impress. of Eng. and its People*, 67.

[2] "Operatives are perfectly right in thinking that if all worked on Sunday, seven days work would have to be given for six days' wages."—JOHN STUART MILL in *Documents of New York Sab. Conv.*

"Sunday is more essential to the *workers* of society than to any other members. The reverent observance of it is a prerequisite to their moral and spiritual growth; and this growth is necessary not only to industrial but to national success."—CHARLES DUDLEY WARNER.

"If the thousands of poor men and women who are compelled to work six days in seven for their own support, could not demand one day in seven as a legal right, they might well ask for it as a mercy."—JUDGE E. L. FANCHER. *Address at Cooper Union, New York, Dec.*, 1883.

multitudes must be drawn upon—an abridgement of their liberty and needed rest. This is already appearing among us. Hundreds of thousands of our fellow citizens are Sunday toilers—toilers seven days in seven—violating a natural law—that other multitudes may use the day for carousal. This is the necessary fact. More shops open for business, more excursions by land and water, more open theatres and concerts; as a result more workers are deprived of Sunday rest. Will toilers never cease from devouring fellow-toilers? Have Sunday pleasure seekers no respect for the rights of others to the day of rest? Then they need to be put under the wholesome restraints of law. Their cry of personal liberty simply means the oppression of fellow workers—depriving them of their needed weekly rest-day. The law should defend the oppressed from all such conscienceless people; should protect them in their weekly day of rest; should make pleasure seeking cease to be a multiplier of Sunday work. A lawless Sunday, or a Sunday with loose laws, puts helpless workers at the mercy of all pleasure seekers. Good Sunday laws are a proclamation of their freedom.

Our Sunday laws are invaded and imperilled by *greed;* not contented with six days work and trade ; seizing and using the seventh for secular ends. Traffic and travel whirl through the day.[1] It is invaded by the silent but steady en-

---

[1] "The desecration of the Sabbath by railroads is an absolute loss to those companies."—WM. E. DODGE.

"If you English people do not take care, the railway system will be a battering ram to break down your Sabbaths"—MERLE D'AUBIGNE.

"Sunday is worth more than Sunday journalism. What Sunday journals displace is worth more than what they supply. They displace rest. They displace the mood of religious thoughtfulness and worship, without which no civilization can be maintained at a high level. The most influential dailies of the world do not issue Sunday editions. Civilization would stand higher than it now does with us, if all Sunday journals were now stopped, as both industrial and moral nuisances."—JOSEPH COOK.

croachments of capital; great corporations running railway trains; smaller capitalists steamboats and coaches; and shop-keepers keeping open stores. All seem to care little for Sunday, and much for dividends. They rob not God alone, but man also. They exact from the toiler seven days in the week. They deprive him of a needed weekly rest-day, that they may drive on the pursuits of business—the schemes of ambition—the clamor for political power. They are breakers of a deep-seated natural law, and are making us a nation of Sunday workers. The tainted breath of Sunday work blows around us widely and disastrously. Proofs of this are not wanting; for the thing is not done in a corner. We see everywhere confectionery and tobacco stores making Sunday sales; saloons, beer-gardens, theaters and concerts open; papers hawked through the streets; steamboats and railway trains running; and all bringing the feverishness of business into the quiet of Sunday life. All this invasion of the day springs from mercenary motives. Sunday quiet, under loose Sunday laws, always goes down before conscienceless greed. Many men of substance, who have the greatest interest in keeping society stable, are its mightiest corrupters. These capitalists are appealed to, not now on the higher plane of Christianity —the supreme motive and force—but on the lower plane of humanity and patriotism. They are violating a stern law of nature; robbing fellow-men of a needed rest-day; lowering the moral tone and fiber of society; making sad forecasts, even a heritage of corruption, for those coming after them. Why will they imperil our institutions of civil and religious liberty? If they will not prize the day above money considerations, the State should compel them to do so. Greed should not be allowed to rob us of a seventh-day rest.

Sunday quiet is a conservator of all that is best in the Republic, giving its citizens a refreshing and toning up weekly; and Sunday desecration is a peril to free institutions, always sending the people down to lower physical, intellectual, and spiritual levels. It would be a happier time, if Sunday quiet breathed over all thoroughfares of trade and travel; over stores and newspaper offices; over city as well as country populations; over high and low, rich and poor, learned and illiterate. Such a Sunday is above any possible commercial value to the State even as to the church. I make this final appeal that such a Sunday may be the heritage of the Republic forever. The appeal goes out to all law-abiding citizens—to Christians, humanitarians, and patriots—to stop violations of Sunday laws—to arrest this widespread and threatening evil—to make Sunday quiet the ruling American usage. The bitter cry of Sunday toilers is ascending against us. Institutions, when decayed from top to bottom, are ready for removal. Avert the decline. Restore the ancient purity. Drive from your Sunday Temple all the trafficking sons of Adam. Fight well this mighty battle. Don't be mere lookers on. Don't study the evil merely from the outside. Plunge into the conflict—into the seething heart of it—and be a heroic worker in the strife. Say to men of greed, "stop business and trade;" to pleasure seekers, "no more Sunday parades and picnics;" and to Government, "no more Sunday mails and delivery." Establish a Sunday quiet that will breathe restfulness all over the land. It will give stability and permanence to our free institutions. It will be security for a noble future. To promote this should call out our utmost seeking—the utmost seeking of every Christian—the utmost seeking of every patriot—the utmost seeking of every humanitarian.

APPENDIX.

I use an Appendix to group together a few things yet remaining to be said. The subject is complete without them. But they are added to be a help to students who may be purposing its wider examination.

SEVENTH-DAY SABBATARIANS.

The Jews stand in history as the oldest. Their high antiquity is known. They reject First and observe Seventh day, because they reject the whole Christian system. Seventh-day is still in all lands the Judaic Sabbath. Yet under the more tolerant civilization that is lifting from them the oppression of centuries, they are beginning to show some signs of yielding; and are pondering the question of conforming to existing social institutions. *The Jewish Progress*, as quoted in *Truth*, New York, Oct. 5, 1884, says: "The requirements of modern society make the abolition of the present (Jewish) Sabbath an absolute necessity." Hatred and blows have not won the Jew. The touch of kindness is having a more persuasive influence.[1]

Traces of Seventh-day keepers appear in Lombardy in the twelfth century—in Germany in the fifteenth century—and in England in the sixteenth century. The German Seventh-day keepers arose by secession from the German Baptists, or Dunkers. Some of them migrated at an early day to this country, and settled in Eastern Pennsylvania. They formed a separate community, but without monastic vows; and recommended but did not enforce

---

[1] Henry Gersoni, in *The Independent*, New York, Jan. 8, 1885, says: "Reform Judaism, among other things, is advocating changing the Sabbath from the seventh to the first day of the week."

celibacy. There have been but a few hundred of them at any time.[1] Some Seventh-day keepers from England, where the cause was having a decaying history, began to appear in Rhode Island about 1665. Several churches were soon organized in Rhode Island, New York and New Jersey. In 1818 they took the name of Seventh-day Baptists. They have now between eight and nine thousand church members.[2] They maintain the divine origin of the Sabbath; but they deny the change that the risen Christ, by use and approval, made in the day. Their criticism here is wholly destructive. They build no Seventh-day Sabbath on the post-resurrection Christ, during that era when all things were made new. They do not even attempt this. The feat is an impossibility. Their sole mission seems to be to tear down the First-day Sabbath— by searching after flaws—by suggesting difficulties—by raising doubts. As destructive critics they are unsurpassed. Their Sabbatism is not built on the risen Christ.

The Seventh-day Adventists are the youngest of all Seventh-day Sabbatarians. They were born of the great Advent craze that collapsed in 1843. They arose out of the wreck. Their date is usually given as 1844. They rapidly grew till most of the Adventists were gathered into the new fold. They now number about sixteen

---

[1] "They are not believed to exceed a few hundreds in numbers, and their ministers may be as many as ten or twelve."—DR. BAIRD.

[2] "Late in the 15th century, 'Seventh-day keepers' appeared in Germany. In England soon after the Reformation they organized as a separate denomination, bearing the name of 'Sabbatarians,' and eleven of their churches existed at the close of that century, of which three only remain. They appeared in this country in 1665, and about 1671 organized a church at Newport, R. I. Other churches were soon organized in that State, and in New York and New Jersey, several of which still exist . . . The name 'Seventh-day Baptists,' instead of 'Sabbatarians,' was adopted in 1818. . . . Their membership in 1885 was 8,591, with 85 ministers and 93 churches."—*Alden's Man. Cycl.*, Art. Baptists.

thousand members. Activity and energy characterize them in history. And their chief distinguishing trait is seen in their persistent effort to undermine the First-day Sabbath.

Seventh-day Sabbatarians—Jews, Baptists, and Adventists—form together about seven-tenths of one per cent. of our population.[1] They are social incongruents; widely diverse in life and faith; but united to break down the Sabbath of Christianity—the Sabbath that the risen Christ, by use and approval, instituted. But the day has less foes and more friends now than in any preceding age of the world.

SABBATIC THEORIES.

Their number is legion. Nearly every writer on the Sabbath has had a theory of his own, both as to the day's origin, and as to its change. All these various theories, however, may be classed with one or another of the four following views:

The Utilitarian View. This is the theory of all opponents of supernaturalism. They regard the original Sabbath as a mere human contrivance—as born perhaps of lunar changes—but certainly an invention of man. They regard the day, in the Christian age, as rising from a spontaneous feeling to commemorate the resurrection of our Lord. Seventh-day keeping is obligatory because it is salutary; binding because a useful and beneficent arrangement; immutable in its claims because required by the convenience of society. This theory rests Sabbatism wholly on expediency. The view is inadequate. It does not account, in any fair way, for the Sabbath in history; for its origin; for its preservation and perpetuity. Opponents of supernaturalism allow themselves, in difficult places, to be satisfied

---

[1] "As to Seventh-day worshipers—Jews, Seventh-day Baptists, and Seventh-day Adventists—they form together but seven-tenths of one per cent. of the population of the United States, and are still fewer in Great Britain."—*The Sab. for Man*, 86.

with very irrational and visionary theories. They seem credulous beyond ordinary men.

The Ecclesiastical View. This confines itself to the Christian age. It does not discuss the original Sabbath, but only the Lord's day. It regards the church as the Sabbath-Maker. The Lord of the Sabbath is dethroned —is pushed aside—is denuded of authority—and the church steps in to occupy his place. Cardinal Tolet says: "The observance of the Lord's day is not a law of God, but an ecclesiastical precept and a custom of the faithful."[a] This makes the Lord's day, not of Christ's institution and approval—not even of Apostolic use and authority—but of church arrangement. Christ will not thus be uncrowned. He asserts his own dignity and right. "The Son of Man," he says, "is Lord also of the Sabbath day." It is his. He made it. He keeps it in unending history. And he will not allow his prerogative and glory to be appropriated and worn by another.

The Apostolic View. This traces the Lord's day back to the Apostles, but no higher. It was born, not of Christ, but of James and John, of Peter and Paul. It arose in Apostolic customs. Whatever was ordered by the Apostles was divinely ordered. The Lord's day was so ordered, and is hence of divine and perpetual authority. This ascription of the day to the Apostles is without warrant in the New Testament. It makes too much of them. It deifies them —puts them in God's place. For in sacred history God alone is the Sabbath-Maker and the Sabbath-Preserver. The Lord's day was not born even of inspired men. It is of higher and nobler original.

The Divine View. This traces the original Sabbath to God, who founded it in the constitution of man and appointed it at the beginning. And it traces the transferrence of the institution, and its change of day in the Christian

---

[a] TOLET. *Insti. Sacerdot.*, 4: 10.

system, to the risen Christ. The Sabbath is thus divine. It was appointed by the Creator to the first man; re-enacted in the Decalogue; and, by Christ's authority, descended into Christian history as the Lord's day. This makes the reason for its keeping twofold; the law in man; the appointment of God; and the twofold mandate is supreme. A seventh of days for rest and worship is of divine obligation and universal authority. In our treatment of the Sabbath, we have to deal with God, not with man; we are responsible to God, not to man.[1]

---

[1] "On the other hand, if the institution of the Sabbath were coeval with creation, a command given to our first parents, and based upon principles of universal obligation; if, in the Decalogue, as a summary of moral law, it is again repeated, incorporated with Jewish institutions, recognized by Christ, observed by Apostles and apostolic men, honored by the primitive church, and handed down to succeeding ages, rooted deeply in every dispensation, and alien to none, spreading widely, and bearing everywhere the prints of holiness and peace, then, we think that, without hesitation, we may claim for the Sabbath the authority which alone can sanction its observance, or give to it permanent obligation."—*Br. Quar Rev.*, 1855.

THE HEBREW WORD FOR SABBATH.

שָׁבַּת occurs, as far as I have been able to ascertain, in twenty books of the Old Testament, and one hundred and fifty times. It is translated into the Septuagint by *anapausis, ebdomas, kataluse*, etc., but is more usually transferred as *sabbaton*. Its translation into the English appears in such words as *rest, to cease*, etc.; but it is more usually transferred and becomes our English word Sabbath. I give here the one hundred and fifty cases of its Old Testament use.

GENESIS.

2 : 2.	וַיִּשְׁבֹּת	κατεπαυσε	He rested.
2 : 3.	שָׁבַת	κατεπαυσεν	He had rested.
8 : 22.	יִשְׁבֹּתוּ	καταπασουσι	Shall not cease.

EXODUS.

5 : 5.	וְהִשְׁבַּתֶּם	καταπαυσωμεν	Ye make them rest.
12 : 15.	תַּשְׁבִּיתוּ	αφανιεῖτε	Ye shall put away.
16 : 23.	שַׁבָּתוֹן שַׁבַּת	ανιπαυσις—σάββατα	The rest of the Sabbath.
16 : 25.	שַׁבָּת	σάββατα	A Sabbath.
16 : 26.	שַׁבָּת	σάββατα	The Sabbath.
16 : 29.	הַשַּׁבָּת	σάββατα	The Sabbath.
16 : 30.	וַיִּשְׁבְּתוּ	εσαββατισεν	The people rested.
20 : 8.	יוֹם הַשַּׁבָּת	ἡμέραν τῶν σάββατων	The Sabbath day.
20 : 10.	שַׁבָּת	σάββατα	The Sabbath.
20 : 11.	יוֹם הַשַּׁבָּת	τὴν ἡμέραν τὴν ἐβδόμην	The Sabbath day.
21 : 19.	שִׁבְתּוֹ		The loss of time.
23 : 12.	תִּשְׁבֹּת	αναπαυσις	Thou shalt rest.
31 : 13.	שַׁבְּתֹתַי	σάββατα	My Sabbath ye shall keep.
31 : 14.	הַשַּׁבָּת	σάββατα	The Sabbath.
31 : 15.	שַׁבַּת שַׁבָּתוֹן	τῇ εβδόμῃ σαββατα	Sabbath of rest.
31 : 15.	שַׁבָּת	σάββατα	The Sabbath.
31 : 16.	הַשַּׁבָּת	σάββατα	Keep my Sabbaths.
31 : 17.	שָׁבַת	κατεπαυσε	He rested.
34 : 21.	תִּשְׁבֹּת	καταπαυσεις	Thou shalt rest.
34 : 21.	תִּשְׁבֹּת	καταπαυσις	Thou shalt rest.

35 : 2.	שַׁבַּת שַׁבָּתוֹן	...καταπαυσις—σάββατα	.........A Sabbath of rest.
35 : 3.	יוֹם הַשַׁבָּת	......ἡμέρα τῶν σαββάτων	.........The Sabbath day.

LEVITICUS.

2 : 13.	תַּשְׁבִּית	.........διαπαυσατε	.... To be lacking.
16 : 31.	שַׁבַּת שַׁבָּתוֹן	...σάββατα σαββατων	............A Sabbath of rest.
19 : 3.	שַׁבְּתֹתַי	....σάββατα	........................Keep my Sabbath.
19 : 30.	שַׁבְּתֹתַי	.........σάββατα	........................Keep my Sabbath.
23 : 3.	שַׁבַּת שַׁבָּתוֹן	...σάββατα αναπαυσις	.........The Sabbath of rest.
23 : 3.	שַׁבָּת	.........σαββατα	.........................The Sabbath.
23 : 11.	הַשַׁבָּת	.........επαριον της πρωτης... .... After the Sabbath.
23 : 15.	הַשַׁבָּת	.........τῶν σαββατων	....................The Sabbath.
23 : 15.	שֶׁבַע שַׁבָּתוֹת	...ἑπτα ἑβδομάδας	....Seven Sabbaths.
23 : 16.	הַשַׁבָּת	.........εβδομαδος	...........................Sabbath.
23 : 24.	שַׁבָּתוֹן	.........αναπαυσις	.... A Sabbath.
23 : 32.	שַׁבַּת שַׁבָּתוֹן	...σάββατα σαββατων	.........A Sabbath of rest.
23 : 32.	תִּשְׁבְּתוּ שַׁבַּתְּכֶם	...σαββατιειτε τα σάββατα	..Celebrate your Sabbath.
23 : 38.	שַׁבְּתֹת	.........τῶν σάββατων	.................The Sabbaths.
23 : 39.	שַׁבָּתוֹן	.........αναπαυσις	...................A Sabbath.
23 : 39.	שַׁבָּתוֹן	.........αναπαυσις	....................A Sabbath.
24 : 8.	בְּיוֹם הַשַׁבָּת בְּיוֹם הַשַׁבָּת	...ἡμέρα τῶν σαββατων	.....Every Sabbath.
25 : 2.	שַׁבָּת־וְשָׁבְתָה	...αναπαυσεται—σαββατα	...The land keep a Sabbath.
25 : 4.	שַׁבַּת שַׁבָּתוֹן	...σάββατα αναπαυσις	.........A Sabbath of rest.
25 : 4.	שַׁבָּת	.........σάββατα	.....................A Sabbath.
25 : 5.	שְׁנַת שַׁבָּתוֹן	...ενιαυτος αναπαυσεως	........A year of rest.
25 : 6.	שַׁבָּת	.........σάββατα	....The Sabbath of the land.
25 : 8.	שַׁבְּתֹת	.........αναπαυσεις	.............Seven Sabbaths of years.
25 : 8.	שַׁבְּתֹת	.........ἑβδομάδες	.................Seven Sabbaths of years.
26 : 2.	שַׁבְּתֹתַי	.........σάββατα	....................Keep my Sabbaths.
26 : 5.	וִישַׁבְתֶּם	....	.........Dwell—safely.
26 : 6.	וְהִשְׁבַּתִּי	....	.........None shall make afraid.
26 : 34.	שַׁבְּתֹתֶיהָ	.......σάββατα	............................Land—her Sabbaths.
26 : 34.	תִּשְׁבַּת	.........σαββατιεῖ	.................Thus shall the land rest.
26 : 34.	שַׁבְּתֹתֶיהָ	.......σάββατα	......................And enjoy her Sabbaths.
26 : 35.	תִּשְׁבֹּת	.........σαββατιει	..................As long as it lieth desolate.

26 : 35. שָׁבְתָה..........σαββατιεῖ.........It shall rest.

26 : 35. בְּשַׁבְּתֹתֵיכֶם בְּשַׁבְּתֹתֵיכֶם..............It did not rest in your Sabbaths.

26 : 43. שַׁבְּתֹתֶיהָ.......τὰ σάββατα......Her Sabbaths.

NUMBERS.

15 : 32. הַשַּׁבָּת...........τῇ ἡμέρᾳ τῶν σαββατων............On the Sabbath.

28 : 9. הַשַּׁבָּת...........τῇ ἡμέρᾳ τῶν σαββατων............On the Sabbath.

28 : 10. שַׁבַּת בְּשַׁבַּתּוֹ...σαββάτων εν τοις σαββατοις......Of every Sabbath.

DEUTERONOMY.

5 : 12. הַשַּׁבָּת..........τὴν ἡμέραν τῶν σαββάτων...The Sabbath day.

5 : 14. שַׁבָּת.............σάββατα..................The Sabbath.

5 : 15. הַשַּׁבָּת..........τὴν ἡμέραν τῶν σάββατων...The Sabbath day.

JOSHUA.

22 : 25. וְהִשְׁבִּיתוּ.......μὴ σέβωνται.................Cease from fearing.

RUTH.

4 : 14. הִשְׁבִּית.........κατέλυσε...................Left thee.

SECOND KINGS.

4 : 23. שַׁבָּת.............οὐδὲ σάββατον.............Nor Sabbath.

11 : 5. הַשַּׁבָּת..........τὸ σάββατον............On the Sabbath.

11 : 7. הַשַּׁבָּת..........τὸ σαββατον............On the Sabbath.

11 : 9. הַשַּׁבָּת..........τὸ σάββατον............On the Sabbath.

11 : 9. הַשַּׁבָּת..........τὸ σάββατον............On the Sabbath.

16 . 18. הַשַּׁבָּת......................................Covert for the Sabbath.

FIRST CHRONICLES.

9 : 32. שַׁבַּת שַׁבָּת.....σάββατον κατα σάββατον...Every Sabbath.

23 : 31. לְשַׁבָּתוֹת........ἐν τοῖς σάββατοις............In the Sabbaths.

SECOND CHRONICLES.

2 : 4. לְשַׁבָּתוֹת........εν τοῖς σαββάτοις.........On the Sabbaths.

8 : 13. לְשַׁבָּתוֹת........εν τοῖς σαββατοις.........On the Sabbaths.

16 : 5. וַיִּשְׁבֹּת..........καταπαυσε.................His work cease.

23 : 4. הַשַּׁבָּת..........τὸ σάββατον.................On the Sabbath.

23 : 8. הַשַּׁבָּת..........τον σάββατον.................In on the Sabbath.

23 : 8. הַשַּׁבָּת..........τον σάββατον.................Out on the Sabbath.

THE HEBREW WORD FOR SABBATH.   211

31 : 3.	לְשַׁבְּתוֹת	...τα σά33ατα...	For the Sabbath.
36 : 21.	שַׁבְּתוֹתֶיהָ—שָׁבָתָה	...τα σά33ατα αυτης σα33ατισει..	Had enjoyed her Sabbaths.

NEHEMIAH.

9 : 14.	שַׁבָּת	...τὸ σά33ατον...	Thy holy Sabbath.
10 : 31.	הַשַּׁבָּת	...του σά33ατου...	On the Sabbath day.
10 : 31.	בַּשַּׁבָּת	...ἐν σά33ατῳ...	On the Sabbath day.
10 : 33.	הַשַּׁבָּתוֹת	...των σα33ατων...	Of the Sabbaths.
13 : 15.	בַּשַּׁבָּת	...ἐν τῳ σά33ατῳ...	On the Sabbath.
13 : 15.	הַשַּׁבָּת	...τοῦ σάββάτου...	On the Sabbath day.
13 : 16.	בַּשַּׁבָּת	...τῳ σάββατῳ...	Sold on the Sabbath.
13 : 17.	הַשַּׁבָּת	...τοῦ σά33ατου...	Profane the Sabbath days.
13 : 18.	הַשַּׁבָּת	...τὸ σά33ατον...	Profaning the Sabbath.
13 : 19.	הַשַּׁבָּת	...πρὸ τοῦ σά33ατου...	Before the Sabbath.
13 : 19.	הַשַּׁבָּת	...ὁπίσω τοῦ σά33ατου...	After the Sabbath.
13 : 19.	הַשַּׁבָּת	...τοῦ σά33ατου...	On the Sabbath.
13 : 21.	בַּשַּׁבָּת	...ἐν σά33ατῳ...	On the Sabbath.
13 : 22.	הַשַּׁבָּת	...τοῦ σά33ατου...	Sanctify the Sabbath day.

JOB.

32 : 1.	וַיִּשְׁבְּתוּ	...επαυσατο...	These three men ceased.

PROVERBS.

18 : 18.	יַשְׁבִּית	...παυει...	Contentions to cease.
20 : 3.	שֶׁבֶת	...ἀποστρέφεσθαι...	To cease from.
22 : 10.	וְיִשְׁבֹּת	...συνεξελεύσεται...	Shall go out.

PSALMS.

8 : 3.	לְהַשְׁבִּית	...καταλύσαι...	That thou mightest still.
46 : 10.	מַשְׁבִּית	...σχόλοσατε...	Be still.
92 : Title.	לְיוֹם הַשַּׁבָּת	...τοῦ προσά33ατον..	A Psalm—for the Sabbath day.
119 : 119.	הִשְׁבַּתָּ	...παραβαινοντας...	Thou puttest away.

ISAIAH.

1 : 13.	שַׁבָּת	...τα σά33ατα...	And Sabbaths.
14 : 4.	שָׁבַת	...αναπέπαυται...	The oppressor ceased.
14 : 4.	שָׁבְתָה	...αναπεπαυται...	The golden city ceased.
16 : 10.	הִשְׁבַּתִּי	...πέπαυται...	Vintage shouting to cease.

17 : 3.	וְנִשְׁבַּת	καταφυγεῖν	Shall cease.
24 : 8.	שָׁבַת–שָׁבָת	πέπαυται—πέπαυται	Ceaseth—ceaseth.
30 : 7.	שֶׁבֶת		To sit still.
30 : 11.	הִשְׁבִּיתוּ	ἀφέλετε	To cease.
33 : 8.	שָׁבַת	πέπαυται	The wayfaring man ceaseth.
56 : 2.	שַׁבָּת	τα σάββατα	Keepeth the Sabbath.
56 : 4.	שַׁבְּתוֹתַי	τα σάββατα	Keep my Sabbath.
56 : 6.	שַׁבָּת	τα σάββατα	Keepeth the Sabbath.
58 : 13.	מִשַּׁבָּת	ἀπὸ τῶν σαββάτων	From the Sabbath.
58 : 13.	לַשַּׁבָּת	τα σάββατα	The Sabbath a delight.
66 : 23.	שַׁבָּת בְּשַׁבַּתּוֹ	σάββατον εκ σαββάτου	From one Sabbath to another.

JEREMIAH.

7 : 34.	וְהִשְׁבַּתִּי	καταλυσω	I cause to cease.
17 : 21.	הַשַּׁבָּת	τῶν σαββάτων	On the Sabbath day.
17 : 22.	הַשַּׁבָּת	τῶν σαββάτων	On the Sabbath day.
17 : 22.	הַשַּׁבָּת	τῶν σαββάτων	Hallow ye the Sabbath day.
17 : 24.	הַשַּׁבָּת	τῶν σαββάτων	Hallow the Sabbath day.
17 : 24.	הַשַּׁבָּת	τῶν σαββάτων	On the Sabbath day.
17 : 27.	הַשַּׁבָּת	τῶν σαββάτων	Hallow the Sabbath.
17 : 27.	הַשַּׁבָּת	τῶν σαββάτων	On the Sabbath day.
48 : 35.	וְהִשְׁבַּתִּי	απολω	I will cause to cease.

LAMENTATIONS.

1 : 7.	מִשְׁבַּתֶּהָ		Mock at her Sabbaths.
2 : 6.	וְשַׁבָּת	σάββατον	And Sabbaths.
5 : 14.	שָׁבָתוּ	κατέπαυσαν	The elders have ceased.
5 : 15.	שָׁבַת	κατέλυσε	Joy of our hearts is ceased.

EZEKIEL.

6 : 6.	מוֹשְׁבוֹתֵיכֶם		Laid waste.
6 : 6.	וְנִשְׁבְּתוּ		Idols—ceased.
20 : 12.	שַׁבְּתוֹתַי	τὰ σάββατα μου	My Sabbaths.
20 : 13.	שַׁבְּתֹתַי	τὰ σάββατα μου	My Sabbaths.
20 : 16.	שַׁבְּתוֹתַי	τὰ σάββατα μου	My Sabbaths.
20 : 20.	וְשַׁבְּתוֹתַי	τὰ σάββατα μου	My Sabbaths.

THE HEBREW WORD FOR SABBATH. 213

20 : 21.	שַׁבְּתוֹתַי	τὰ σάββατα μου	My Sabbaths.
20 : 24.	שַׁבְּתוֹתַי	τὰ σάββατα μου	My Sabbaths.
22 : 8.	שַׁבְּתוֹתַי	τὰ σάββατα μου.	My Sabbaths.
22 : 26.	וּמִשַּׁבְּתוֹתַי	απο των σαββατων	From my Sabbaths.
23 : 38.	שַׁבְּתוֹתַי	τὰ σάββατα μου	My Sabbaths.
30 : 18.	וְנִשְׁבַּת	απολειται	Shall cease.
33 : 28.	וְנִשְׁבַּת	απολειται	Shall cease.
34 : 10.	וְהִשְׁבַּתִּים	αποστρύψω	Cause them to cease.
34 : 25.	וְהִשְׁבַּתִּי	αφανιῶ	Will cause to cease.
44 : 24.	שַׁבְּתוֹתַי	τὰ σάββατα μου	My Sabbaths.
45 : 17.	וּבְשַׁבְּתוֹתִי	ἐν τοῖς σαββατος	The Sabbaths.
46 : 1.	הַשַּׁבָּת	τῶν σαββάτων	On the Sabbath.
46 : 3.	בַּשַּׁבָּתוֹת	ἐν τοῖς σαββάτοις	In the Sabbaths.
46 : 4.	הַשַּׁבָּת	τῶν σαββατων	Sabbath day.
46 : 12.	הַשַּׁבָּת	τῶν σαββατων	The Sabbath day.

HOSEA.

2 : 11.	וְשַׁבַּתָּהּ	τὰ σάββατα αυτης	Her Sabbaths.
2 : 11.	וְהִשְׁבַּתִּי		Cause—to cease.
7 : 4.	יִשְׁבּוֹת		Who ceaseth.

AMOS.

8 : 4.	וְלַשְׁבִּית		The poor—to fail.
8 : 5.	וְהַשַּׁבָּת		The Sabbaths.

THE GREEK SABBATON IN THE NEW TESTAMENT.

The Greek *Sabbaton* is used 70 times in the New Testament; is translated 60 times *Sabbath;* 9 times *week;* and 1 time *rest.* It always means *Seventh* day. Its cases of use here follow. They will be helpful for reference to students of the Sabbath question.

MATTHEW. 11 times.

Jesus went on the Sabbath day	τοῖς σάββασι	12: 1.
Not lawful..on the Sabbath day	ἐν σαββάτῳ	12: 2.
On the Sabbath day	τοῖς σαββασιν	12: 5.
Priests..profane the Sabbath	τὸ σάββατον	12: 5.
Lord even of the Sabbath day	του σαββάτου	12: 8.
Is it lawful..on the Sabbath day?	τοῖς σάββασι	12: 10.
Into a pit on the Sabbath day	τοῖς σάββασι	12: 11.
To do well on the Sabbath day?	τοῖς σάββασι	12: 12.
On the Sabbath	ἐν σαββάτῳ	24: 20.
In the end of the Sabbath	ὠψε δε σαββάτων	28: 1.
First day of the week	εἰς μίαν σαββάτων	28: 1.

MARK. 13 times.

On the Sabbath day	τοῖς σάββασιν	1: 21.
Corn fields on the Sabbath day	ἐν τοῖς σάββασιν	2: 23.
Why do they on the Sabbath day?	ἐν τοις σάββασιν	2: 24.
The Sabbath..for man	τὸ σάββατον	2: 27.
Not man for the Sabbath	τὸ σάββατον	2: 27.
Lord also of the Sabbath day	του σαββάτου	2: 28.
Heal on the Sabbath day	τοῖς σάββασι	3: 2.
To do good on the Sabbath day?	τοις σάββασι	3: 4.
Sabbath being come	γενομένου σαββάτου	6: 2.
Before the Sabbath	προσάββατον	15: 42.
Sabbath was past	διογενομένου του σαββάτου	16: 1.
First day of the week	τῆς μίας σαββάτων	16: 2.
First day of the week	πρώτῃ σαββάτου	16: 9.

LUKE. 20 times.

On the Sabbath day	των σαββάτων	4: 16.
Taught..on the Sabbath day	ἐν τοῖς σάββασι	4: 31.
On the second Sabbath	ἐν σαββάτῳ δευτεροπρώτῳ	6: 1.

THE GREEK WORD FOR SABBATH.

LUKE—Continued.

Not lawful..on the Sabbath day	ἐν τοῖς σάββασι	6:	2.
Lord also of the Sabbath day	κυρίος..του σαββάτου	6:	5.
Another Sabbath	ἐν ἑτέρω σαββάτω	6:	6.
Heal on the Sabbath day	ἐν τῷ σαββάτῳ	6:	7.
Is it lawful on the Sabbath day?	τοῖς σάββασιν	6:	9.
Teaching..on the Sabbath	ἐν τοῖς σάββασι	13:	10.
Healed on the Sabbath	τῷ σαββάτῳ	13:	14.
Not on the Sabbath day	τῇ ἡμέρα τοῦ σαββάτου	13:	14.
Each one of you on the Sabbath	τῷ σαββάτῳ	13:	15.
Be loosed..on the Sabbath day	τῇ ἡμέρα τοῦ σαββατου	13:	16.
Eat bread on the Sabbath day	σαββάτω	14:	1.
Heal on the Sabbath day	τῷ σαββάτῳ	14:	3.
On the Sabbath day	ἐν τῇ ἡμέρα τοῦ σαββάτου	14:	5.
Fast twice in the week	νηστεύω δις τοῦ σαββάτου	18:	12.
The Sabbath drew on	σάββατον	23:	54.
Rested the Sabbath day	τὸ..σάββατον	23:	56.
First day of the week	μιᾷ τῶν σαββάτων	24:	1.

JOHN. 13 times.

The same day was the Sabbath	σάββατον	5:	9.
It is the Sabbath	σάββατον ἐστιν	5:	10.
These things on the Sabbath	ἐν σαββάτω	5:	16.
Broken the Sabbath	τὸ σάββατον	5:	18.
You on the Sabbath	ἐν σαββάτῳ	7:	22.
If a man on the Sabbath day	ἐν σαββάτῳ	7:	23.
Whole on the Sabbath day	ἐν σαββάτω	7:	23.
It was the Sabbath day	ἦν δὲ σάββατον	9:	14.
Keepeth not the Sabbath day	τὸ σάββατον	9:	16.
On the cross on the Sabbath day	ἐν τῷ σαββάτῳ	19:	31.
That Sabbath day was a high day	του σαββάτου	19:	31.
First day of the week	μιᾷ τῶν σαββάτων	20:	1.
First day of the week	τῇ μιᾷ των σαββάτων	20:	19.

THE ACTS. 10 times.

Sabbath day's journey	σαββάτου ἔχον ὁδόν	1:	12.
On the Sabbath day	τῇ ἡμέρα τῶν σαββάτων	13:	14.
Read every Sabbath day	πᾶν σάββατον	13:	27.
The next Sabbath	τὸ μεταξύ σάββατον	13:	42.
The next Sabbath	τῷ τὲ ἐρχομένῳ σαββάτῳ	13:	44.
Every Sabbath	πᾶν σάββατον	15:	21.
On the Sabbath day	τῇ τε ἡμέρα τῶν σαββάτων	16:	13.
Three Sabbaths	σάββατα τρία	17:	2.
Every Sabbath	πᾶν σάββατον	18:	4.
First day of the week	τῇ μιᾷ τῶν σαββάτων	20:	7.

FIRST CORINTHIANS.   1 time.

First day of the week............κατὰ μίαν σαββάτων,......16: 2.

COLOSSIANS.   1 time.

Nor of the Sabbath days...........ἢ σαββάτων...............2: 16.

HEBREWS.   1 time.

There remaineth therefore a rest....σαββατισμός...............4: 9.

These are now the 70 New Testament uses of the Greek *Sabbaton*. I reproduce its 8 uses, where it is translated " the first day of the week."

The first day of the week.......εἰς μιαν σαββάτων.......Matt. 28: 1.
The first day of the week.......τῆς μιας σαββάτων......Mark 16: 2.
The first day of the week.......πρώτη σαββάτου.........Mark 16: 9.
The first day of the week.......μιᾷ τῶν σαββάτων.......Luke 24: 1.
The first day of the week.......μιᾷ τῶν σαββάτων........John 20: 1.
The first day of the week.......τῇ μιᾷ τῶν σαββάτων....John 20: 19.
The first day of the week.......τῇ μιᾷ τῶν σαββάτων......Acts 20: 7.
The first day of the week.......κατὰ μίαν σαββάτων.....I. Cor. 16: 2.

www.ingramcontent.com/pod-product-compliance
Lightning Source LLC
Chambersburg PA
CBHW031833230426
43669CB00009B/1331